The GI Bill Boys

Library of Congress Cataloging-in-Publication Data

Suberman, Stella.
The GI Bill boys: a memoir / Stella Suberman.
    p. cm.
Includes index.
ISBN-13: 978-1-57233-855-5 (alk. paper)
ISBN-10: 1-57233-855-5 (alk. paper)
 1. United States—History—1933–1945.
 2. United States—Economic conditions—1918–1945.
 3. Depressions—1929—United States.
 4. New Deal, 1933–1939.
 5. United States. Servicemen's Readjustment Act of 1944.
 6. Veterans—Education—United States.
 7. Suberman, Stella.
 8. Suberman, Jack.
 I. Title.

E806.S86 2012
973.91—dc23   2011041686

The GI Bill Boys

A MEMOIR

Stella Suberman

The University of Tennessee Press • Knoxville

CONTENTS

ILLUSTRATIONS

INTRODUCTION

For those of us who follow presidential political campaigns, 2008 was a wildly exciting election year, and one without precedent. With no vice-president awaiting a turn, the presidency was an open seat, and the contest for the Democratic nomination was between—*what?*—a woman and—*what? what?*—an African American. I had grown up in a family where intense interest was paid to all political events, no doubt more than some warranted, but we all knew that this one deserved the attention being lavished upon it. My father would have said, "Pay attention, children. Here's one you'll tell your grandchildren about."

And yet on one particular 2008 morning I became aware that another story—a totally unexpected one—was seriously beckoning: Congress was debating the GI Bill? I thrust my paper at my husband Jack as we sat at the breakfast table and said, "Look here. Could it be *our* GI Bill? The GI Bill of World War II?" Jack didn't look, just kept his nose in his paper, and as one who never let a teachable moment go to waste, said, "Here's an idea: why don't you just read the story?"

I read the story and was hooked. Despite that the debate in Congress was not about our GI Bill, the 1944 one, but about the current Montgomery bill, the one named for Gillespie V. Montgomery, the Democratic congressman from Mississippi who, in 1984, had revamped our bill, I read every word and wanted more. Our GI Bill may not have been the star of this particular congressional show, but it was a show that became more and more meaningful to me.

I learned from newspaper reports of the Senate debates that vast differences existed between the old bill and the Montgomery one. The newer bill seemed to me a coy sweetener designed to encourage enlistments, whereas the GI Bill of World War II had been a straightforward reward for a job well done. It seemed that if, in their quest to reenter civilian life, World War II veterans had been provided a smooth road, current veterans were on a road pocked with potholes.

In recent years, I had not been thinking of current or past G.I. bills, but when Senator Jim Webb of Virginia introduced the enhanced bill, when he said, " . . . let's give them [the recent GIs] the same educational chance that the greatest generation had," I understood that he was referencing the first GI Bill, and I began to remember, both generally and specifically, our own 1944 GI Bill.

As the year 2008 became 2009, certain events, eerily similar to those that had taken place years before that first GI Bill was even a memorandum on President Roosevelt's desk, were suddenly popping up all around: Again the nation was in a fiscal emergency; again we were harking back to the Great Depression, and in a wry homage to that calamity, we were calling this new crisis the Great Recession. Stock markets were plunging world-wide; foreclosures were rampant; banks were closing; legendary industrial and commercial giants were imperiled; jobless men and women sought work; college graduates were back living with the folks. Fireside chats were recalled; the old New Deal alphabet soup was recited; our new president was reading up on Franklin D. Roosevelt, and the last president was being compared to Herbert Hoover. Agitation began for a committee to investigate the bankers and Wall Street executives who brought on the financial crisis. Like the Pecora Committee of 1933? Hadn't I seen this movie? Actually, I had been an on-the-spot witness to it. As had my husband, Jack.

As these events resonated, I soon convinced myself that a memoir I had written, *When It Was Our War,* was asking for a sequel. The original book, published by Algonquin Books, told of how my husband and I had lived our lives during "our" war—World War II—but it had not dwelled on the dark days of the Depression; and it had told nothing of that period in the war's aftermath when the Depression, having beaten a wartime retreat, was threatening a resurgence; and no mention had been made of our lives as we had lived them under the GI Bill. And, I thought, wouldn't a book that delved into these matters shed some welcome light?

I thought this, in fact, at almost the very moment the proponents of the enhanced bill got the win. When Senator Webb proclaimed that current veterans now had "the same opportunity for a first-class educational future as those who served during World War II"—I wondered if he had been read-ing my mind. Wasn't that the rationale for my proposed sequel? Wasn't it true that without "our" GI Bill, that "first-class educational future" would have been extremely doubtful for most World War II veterans?

* * *

When Jack came out of the service, we had been married for three years, we had a son, and we were among those for whom a future was a daunting mystery. Jack had been in college before the war, but like many young men he had enlisted immediately after the Pearl Harbor attack, in his case a semester before graduation. Even if he had possessed a diploma, however, it would not have served him. A job seeker with an undergraduate degree in English literature? If, during the Great Depression, there were few job openings in any field, there were virtually none for young men with so impractical and unusual a degree; and indeed even after the war, when the Depression threatened to return, such a degree would have been a source for wry joking. And so when Jack returned from war, if he had asked the future for some kind of work more satisfying than the meager offerings of the Great Depression, the future might ask what he had to offer. It might say to him: What are your qualifications, your marketable skills, your profession? And Jack, like many of the returning veterans, would have had to answer that he had none. In that tense period after the war, it seemed that in the quest for a future, not much was on offer, and we could only ask for something wonderful to turn up.

Something wonderful was indeed out there and waiting to make its presence known. It was a bill officially called the Servicemen's Readjustment Act, to be known forevermore as the GI Bill, and it came to us because some who were in a position to effect changes had set themselves to remembering World War I and its spawn, the veterans' 1932 Bonus March on Washington, and to remembering the Great Depression. With this in mind, I thought to begin my new memoir with our lives as we lived them during that Great Depression and to end the memoir with our lives under the GI Bill.

It must be said that the GI Bill was not, in fact, the solution for all, and some did not choose it, and some who did failed along the way. Moreover, those who chose it were not waved through tollgates; sometimes heavy tolls were to be paid. But it must also be said that for those who took advantage of the bill to go back to school, to open a business, to learn a trade, to become a professional, it made all the difference. For Jack and millions of other returning World War II veterans, the GI Bill was at their backs and a meaningful future lay ahead

In the end, the GI Bill, that bargain between America and its returning World War II veterans, can be said to have brought forth a brand new America. Out of the suffering of the veterans of the First World War, out of the blight that was the Great Depression, out of a country at the cross-roads, America was able to reinvent itself. If America had been a country of two classes, it would now be a country of three; and the newly robust middle one would threaten to chase the others off the pie chart. What had begun as a welcome home message—a "well-done"—from America to its returning World War II veterans had become the instrument that brought America to its grand place in the world.

The bargain was, from the beginning, a bargain of the most satisfying kind, for it was win-win. It told the returning veteran that America was prepared not only to ease his reentry into civilian life—to assist him in making the transition from the battlefield—but also to ensure an ex-soldier's life would be a rewarding one. It told the sixteen million veterans that they would not be demobilized to a place on bread lines or on corners selling apples. It promised that they would not become forgotten men. And those who took the offer agreed, in turn, to use it wisely.

Some twelve million GIs took the offer. According to government figures, the education and training classes alone attracted more than nine million, of which more than two million attended colleges and universities, and some seven million received lower school or on-the-job training.

There are more figures to think about. By the time GI Bill eligibility for World War II veterans expired, the United States had 450,000 trained engineers, 240,000 accountants, 238,000 teachers, 91,000 scientists, 67,000 doctors, 22,000 dentists, and more than one million other college-educated individuals. The G.I. Bill was instrumental in the founding or expansion of our great public universities as well as in raising the quality of private ones.

And how fared those billions of dollars invested in the GI Bill? It turned out that each dollar invested in veterans' benefits brought to the nation an eightfold return.

* * *

Wishing to be a reliable memoirist, I have not just relied on my own recollections. I have conferred and consulted, reread letters, and confirmed stories that through the years have been told and retold. Still, I know very well that others who were also eyewitnesses to the events recounted here will quarrel with this and that, and I understand how recollections can differ. But this memoir is my way of looking at all of those events, my take on the adventures and the adventurers, and I claim my right to seeing them my way.

1

Moving into the Depression

THE PRE-DEPRESSION YEARS

Before Jack and I met, we had lived in very different circumstances. Even the words we used for our basic biographies were different: Jack was born and *bred* in New York; I was born and *reared* in a small town in Tennessee. In addition, Jack came out of the New York Jewish middle-class tradition as the son of a fur importer; I came out of the southern "Jew store" tradition as the daughter of the owner of a modest dry goods establishment. It might be said that Jack's Depression story had big-city notes, and mine had small-town southern ones. Still, they had the same underpinning: the businesses of both fathers had gone bust.

Jack and I, like all of our generation, became Depression kids. The Great Depression had been with us for just about half of our young lives, and even if Jack and I had become Depression kids in different places and were born into different social and economic groups, we were both profoundly familiar with this sinister force and its soul-trying deprivations and restrictions. Still, Jack and I could not be said to have "suffered" as had so many other Depression kids. The Great Depression may have bent our families but it did not break them. Even if the means of both families had declined in substantial ways, the means had not entirely disappeared, and what was left of them provided not only the necessities but a little something beyond. Still, during those desperate years you had only to be alive to recognize the depth of the want and despair around you and to be devastated to know that the term "no means at all" applied to one-third of the nation. As my mother would say, tearful as always at the thought of need, "So many people don't have what to eat, don't know where to turn." It's true that my mother cried easily—my father would tease and say, "Mama cries when somebody misses the bus"—but he didn't tease her when she cried over the misery the Depression had wrought.

And so despite that we were never truly—as Jack would say—*kayoed* by the Depression, we knew it intimately. It was ever there, in the background, or hovering overhead, or staring us down. We knew it was a thing of epic proportions, but considering that we had no other depression to compare it with, we didn't call it the *Great* Depression, just the Depression. We used the word as a noun—"the Depression"; and we used it as an adjective—"a Depression job," meaning a job not worthy of one's accomplishments, or "a Depression thing to do," like your mother using milk instead of cream in her coffee, or you never being allowed to throw anything out even if you couldn't stand to look at it another minute.

IT'S A LOVE MATCH

The grip of the Great Depression was still holding on when Jack and I met in Miami during the winter of 1940, when I was eighteen and a sophomore at the University of Miami, and Jack was twenty and a junior at the University of Florida. Our meeting went something like this: 1. introductions; 2. a few exchanged words; 3. game over. Young as we were, we seemed to know almost at a glance that we need look no further, that we had found our life partners and forget about it.

How did it happen like this? Perhaps we were prescient. Or perhaps the fact that Jack was a varsity basketball player at Florida's flagship university went right to my head. As for Jack, the familiar accents of New York had become *too* familiar, and he found something refreshing in a southern one and decided to hold on. Or maybe Jack found me easy to tease and enjoyed trying out his terrible southern accent on things like, "Lord-a-mercy, derned if that don't look gooder'n pie." Or maybe I thought him "just so fascinatin'," with his casual knowledge of all things New York, a city that was regarded by my family, with the very vocal exception of my father, as one of the two glamour capitals of the world, the other being St. Louis.

From the moment Jack had first taken my hand as we sat watching a movie, we understood that we were "going steady," as we then called a committed relationship. Jack would joke that we had a "mixed marriage," by which he did not mean the usual—that one of us was Jewish and the other not—but that he was from the North and I from the South. The significance of these geographical differences was a matter of some conjecture between us, and I would maintain that Jack's being from New York City accounted for his being outspoken and outgoing and accustomed to declaring himself candidly and forcefully; I, on the other hand, being southern, was inclined to keep any deeply held feelings and opinions to myself—especially ones that might offend. I had fallen in with the southern belief that a face-to-face insult was akin to committing a sin, and though I didn't know if I believed in "sin," I believed in being polite.

New Yorker or Tennessean, we both enjoyed being with people and having lots of talk around us. Jack's way with talk tended toward discussion and debate and was carried on with those who could discuss and debate right back, and mine took the southern way and tended toward rattling on about almost anything and with almost anybody. Jack had a take on this. "Southerners don't really talk," he would joke to me. "They just interview each other and award compliments."

We were different in other ways. Jack was the oldest of the family's three siblings, and he was very clear on his right to prevail; I, conversely, was my family's youngest, and I had to defer to three elder siblings before I could (read: *might*) get my way, and it's possible that this oldest child/youngest child dynamic played a large part in Jack's and my relationship. Still, in those moments when I thought Jack was being as stubborn as a Sunday mule, which in my hometown of Union City meant you were really, really devoted to your own opinion, I didn't say, as some southern women might, "All right, sugar. You know best"; I went right ahead and pitched a fit. I pitched several of these fits, and in an interaction with Jack some years later, I would pitch a fit with a tail on it, which in Union City parlance meant a very lively fit indeed.

Still, we were alike in more ways than we were different. We were told that we "favored" each other, as the southern expression went, which meant we looked alike. Although Jack's eyes were blue—"blue as Miami Beach seas," I would say in my head—and mine brown, we were both dark haired, and among our families and friends we were considered tall. Well, Jack *was* tall. In those days, his six foot two qualified him as the basketball team center who would execute at center court the jump ball required after every basket, a rule that often led to a final score of something like thirty to twenty-eight.

We both liked sports, movies, and books. He and I understood that we both had respect for the Golden Rule, though we probably used it sometimes as a shield against a serious discussion of religion, or rather of the existence of God, a concept that Jack didn't hesitate to deny and that I was making up my mind about. On the question of where on the political spectrum we stood—an issue that could have been a deal breaker, politicized as I had been by my father and Jack by his—our views were happily identical.

Was an athlete who loved books an oxymoron? If this was the conventional wisdom, Jack flouted it, and I compared Jack's lifestyle—competing in sports and reading books—to that of the American Indian. "You go out on the warpath," I told him once, "and then you settle back in the wigwam to do a little basket weaving."

I knew, as did everyone who knew us, that Jack's love of books went beyond the usual. He read any and all books as if all were written by the gods, sometimes by the greater ones, sometimes the lesser. Even books with less than a claim to literary excellence received his ardent attention. I was no slouch when it came to books, but I had to concede that vis-à-vis Jack, I was overmatched.

Would we marry? We didn't talk about it because there was no point in talking about it. We were only too aware that no "good Jewish boy" ever married before he could support a wife, so we just accepted that we would if we could. We had taken "The Love of My Life" as our song, and as the one of us truly devoted to pop music, I took the lyrics to my heart, and I knew that if Jack Suberman had asked me to "square [his] blunders and share [his] dreams," I would have said "yes" before he had cleared his throat in preparation for the question, even as I knew that at that point in our lives, the "dreams" of the song were just that.

Still, thoughts of marrying Jack filled my head, and I often fantasized how our married lives would proceed. Having known from our first date that Jack was a reader—he was at that point in the middle of Thomas Wolfe's *You Can't Go Home Again,* a book that when I read it days later slightly unsettled me with its insistence that a war was on its way—little by little I had dreamed myself into a future based on this love of his. The fantasy took Jack and me into a college town—an appropriate place, I thought, for a book lover to operate from—and I had Jack strolling around on a leafy campus in a tweed jacket with leather patches on the sleeves, pipe in hand, dispensing wisdom right and left. "You remind me," I said to him one day, as I floated away on a reverie, "of a wise, and witty Mr. Chips," and his answer was to laugh and say, "What? I remind you of that prissy little twerp, Robert Donat?" When I thought about it, I realized that the movie's Mr. Chips was an unmistakably effete actor, with an unmistakably effete way of moving and speaking, and was that my Jack? No, it wasn't, and what had I been thinking?

I knew very well that this leather patches idea was a fantasy and not a plan. I was not so out of touch with reality as to be unaware that it did not qualify as a strategy for our future. Nor was I so deluded as to believe that I had the power to make my fantasy come true. How could it happen with the Depression hanging over us? Who or what would pay for the required graduate degrees, even the tweed jacket and the leather patches? And not to be discounted, where was the guarantee that Jack would go along with my fantasy? Just because I was enamored of it? Would Jack, as a firm believer in his right to prevail, let me take the lead in the important matter of his career? I'd have to say it was at best problematic.

I didn't dwell on it. The Depression had taught me about pie in the sky, and I knew it would take something wondrous, amazingly wondrous, for this luscious slice to appear on my plate. Still, though I never mentioned my fantasy to Jack, I clung to it.

In 1940, the year Jack and I met, we were still at the mercy of the Great Depression, Roosevelt was president, World War II had not yet happened, the GI Bill was not yet heard from. The Depression being front and center, Jack and I talked about it a lot. Jack called the Depression "a tyrant," as if it was a living, breathing creature, and when he would say that we all "interacted" with it, I realized the truth of what he said. Wasn't I always arguing with it? Didn't I persist in asking, "Will you permit this?" and "Is that within your strictures?" The presence was a repressive thing, a hateful thing, and when I wondered if it would at some point go away and leave us alone, Jack would say, "Only when something more powerful throws it off a cliff."

The trouble was that when something more powerful came along to throw it off a cliff, it turned out to be a terrible war. And after the war's end, who could guarantee that the tyrant would not climb back up to begin the whole detestable thing again?

But those things would happen later in our relationship, and the stories about them would have to wait. For now, during our first times together, we would tell each other a lot of stories about the Depression—how we lived those years before and after it—and though they often centered around unhappy events and outcomes, there were happy ones as well.

* * *

Because Jack and I came from places that might be on different planets, the question of how it was that this New York boy and this Tennessee girl found each other in south Florida might arise. And the answer is that the Depression had picked their families up and dropped them there—the Subermans in Miami and the Kaufmans across the causeway from Miami, in Miami Beach.

2

The Jew Baby

In comparing notes on "how it was," on how our lives had proceeded before the Depression came, Jack and I gave each other equal time, even if I had first to overcome Jack's notion that his Biggest City stories were more significant, definitely more interesting than my Small Town ones. Still, to my surprise, Jack in the end proved to be a good listener and a crack interrogator.

As we talked, we understood that our experiences before and after the Depression basically resembled each other in only one way, and that was that we were both offspring of once-comfortable middle-class Jewish entrepreneurs. But there the similarity ended. Jack's father was, after all, a savvy New York wholesaler of fur skins, and mine was a tactful Union City, Tennessee, retailer with a store that sold everything from shoelaces to men's Sunday suits and women's Easter hats. But no furs, definitely no furs. Indeed, if a customer had walked into our rough-and-ready store and said, "Can I see something in a mink or sable?" my father would have alerted the Tennessee Home and Training School for Feeble-minded Persons in Nashville to come get her.

* * *

I told Jack that before I was a Depression kid, I was a "Jew baby," and to my surprise I discovered that the boy that I thought knew everything didn't know about Jew babies, or even about Jew stores. And so I explained to him that Jew stores were modest dry goods stores catering to the lower economic elements of the town—to blacks, farmers and sharecroppers, and factory hands—and operated by immigrant eastern European Jews; they were in almost every small southern town, and a "Jew baby" was what southern townspeople called a child of "Jew store" owners. When I told Jack what I knew about Jew store history, which was that they had dotted the whole of the southern landscape in the 1920s and 1930s, it turned out that Jack had in fact heard of Jew stores; he just didn't know they were called that. "Come on," Jack would say to me, "were you so polite that you couldn't tell people to stop using that terrible expression?"

Through the years I came to know that terms like "Jew lawyer" were considered unambiguous signs of anti-Semitism, but "Jew store" and "Jew baby"? I explained to Jack that since among southerners a face-to-face insult is considered a sin, to which Jack would add, "At least if the face is white," I could only assume that no insult was intended.

I do know that aside from a very few disagreeable incidents, my family got along extremely well in our little town in northwest Tennessee, and we were eventually comfortable enough to call ourselves "Jewish southern-ers" or "southern Jews" depending on the circumstances, although I must admit that saying "Jew southerners" never entered our minds. Still, when I would say how comfortable we were in our little southern town, the New Yorker in Jack would show up—that part of him that didn't quite trust gen-tile displays of goodwill toward Jews—and he would say, well, generous thoughts in prosperous times do not prove very much. And indeed, when we came to Union City, times were prosperous indeed.

THE GOOD YEARS

My parents had come to Union City in 1920 with my mother, my brother Will (in Union City he was called "Willie"), and my sister Minna ("Minnie" in Union City) to open our store—Kaufman's Low-Price Store—and my sister Ruth and I were born there a few years later. My father had brought the family from New York by way of Nashville, where he had been hired as a clerk in a Jew store, and a man oddly named Johnson (oddly because "Johnson" is a name definitely not typical among Jews) took him under his wing. We always figured that, like many immigrants, Mr. Johnson carried such a surprising name because he had come to America via Ellis Island and the official there could not spell Schlomo Ehrenplotz (or whatever was Mr. Johnson's real name) but could spell "Johnson," so Johnson it was. At any rate, Mr. Johnson was a part-owner in a St. Louis wholesale house and as such was ever on the lookout for a town that needed a Jew store, because a Jew store guaranteed him another customer. Mr. Johnson was also on the lookout for an energetic young family man who could run one. Having noted that my father was a young man full of life, and having also noted that the Brown Shoe company was opening a factory in Union City, Mr. Johnson declared that he would stake my father to a Jew store there, and my father agreed before the words had left Mr. Johnson's lips. As my father would say, "Who could turn down such an offer? Had I ever had such an offer?" Well, no, he had not. Not in his little *shtetl*—his village—in Russia, certainly not in New York. Through all the years afterward, Mr. Johnson remained a family hero. It doesn't matter that his first name is lost to me in the mists of time: he was always called, and with deep admiration, just "Mr. Johnson."

Our store in Union City was on First Street, and we lived most of our Union City years in a house on Fifth Street. The whole of the town was pretty much comprised of the east-west area between those blocks and a few north-south ones, together with the streets of Niggertown, as it was called, on the other side of the railroad tracks.

Jews were a distinct rarity in Union City—home as it was to five thousand or so Protestants, of whom more than half were black—though a few Jewish people, often peddlers in wagons, had come in and out through the years. And if we were comfortable there, I later learned from my parents and older siblings that much had to be done before comfort set in. I was always interested in the story of how the townspeople reacted to our coming. Townspeople would tell my mother that they had initially felt only disappointment. It seems they had hoped—*finally!*—to see Jews with horns, and when neither my brother nor my father filled the bill, they set themselves to hoping for the best, and the best was that Will would grow his in time.

Confused feelings about us also came from their strict reading of the Bible. Should they love Jews as the blood cousins of Jesus or should they hold them in contempt for crucifying him? Didn't Matthew 27:25 report that the Jews themselves said, "His blood is on us and on our children," and didn't this mean that Jews were to be cursed forever? It was something for each Bible-reader to settle in his or her own way, but we never, as far as I knew, felt any significant fallout, not even from the nightriders, our spin-off of the Ku Klux Klan.

I had joined the townspeople in a few of their more questionable attitudes, and I did not hide these from Jack. In Union City I seem to have accepted without question that whites were in the "catbird seat"—that exalted construction in which our native gray catbirds enthroned a mate/king—

and I did not ask why the blacks, whose numbers were larger than the whites, were not the ones occupying those seats. It had also seemed to me nothing but natural that the place of blacks was as domestic servants or as hired help when burdensome, often repugnant, tasks needed doing. With this kind of rationale, was it any wonder that Jack opened his eyes wide and, as if he was giving me information I needed to have, said, "You know what you are, don't you? You're a racist." And when I protested that I wasn't—was I ever, ever ugly to blacks?—did his opinion soften? I'd have to say it did not. He just said, "Boy, do you have a lot to learn."

Our acceptance in Union City was further assured in 1927 when my father was asked to serve on the Obion County Democratic Party Committee. When the chairman of the committee had intoned, "Morris Kaufman, you're just the one to go out and get us some votes and some money," my father, being a "Double Dyed, Capital D Democrat"—as then in the South we called staunch supporters of the Democratic Party—had not only taken up the challenge with his usual *zutz*—his hustle—but very much appreciated the message of the appointment, which was that he had been accepted as part of the town. And he proceeded to work hard to fulfill his committee duty to elect the Democrat Al Smith.

Did the committee appoint my father because they thought he was in a good position to get votes because he was a store owner to whom many townspeople owed money? Or because he was a well-to-do entrepreneur who was himself likely to contribute? Or, as Jack offered, because he was a Jew and Jews were "known" to be personally persuasive about money matters?

Whichever reason applied, we in the family didn't care. As a Jewish family in a thoroughly Protestant town, we just appreciated the honor. And when the committee confirmed the honor by addressing my father as "M. A." for Morris Aaron, which were his first two names, he knew he was in, for in the South referring to someone by his initials was an unmistakable sign. After this transformative appointment, politics and world events moved up in my father's list of passions to just behind his family and his little store on First Street.

All this is not to say that the 1928 election went smoothly for the Obion County Democratic Committee. The trouble was that the Democratic candidate, Alfred E. Smith of New York, was a Catholic, and if Obion County, which included Union City, was any criterion, RomanCatholics (always pronounced in Union City as one word) were anathema to southerners. As it turned out, despite my father's best efforts, Obion County (perhaps including members of the Obion County Democratic Committee) and the whole of Tennessee in fact joined other southern states to reject the Democrat, Al Smith. The Solid South had become the Porous South and a Republican named Herbert Hoover was in the White House.

My father was celebrated for having a Jewish saying—and some non-Jewish ones—for every occasion, and in his outrage at Hoover's election and at Republicans in general, he made up a new one in an attempt to sum up, as he saw it, the difference between Democrats and Republicans. "Democrats think little people deserve more than they get, and Republicans think little people get more than they deserve" was the way he put it. And if, through the years, every once in a while he would ask me if I could still remember his saying, I would always answer yes, Dad, I do. And when I asked Jack if he felt like joining my father and me in the thought, he laughed and said, "Absolutely."

I'm sure we Kaufmans took our love of politics to the extreme, but politics, as I was to learn whenever we got together with other Jew store families, was a big thing among Jewish people, perhaps because they often had a lot to lose or to gain from how issues were decided. Jack said it was the same among his parents' crowd, that when an issue was up for a vote, they too would first ask if it was good or bad for the Jews. "They just took it for granted," Jack said to me, "that Jews had a stake in it somewhere." In Union City, my father would joke about this state of affairs, and when the Tennessee state legislature was trying to decide on the state flower, my father laughed and asked, "So what do you think? Is the sunflower or the passionflower better for the Jews?"

* * *

With time, as I told Jack, we grew more and more at home in Union City. My father's store prospered; I and my siblings had friends; my mother had her much-admired garden and her neighbors. We felt we were not only tolerated but liked, and we had confidence that being Jewish was not in the end disqualifying. Happy times. A good living and a good life. Jack would say it was the same for him, except, he would add, "We seem to have lived on another planet."

It was a good living and a good life in Union City not only for the Kaufmans. It was the 1920s, and the whole town was in a very good mood. Paychecks went into pockets every Saturday without fail; townspeople stopped each other on the street before going to the picture show on First

Street and talked about what they had just bought—a new kind of fertil-izer from Suggs Feed and Seed, some Rudy Vallee records from Redfearn's Drug Store, Easter Sunday organdies from Kaufman's Low-Price Store, and sometimes if they had a mind "to put on the dog," a string of real pearls from Morgan-Verhine, the department store that passed for posh in our town. Stores on First Street were busy; clerks said "Be with you in a min-ute" to waiting customers. Brisk sales were the norm.

It was a time when townspeople took time to talk local events, to gossip, and, with more-or-less good nature, to argue. The Great War, which had ended in 1918, was always up for a good going-over, and Kaufman's Low-Price Store was for many the setting of choice for exchanging opinions. Only a few Obion County farmers had served in the Great War—farmers having been designated as necessary to the war effort—but many nonfarm-ers had actually been on active duty. And so stories—and opinions—varied.

My father would bring it all home. One of the farmers, one who had been given a deferment so he could stay home and grow a lot of cotton, came daily into the store chiefly, it seemed, to defend his contribution to the war effort—"You tellin' me them boys didn't need no uniforms?" he would shout at whoever might think the boys didn't. His claim of "purt near" serving in the war would be countered by an ex-infantryman who had returned from service and was now trimming leather at the shoe fac-tory. As my father told it, the ex-infantryman would pound on a stack of fabric bolts and hint that his fellow townsperson farmer was unqualified to discuss anything about the war. "Was you at Belleau Wood?" he would shout at him. "Was you in the trenches?" Of course the farmer had not been at Belleau Wood; he had been, as the ex-infantryman would point out, "pickin' the weevils out of yer dad-blasted cotton." Through all this thrust and parry, my father would maintain the affable persona that all Jew store owners possessed and would decline to offer support either way. After all, he was a businessman and they were both good customers.

Through the years, I seemed to have learned a lot about the Great War and the men who fought in it. Ruth and I knew their songs, and in parlor concerts, we sang "Keep the Home Fires Burning" and "K-k-k Katy" and "Over There." I had thrilled to many a tale of heroic struggles on the west-ern front—at Verdun and Ypres and the Somme. But I had also listened to horror stories of the soldiers living in slimy, roach-infested trenches and of their suffering from a condition known as "shell shock" that came from the thunder of artillery barrages. And how often did I hear of the blindness that was caused by something called "mustard gas"?

One story spoke to me in a more personal way. Wrapped as it was around the everyday subject of personal hygiene, it was a lighter story and an appreciably less significant one, but I liked it because I could personally relate to it. As the story went, the Red Cross had come to a battlefield to pass out supplies, and one of the soldiers had asked for a toothbrush. He apparently hadn't brushed his teeth in six months, and by now, he was reported as telling the Red Cross people, "My mouth feels like a family of pigs is making their home in it."

Sadly, the Red Cross had no toothbrushes, and the soldier went back to the trenches and apparently to all those pigs. I guess I took such notice of this particular story because it was so timely: in my class in my four-room Union City schoolhouse, Westover, we had had a lesson on the importance of toothbrushing, and when we were called upon to give our own experience, one of the boys had said that if you want to brush your teeth, you "jes wet your finger, slap some grits on it, and scrub like the dickens." It was one of the stories I told Jack when we first met, and he joked, "Well, it's a good way to make use of grits without having to actually eat them." I took great umbrage at this. Not like grits? *Laugh* at grits? Well, I never.

In those pre-Depression times, "totin' privileges" for blacks were generous, and no consultation was needed. I explained the custom of "totin' privileges" to a mystified Jack as our Negro maid Willie Arnold had explained it early on to my mystified mother, how it was a custom that allowed the cook—as a domestic servant was called in Union City, whether she cooked or not—to take home leftovers, and how it was not unusual in those halcyon days for the cook to go home with something substantial—maybe a ham bone showing a goodly residue of meat or a handful of strawberries only slightly crushed.

It was a time when my parents could send my brother to college without much thought of expense. When our Uncle Henry—the one college-educated member of my mother's family—wrote that Will should be college educated, when he said, "After all, Morris can afford it," my parents agreed and sent Will to New York, to the private New York University. And yes, my father could afford it.

It was even a time when my father could think about taking a real vacation—leave the store for a while in the hands of his trusted clerk, Bob MacGowan, and take the family maybe down to Florida. He had been interested in reading about the Boom, the 1920s Florida land extravaganza when Florida land sales were so out of control that underwater lots were selling, as my father would say, "like they were growing diamonds." We had all seen the Groucho Marx movie, *Cocoanuts,* and Florida had been pictured there as the logical abode for the zany Groucho, which made it even more attractive as a pleasure spot. But when the Boom, as the Florida explosive land speculation was called, eventually turned into the Bust, my father stopped thinking about vacationing in Florida. Residential developments could fail? Planned cities could stop construction? Investors could be wiped out? My father felt that something sinister was in the air, not only in Florida but in America. He thought maybe Florida was the canary in the mine, and when the canary had fallen off its perch, it was perhaps a signal that prosperity was falling off its perch as well.

But what did it have to do with me? I surely had the sense—a seven-year-old's sense—that all things were going along just as they should. Did I have questions, doubts, anxieties? If I did, they were forgotten in the joys of the next moment. No doubt my thought was that unless somebody was down with the measles or with a bad case of impetigo, there was not much to worry about. Pleasantness and abundance floated about me like the lilies on Irene Foster's backyard pond. So when a headline in the *Memphis Commercial Appeal* announced on Wednesday morning, October 29, 1929, that the New York stock market had collapsed, it seemed a curious time for such a thing to happen.

THE DEPRESSION COMES TO UNION CITY

In the first throes of the October news, Union City had held fast. Most townspeople clung to the thought that talk of a depression could be only a rumor or, if true, was relevant only to New York City. My father invoked his maxim about the presence of God—that God was just a rumor agreed on by everybody—and he would proclaim to us, in his way with the language, "A depression might only be in New York, and New York never even heard tell of Union City." My father had learned much of his English as a young bachelor in Savannah, Georgia, where "Teach English to Morris Kaufman" had been a project for an Episcopal church women's group yearning to be useful, and his language was typically fitted out with a dollop of southern, and he would say, "Who says we got to giddy-up to New York's tune?" My father never felt the need to apologize for his lack of love for New York. After his arrival there as a poverty-stricken immigrant, the city had shown him no sign of welcome and had indeed driven him to flight. It's true that he had found a soft landing in the South, but he had never let go of the thought that New York was a cold, cold city.

The Depression may have been New York's problem—and Jack was eager to tell me all about it—but it soon became Union City's as well. Without so much as a by-your-leave, the Depression found the road sign that said "Union City Town Limits," made itself at home on First Street, and proceeded to swallow store after store. Union City had begun its fall into hard times, and Kaufman's Low-Price Store was about to suffer an almost mortal wound.

My father told it to the family, blow-by-blow: the five-and-ten on First Street finally made good on its threat to close; the store next to ours, where my mother bought her made-to-order corsets with the whalebone stays, shut its front door and never opened it again. My father's report on Morgan-Verhine's, that icon of reckless spending, was scary: from across the street he had watched as Morgan's customers dwindled to maybe one or two a day, and Jack said, when I told him this, "Did your father indulge in a little schadenfreude at this?" Schadenfreude? After Jack, taking advantage again of a teachable moment, explained the term to me—that it meant getting pleasure at the misfortune of others—"How could he?" I said, "He wasn't doing very well himself."

Morgan-Verhine's problems were symptomatic of the new times: reckless spending had gone out of style. And if my father and Mr. Morgan had only minimally communicated in the past, Mr. Morgan was now seeking my father's advice. He confided that he was considering giving "the coloreds" the privilege of charging, which led my father to express to us that it was a good example of Mr. Morgan's *goyische kopf,* his gentile head. A *goy* could get by in good times, sure, but when times were bad, where was the *seckle,* the ingenuity? It took a Jew, my father would say, to figure out the ins and outs, though the ins and outs were proving hard for my father to figure out as well.

Still, my father felt that he should offer some advice and told Mr. Morgan that to depend on colored trade was to depend on birds dropping down gold. And it was true that if the white people of Union City were feeling a hard pinch, the black people were taking blows. Our cook, Willie Arnold, would say things to my mother like, "We never been eatin' high off the hog, and now we gots to be eatin' so low there ain't no way to get at it." Willie Arnold stories always made Jack laugh, and he would say that when the time came to claim civil rights, Willie Arnold would be directing the troops.

And so in Union City I became ever more mindful of the Depression and ever more apprehensive. How could I not when the neighbors told one pitiful narrative after another and I took every word on board? When Mrs. Cummins down the street was selling off everything she owned, including the silver table setting she had inherited from her husband's grandmother with the "C" on every single piece? When Kaufman's Low-Price Store was down to a staff of my father and Mr. McGowan? How could I not be alarmed when my father reported that the canvas bag with the week's deposits he carried to the bank every Saturday night held fewer and fewer dollar bills? How not to murmur "oh no" when my father said, "I don't need a bag no more. All I need is an envelope"?

I knew that our store had never been the place for reckless spending, but where were our thrift-minded regulars? Colored trade had become irrelevant, and the farmers and the farmhands were at the mercy of farm prices declining by the hour, which meant that our regulars were down to the factory workers. And so when my father brought home the news that the shoe factory might close, I felt a fear beyond all other fears. *The shoe factory?* The engine on the hill that made Union City's wheels go 'round? Yes, the shoe factory. And now I watched while the spirits of my father—my ebullient, confident father—flagged and while his usual look, the one that said, "Don't worry, I got it covered," went missing.

Some of the factory hands had already been laid off and were now milling about town looking for work. A few found jobs as city hires, and when my father would say, "And so what?" I knew what it meant. What it meant was that city hires could expect city wages, which had never been more than paltry and were now down to rock bottom like everybody else's; and the jobs were temporary ones—fixing one of the brick walks around the courthouse or shoveling roads after a snow. When Jack expressed surprise that snow fell in Tennessee, I would explain that although it sometimes did, it sometimes didn't, and the hires therefore had no guarantees. A few of the let-go factory workers found jobs harvesting crops, but didn't harvesting last only a few days? And, anyway, who said farmers were hiring?

At our house, the family knew the Depression in many ways, and my mother adapted very well. We all said that my mother had three kinds of corpuscles in her blood—red, white, and frugal—and taking easily to the new thrift requirements, she would cry, "Still good!" when one of us tried to throw out a garment that we felt had given its all.

My mother came by her frugal corpuscles naturally: she was an immigrant child from Russia who had worked as a youngster in the downtown New York factories, and money was to her the result of hard work, and acquisitions were subject to a somewhat rigorous test of value. She was not, however, a textbook penny-pincher, and when she applied her value yard-stick, it was in terms of not only need but pleasure. If, pre-Depression, I had held my breath over a totally unnecessary organdy dress with a huge sash that had just arrived from the St. Louis wholesale houses, my mother, ever-mindful that we were not among those able to "strut their stuff" at Easter, would take it home and plan a party at which I could wear it, and to heck with the prospective sale. And now, the Depression having made its demands, her yardstick simply asked a little more in the way of value. Sometimes she would try to impress us by reciting something in her own way with the language, which, early on, was a mélange of a bumpy English flavored with Yiddish and later infused with southern, and in trying, for example, for the aphorism, "Take care of the pennies and the dollars will take care of themselves," she would tell us, "If you *gefeln* the pennies, the dollars will *lib* you." In plain English, if you like the pennies, the dollars will love you.

* * *

The Depression was, in truth, on our very doorstep. Men on the move look-ing for work jumped off the freight trains—"riding the rails," they called it—and came daily to our back door. They preferred a job to a handout—"You got something needing done?" they would ask—and my mother al-ways found something for them to do. They might take a hoe to a patch of ground as yet untilled, or tote coal from the shed to the bin, or patch a screen door, and when the men were getting ready to leave, my mother would send me out to them with a sack of food, and I would go out with a few boiled sweet potatoes, a half-loaf of bread, two or three hard-boiled eggs, or maybe a jar of tea.

When I handed these things over, I would say, "Here's your sack for the road," and my southern manners would kick in—Jack would say that I went into "interview mode"—and I would ask them where they were from or where they were going. And when Jack asked me, "Well, where *were* they going?" I told him that in time I stopped asking the question, for I knew pretty quickly that they were going nowhere, just moving along from one town to the other, from one handout to the other, maybe stopping at an im-provised roadside campsite where they would mill around with others like themselves. I may at that time have been a mere eight-year-old, but even an eight-year-old can figure out that these men had no destination in mind, just the hope that the next town—any town—would have a job for them.

We had always bartered, mostly for fun, but bartering now went from an amusing diversion to a serious negotiation, with solemn thought given to such things as the value of a hen versus a boy's outgrown Sunday suit. Anything "new" in the way of dresses was homemade, fashioned from maybe an old curtain and run up on the home sewing machine. When the batting of my bed quilt began to escape, there it suddenly was on my mother's sewing machine being reincarnated into a skirt for my sister Minna.

We might occasionally try to joke about the Depression, but it would be the kind of joke that had at its core the plight of a suffering soul. We knew that blacks often indulged in this practice, what was called "hard joking," but now everybody was doing it. It had become a Depression thing. My father tried his best to come up with such jokes, and he might wryly remark that out-of-work factory hands were making a living by fixing each other's wagons, or—"Ain't it a doggone shame?"—the town banker was giving up his annual holiday in Hot Springs, Arkansas, and making do with a back-yard tub and a rubdown from his wife.

Our bank, the Commercial Bank and Trust, was still open on First Street, but a lot of the state banks had closed. Our weekly paper, the *Union City Messenger,* which had hitherto chiefly kept us informed about the re-oiling of the Dyersburg Road or Mrs. Chalmers's tea for her visiting cousin, was now showing photos of depositors in other Obion County towns waggling their deposit books at the closed doors of their once friendly bank. Occasionally my father would recognize a Kaufman's customer and he would shake his head and say, "A good man. And it looks like the bank's going to go down and take his money with it."

Domestic servants—of which most every white family had at least one—were not let go, but they often went home on Saturday payday not with their usual dollar but with a dime or a quarter. At a neighbor's house, I would often hear Miz Upchurch (usually "Miz" for a married lady's honorific, but often "Mizriz") or some other Miz telling her cook some version of "I'll get something to you next week."

Totin' privileges were now strictly monitored and less generous. The cook might be handed a flour sack holding a tablespoon or so of flour or a lard can with a tiny swirl of the white goo at the bottom, but she often went out the back door heading for home with only a cracked pot or a jar containing remnants of its original contents, usually jelly, under the lip. If in her totin' privileges sack she had a jar of fruit or vegetables put up by her mistress, it was not now a bonus but a part of her wages. The cook knew not to demand, not just from long habit but because she too was aware of "the Depress."

My father's five-foot six-inch frame held very large opinions, and many related to the Depression. I was his most loyal listener, and I seemed to have taken listening to my father as my family assignment, as it was Ruth's to water the houseplants. After the Depression came to us, the number and noise level of his attacks on Republicans shot skyward, mostly aimed at the sitting president, who was the face of those reviled creatures. "It would never happen if you had a Democrat in there," he would shout, even if only into the open newspaper in front of him. "Democrats know who needs and who don't," he would say. "You get a Democrat in there, you'll see the difference." And then would come a bit of his political philosophy: "Those Republican guys don't care about us *nebbisches*, us little guys. They care only that their rich friends get richer. Am I right, or am I right? " Even if confused by the phrasing but knowing what he wanted to hear, I would say, "Yes, Dad, you're right."

As recognition of my loyalty, my father would try things out on me. I was eight years old, and it was a year after the Depression had entered our lives when my father tried me out on the Smoot-Hawley Tariff Act, a bill that in an attempt to lessen the effects of the Depression raised tariffs on imported goods. "What a bunch of *kalichers*," he would say, meaning that the lawmakers were so ignorant of how business worked as to be like greenhorns, a word he had gotten very accustomed to in New York. "Do they expect countries not to turn around and for spite stop buying from us?" he would ask me. And Jack, listening to me, would say, "Are you expecting me to believe that you could discuss this at eight years old?" and I would say, well, at eight years old, I may not have understood about tariffs and trade, but I understood about people getting mad when they thought somebody had been ugly to them. And when my father said, "The joke's going to be on us," I told Jack that I understood that as well.

UNION CITY ENTERTAINMENTS, DEPRESSION-STYLE

If our entertainments had always tended toward the simple, after the Depression set in, they got even simpler. We bought almost nothing in the way of toys and managed to fashion any new ones from sticks and stones, and we played baseball with a sad little ball skinned to the core. If a doll's dress was torn, we didn't go to the store and buy a new one, or maybe two because our doll was something of a fashion plate, we made do with flour sacks. When the left eye of my favorite doll, Janine, no longer blinked, I fashioned a flour sack bandage and would say to my friends, "Lord have mercy, poor Janine's got the pinkeye real bad."

For home-grown entertainments, the house parlor in Union City (the "front room") was the usual setting, and in ours, we diverted each other with the piano playing of Minna, and Will's readings (in an oratorical way) from some popular science magazine he had gotten hold of, and Ruth and I contributing in any way possible. Mainly Ruth and I waltzed around in what we hoped were classical dances, taking turns at draping ourselves in the piano shawl. Jack had a good laugh at this, and when he said, "You probably thought you were doing Isadora Duncan," I had to admit that we did. Of course we had never seen Isadora Duncan, that queen of the emotionally wrought dances sweeping the country, but we had seen her impressionists when the annual Chautauqua show came to town to enlighten us with cultural and educational presentations, and we thought we had her down to the last leap and farewell wave.

What else did Ruth and I do? Well, we gave recitations, serious and dramatic ones, with our eyes fixed ever on the heavens—well, on the ceiling, which in our little house was so low, heaven was there for the touching. And we worked up a minstrel show act in which we were endmen who told jokes in the black vernacular, with Ruth performing as "Rastus" and me as "Rufus."

When we collaborated in these home entertainments, Ruth and I, only eighteen months apart, were doing what was expected of us, which was to do everything together. Only in looks did we depart from one another. Although Ruth's hair was brown like mine, it was straight and mine was curly, and her eyes were blue like my father's and mine dark like my mother's. After I was born, our Union City mentor, Miss Bookie Caldwell, with whom we lived in the early Union City years, pointed out that I was now the "young 'un" and Ruth was now the "knee baby," and, as such, we were expected to be always together. My mother accepted this, though she often thought our mentor held some pretty peculiar views. But she accepted most of what Miss Bookie said, chiefly because Miss Bookie had gone to college. "A girl in college," my mother would say after Miss Bookie had regaled her with tales of college life. "Whoever heard?" And she might well have thought, "Whatever for?"

I had one entertainment, however, that was uniquely mine, and that was attending school before I was officially eligible. Perhaps my mother was heeding Miss Bookie's dictum that Ruth and I were supposed to be inseparable; but whatever the case, my mother sent me off to school with Ruth—in Union City, official rules were made to be waived—and, unregistered, I sat beside her at her little desk and proceeded to learn what she learned, though sometimes she learned what I learned. I don't know how Ruth felt about it, but there being no pressure on me at all, going to school was a most enjoyable thing to do.

Most everybody had a radio, and because radios didn't use much electricity, we listened to them every night. Competition among owners was keen. A set of new idioms came along with the advent of radios, and my father would say to the competition, "My Atwater-Kent *brought in* Philadelphia last night. Your DeForest *bring in* anything besides *static?*" My mother was taken with KDKA's featured performer, a singing pianist called Little Jack Little, and she talked about him so much that she fell into substituting his name for the phrase "little by little," and when she would ask, "You think times is getting better?" my father would answer, "No, Rebecca, not even little-jack-little."

On the occasional Sunday afternoon, our search for diversions that didn't cost anything often found us at an event called "the auction." When one had been advertised, the Kaufmans, along with almost the whole town, went out to the venue and watched. The auction might be targeting a farm long overdue on its mortgage or some other obligation to the bank, and the bank would have set up shop on the farm to auction off everything in sight. Piles of farm equipment sat in the front yard, and in the background the little farmhouse awaited its fate. After the land had been auctioned off, the stock went next, and then the machinery, and then the house. They were all hard sells. A lot of dickering took place, and the farmer/owner would look on, perhaps wondering why nobody seemed to care that he was losing his farm. After one sale—a family farm owned by one of our customers—my father said, "Whoever's got the farm, they got also a piece of a good man's heart."

THE PICTURE SHOWS

The most popular venue for distraction, however, was the picture show on First Street. Movies were an integral part of our Saturdays and were the only distractions for which we were willing to part with money. Going to the movies was the one pre-Depression experience that Jack and I totally shared. Every movie I had seen, he had seen; every movie star I knew, he knew. We had thrilled to the same serials, those little showpieces of evil and derring-do that left us hanging from one Saturday to the next.

Jack and I noted a few differences, however: in New York a ticket cost ten cents; in Union City it was a nickel, and in Union City my friends and

I worked hard to get one. Because nickels didn't grow on trees, or, as my mother reminded us, come out of our ears (as my father would have us believe when he did his magic tricks), we each had our own way of earning them. Hal Semone across the street had a little business sweeping dirt yards. Ruth and I and my best friend, Doris Johnson, stood in front of the U-Tote-'Em Grocery Store and sang songs and kind passersby threw us pennies. My sister and I had an allowance of a nickel a week, but that went to buy the candy corn that accompanied us into the picture show, so we had to work hard for that other one.

For some in Union City, the newsreels that preceded every movie were their only source of information. Many Union City families had for economic reasons stopped delivery of the newspaper—after all, two cents was two cents—but in our family, my father insisted that we continue our delivery, and he said over and over, "This is the best two cents we'll ever spend." That reading newspapers was an indispensable part of living your life was a lesson learned by all the Kaufmans. And Jack's family, Jack would say with a laugh, would no more give up the *New York Times* than give up the *schmear* of cream cheese on their bagels. The fact remained, however, that it was up to the newsreels to provide many with their only acquaintance with national and world events.

Jack would say that in addition to being entertaining, movies gave us a picture of our world and a sense of where we were in it, and I thought this sounded about right. Movies gave us yardsticks. Good or bad, serious or comic, they spoke to us. The movies at the very least helped us to escape, and they did this in various ways. Movie romances took us out of our gloom and into the arms of movie idols like Rudolph Valentino, the Italian actor who passed as a scimitar-wielding Arab sheik; or men (and boys) melted into the come-hither eyes of Theda Bara. My own true love was the pubescent star Jackie Coogan, and dreaming of him took my mind off not getting a new set of pencils when I started the third grade. Slapstick comedies provided us with characters worse off (more luckless, more hapless) than ourselves, and when, like us, the fat/skinny comedy team of Laurel and Hardy fell prey to Depression indignities, we were only too familiar with those indignities ourselves, and we laughed heartily at their attempts to outwit them.

Gangster films came on the scene because gangsters—usually bank robbers—were suddenly big news. James Cagney showed us a really bad guy (but not all bad, because didn't he love his mother deeply?) in *The Public Enemy,* though he was not a true gangster, just an "ordinary" robber and murderer. When Jack and I talked about the movie, we of course compared notes on the scene that had everybody talking, the one in which Cagney showed his displeasure with his girlfriend by grinding a half-grapefruit— "Just screwed it right in," Jack joked—into her face. Still, gangster films had a hard time being escapist. How could they take us to a happy place when their grim atmospherics mirrored the ones in our lives?

Films about the upper classes were so abundant that we knew upper-class lifestyles as well as we knew our own. I had learned the word "ritzy" somehow, and I used it often. I might have been unaware that the ritziness derived from an art deco sensibility, but I was well aware that movie characters dressed themselves in ritzy attire and lived in ritzy mansions featuring sweeping marble staircases and porthole windows. The ritzy characters were most often mean-spirited, but sometimes they were generous, and if they were, I cherished them. How grateful I was to Ann Harding—the actress of supernatural elegance and decency—when she detected fine qualities in a servant's son and prevailed upon her husband to help the boy escape the fate the Depression would inevitably visit on him. Miss Bookie Caldwell was not impressed and she would say of the movies' depiction of noblesse oblige, "I swan, that goody-goody stuff just turns sour on my stomach." I had stores of tales about our mentor and I told them all to Jack, who was delighted with them, and delighted with Miss Bookie and her attitudes. He finally gave Miss Bookie the ultimate accolade and awarded her the title of the "sage of Union City, Tennessee."

If we had a ritzy class in Union City, I didn't know anybody in it. Miss Bookie Caldwell was not ritzy. Having lived in her house, I had certain knowledge that the house was not ritzy either. It had no marble staircase or port hole window, just an ordinary Union City thing—a front porch with a floor that undulated so extremely that Miss Bookie Caldwell declared she got seasick just setting foot on it.

Movie colleges were seen often. Chiefly they were private ones with imposing Gothic buildings situated on verdant campuses, and those who attended these picture-perfect places of learning wore "beanies" on their heads and rode around in "jalopies," with "leapin' Lena" and "I'm available" painted on them. Still, the high school graduates in our town knew that the silver screen held the only colleges they would know. If any of the town's young people had been hoping to join that select Union City circle of the college educated, it was a hope that sank without a trace. No one in Union City was thinking about going to college. Which of us had the money? True, my brother was in college, but now when my father signed off on Will's check each month, he never failed to turn to us and say in a rueful voice, "Who knows if I'll be able to write the next one?"

THE DEPRESSION HAS THE LAST WORD

By late 1930, it was obvious to my father—and to all of us—that things weren't getting any better and that Kaufman's Low-Price Store was barely alive. Our store may have offered prices that better suited the new economic realities in the town, but it was clear to anybody who knew the retail business that the business was on its last legs. We were now closing early on Saturday nights, and most of the stock, even Easter dresses and men's work shoes that had always flown out the door, were overstaying their welcome. At this point, "something new for Easter" meant not a new organdy dress but just a new flower for last year's hat. And men's work shoes, once the store's mainstays, were now not being replaced but being repaired, and in various ways, usually with soles devised of odd pieces of linoleum. In truth the whole of Union City had continued to founder, and what had kept the town more or less afloat—the shoe factory—was down to a skeleton force and showing signs of working its way down to no force at all.

If the shoe factory went bust, my father said it would surely take all of Union City's commercial life with it, and as usual seeing himself as an idea man, he went about his days trying to come up with something that might keep the shoe factory going. What he finally decided on was a pledge drive. "We'll get people to come and pledge to help," he explained, unhelpfully, at least unhelpfully to me. When I finally got the picture, I understood that there would be a town meeting, and townspeople would promise to lend the factory money, and the factory would promise to pay it back. The meeting would be held in the school auditorium, with my father as master of ceremonies.

It was an exciting event. The whole town turned up, and pledges were shouted out, and when the pledging slowed, my father stepped in. Even with his reduced account in the First National Bank, he agreed to match every pledge with a 50 percent pledge of his own. This was all right with me. The factory had made the promise to pay back, and from what I knew about promises, you had to keep them. So I felt that my father's money would be safe in the factory's hands.

My father was a very good master of ceremonies. He knew his crowd, and he knew how to tease them into a good mood and would ask things like, "Who wants to see a tightwad Jew spend his money?" In addition to attracting a renewed shower of pledges, such self-deprecating jokes invariably brought the house down,

But if I thought we were surely saved, when I looked at the factory owner standing on the stage with my father, I knew we were not. Although my father was ever-smiling, the owner was grim-faced, and I knew that the pledge drive had not made much of a difference. And in the months that followed, we learned that the pledges had only managed to keep the factory's nose above water. "It's going to sink," my father kept saying, "and who's going to provide for this town when the factory goes down?" He didn't say that if the factory went down, his loan would go down with it, and although it was not much of a loan, money it was. And it was at this moment that my father began to think of leaving Union City. Although at first he tried to keep the thought out of his head, when one of my mother's imperatives came charging in, he was suddenly beleaguered.

Throughout our stay in Union City, my mother had two abiding imperatives, and the first had been fulfilled. It came on the first of the rare times that my mother departed from my father's opinion and had one of her own. Her opinion was that Will should have a bar mitzvah, and to have one, he should be sent to New York to live with our grandparents, and never mind that my father thundered, "Send him to New York? For what and for why?" My father was angry, we all remembered, so angry that Will said he could see him "glowing in the dark." Nevertheless, Will went to New York, had his bar mitzvah, and came back home with six pen and pencil sets and a mound of variously denominated gold coins to show for it.

Will also came home a celebrity. With his newly acquired knowledge of Hebrew, he was now in demand for preprandial blessings at Sunday dinners. As my brother told the story, the father of the family would ask for quiet and say, "Listen, children, listen to Willie. He's speakin' the language of our Lord." Having learned a few things at the New York Hebrew school he had attended, Will knew that the language of their Lord was not Hebrew but Aramaic, but he had said nothing. When Jack, reacting as usual to what he figured was a teachable moment, asked me why Will had not made the correction, I told him that Will would never do such a thing. "Will was very much the southern gentleman," I told Jack, "and southern gentlemen don't want to be accused of 'puttin' on,'" "puttin' on" being an expression in much use in Union City meaning as it did "showing an undeserved sophistication."

As the Depression showed no signs of retreat, my mother's second imperative now moved to the front burner. We all knew this second imperative—through the years we had heard about it, teased about it, got tired of the jokes about it—and it was that her daughters have Jewish husbands.

From her earliest days in Union City, my mother had kept an eye out for Jewish suitors, and hoping to flush one out, she had made it her business to beat bushes near and far. Now, with Minna coming into marriageable age, she grew frantic, having found no suitable son-in-law nesting in Tennessee bushes. Actually, my mother had whacked at the bushes of neighboring states as well, only to find that she was too late, and the quarry had flown: he was already engaged, had gone off to New York, or, if he was planning to go into the family business, that venture, like ours, held no promise of supporting yet another family.

My father would tell my mother to stop looking and settle for some "nice Union City boy," which only set my mother to crying out not only in protest but in some terror. "Our daughters not marry Jewish boys?" she would cry, "What are you talking?!" After which, my father would counter—unsurprisingly, if riskily—with, "Our daughters wouldn't be happy with gentile ones?" And it was at this point that my mother would charge into the backyard and smite the weeds that had had the nerve to make themselves at home in her garden.

So where, oh where, could Jewish boys be found? The answer of course was in New York. It was a most satisfying solution to my mother, for in one fell swoop, it would answer three of her needs: she would again have Jewish people around her, we girls would have Jewish boys—"so many I can't think about it"—to choose from; and she would again have her college boy in her arms. In the face of my mother's deeply joyful anticipation, my father could only shake his head and stop arguing.

In the end my father sold Kaufman's Low-Price Store to his clerks (for nothing, my father said)—the full-time Bob McGowan and the part-time Gaither Jones—who, we learned later, sold it after a few years to the Black and White chain, and we said our goodbyes to the cotton fields of Jew-less Obion County and the five square blocks that was (white) Union City and took ourselves off to the Jewish hotbed of New York City.

And so we left the South—the South we had lived in so agreeably. And though we might have said we left it for many reasons, we didn't fool ourselves. Although my father had insisted that we were leaving Union City "to keep Mama from pitching a fit," we all knew that the Depression was what did it. With Kaufman's Low-Price Store no longer a goose laying golden eggs, and showing no promise of ever doing so again, the Depression had told us in no uncertain terms that it was time to go.

I looked forward to New York. I wanted Will not to live with our grandparents anymore but with us, and I wanted to "trip the light fantastic." I had heard about this "fantastic" when my mother sang "The Sidewalks of New York" as she sat at her sewing machine rerouting another hand-me-down, and though I had no idea what a "fantastic" was, nor had my mother, I was keen to find out.

3

New York, New York, a Wonderful Town?

WE SET UP SHOP

Will met us at the train station in Manhattan and took us immediately on the subway (!) to my grandparents' apartment in the Bronx, where we were to stay until we found our own place. My father, however, was not eager to move out. It was the inevitable signing of a lease that bothered him; it seemed to him both an act of unwelcome bonding with New York and an act of disloyalty to Tennessee. As he saw it, Tennessee had made a good life for him and his family; and with a little Jew–store owner savvy, he had seen to it that we had all been happy there. Although mindful of our status as outsiders, he saw us as unthreatened, and he had often looked up and down First Street and said, "Anybody seen any Cossacks around? No? So let it be."

My father's distaste for New York stemmed from his arrival there as an immigrant. He had come over as an eighteen-year-old with a head full of expectations and his *mazel* and his *zutz*. He had listened with "a heart going so fast like a steam engine," as he himself described his joy when the people in his *shtetl* told him that in New York the streets were paved with gold, that he would have a big bed to sleep in, and a fine suit for the big job he was going to get. And when he got to New York? He saw that streets were lined not with gold but with trash, and no big bed for sleeping but an old blanket on the floor in the corner of the apartment rented by a member of his *mishpoucha*, the extended family, who in this case was a cousin of a cousin-in-law. And his expectations? His expectations had turned literally to dust when his first job was delivering coal, a job which paid fifty cents a day and all the coal dust he could carry home.

My father blamed his unrealistic expectations on his *shtetl* dwellers and their rumors. "All what they told me was nothing but *klangs*. Did they see? Did they know?" he would ask, to which his own answer was: "Of course not. It was just rumors," which was similar to his answer about the existence of god. It wasn't long, he would say, before he knew that New York was as cold and unwelcoming as the office of the Russian authorities in his *shtetl*.

Still, we had to live somewhere in New York, and we found an apartment in one of those big brick apartment buildings typical of the Bronx. The apartment had been advertised for rent with a Depression "concession" as a sweetener, which was two months' free rent in exchange for a year's lease. To the extent that my father would allow, I was keeping track of the money my father had when we came out of Union City, what he called "carfare"—"enough to take the subway back and forth looking for something to do," he would say—and I wondered if it would cover our rent. I was assured when my father swallowed the sweetener, handed the owner some of his "carfare," and rented us an apartment in the west Bronx.

As I discovered later, our apartment was in a section of the Bronx where, in a nice coincidence, Jack and his family had lived in their "apartment with *two bathrooms*," which his mother would later tell me about with such pride. And when Jack and I talked about it, we decided that it was possible that he had played stickball in front of my building. And could it have happened that we had walked on the same sidewalk at the same time? Had we looked at each other? If so, had he given me that smile—the one I had seen that first moment in Miami, the one that had made me want to grab him and hold on forever?

Our apartment was on the sixth floor in that Bronx building, and we got to it by elevator, and that elevator was the inspiration for the first of many letters I wrote to my best friend Doris in Union City. Even as I knew I would be accused of puttin' on, I would have even so been unable to resist flaunting that elevator. And I would have gone further: I would have told her, in an even grander show of puttin' on, "You just got to have an elevator if you live on the sixth floor like we do."

* * *

From the very early days, it became clear to me that the "light fantastic" did not mean that all was bright and beautiful in New York. No, in these days of the Depression, New York could be very dark indeed, and we had evidence of this even as we were moving into our new home. There it was, as if putting us on notice—a pile of furniture heaped about on the front side-walk of our new building. Had these sofas (or "divans," as we called them in Union City), these bureaus (Union City's "chestadraws"), these kitchen chairs—had they fallen out of a window? "They're there because somebody got behind on their rent," my father told me, "and then somebody will come and take it away." I wasn't familiar with "getting behind" on rent, and I wondered if we might do that ourselves. I thought about the money my father had received for the store and the sum still in the First National on First Street in Union City—would it be enough to keep us from "getting behind"?

It was no comfort to me that when my father spoke of "losing the store," as he called it, he spoke in an angry voice, as if somebody or some*thing* had been ugly to him. Nor was there comfort in the pledges my father had made to the shoe factory. He had fulfilled his part and given the loan, and the factory was paying back, but "in such dribs and drabs," my father said, "I can maybe buy a postage stamp once a month." And what if the factory just closed the doors for good and said to heck with my father's loan?

In New York, unlike in Union City, signs of the Depression came to us in the Bronx not in homeless, jobless men knocking on our back door—our apartment actually did not have a back door—but in the window signs in the neighborhood stores that said "No jobs here," or "No help needed." If a job was come by, a bartering deal was set up in which the men put in their time as general handymen in exchange for produce, a slice of meat, or a piece of cheese. When Jack and I talked about it, he pointed out to me that in some ways it was New York's variation on the South's totin' privileges. "It's the same," he would say. "Just substitute salami for fatback."

SURVIVING NEW YORK

After our arrival in New York, Ruth and I were sent almost at once to an elementary school near the Bronx reservoir, a mammoth edifice of brick and mortar and called, in the New York City bureaucratic way, P.S. 86, and I was assigned to the third grade and Ruth to the fourth. In Union City, our bucolically named Westover Elementary was a cottagelike building of four classrooms, and when you got to the fifth grade, you transferred from Westover to our one school of higher learning. And here we were in P.S. 86, a building so large, its occupancy so great, that when I wrote Doris, I probably wrote, "Lord, Doris, P.S. 86 is just so big, it makes Westover seem like the Sunshine Girls," the Sunshine Girls being a preschool class of about a dozen of us Union City girls who daily met in the basement of the Presbyterian church to paste wallpaper on empty jars and call them vases.

On our first day at P. S. 86, Ruth and I were sent to the speech clinic, where we sat with the Chinese girl, the Hungarian girl, and the Italian boy. The clinician called us immigrants—yes, *all* of us—and she said she was aware that we were in New York because we were trying to escape the Depression in our own countries. Ruth and I did not mention that we were from *our* country, the same one the teacher was from, and when she never corrected herself, we had every feeling that she thought the South was indeed a foreign country. But protest was out of the question: we were Tennesseans who knew our manners. And so Ruth and I sat with our fellow immigrants learning to speak proper (read: New York) English.

It was clear that the clinician thought Ruth and me particularly frustrating. If we could speak English, why couldn't we speak it right? One pronunciation seemed to give her particular pain, and "Girls, girls!" the clinician would cry. "Not *choklit!* It's *chawklit!*" Ruth and I, working our southern manners to the limit, tried to cooperate, and we said it her way as best we could. But when we were not in the clinic, did we say *chawklit?* I'd have to say no, we did not. And in a note to Doris I no doubt said, "Lord have mercy, Doris, that clinic lady thinks we're as dumb as a bucket of rocks."

As for twenty-year-old Will, just as we were arriving in New York, he was due to graduate from college. He had opted for a degree in engineering despite the hostility in the profession toward allowing Jews in; in other words, he loved the profession even if it didn't love him back. But if getting a job was doubtful, it was also problematic that Will would graduate at all. Graduating depended on tuition bills being paid, and gone were the days when my father received Will's tuition bill and sent the requested check back in the return mail. He now had to find a solution. In the end, my father paid his last tuition bill by spreading out the final payment, and Will duly graduated.

Now Will had to figure out how to get a job. Maybe to outwit the prejudice by pretending his name was German and not Jewish? Maybe by adding an extra "f" or an extra "n" or maybe an extra both? But my father, remembering that his own name had been "Plotnikoff" before he had changed it to "Kaufman" in Savannah, said, "Enough with the name changing," and that was that.

So what was Will going to do? Somehow my father found for sale a repair shop for taxi fleets. The asking price was so cheap that he bought it with just a bit of his carfare stash. Will, who liked fooling around with engines, therefore had a job, even if a high-toned "engineering" one it wasn't. But did my father like the taxi repair business? No, he did not. He would say, "What's a born sal-es-man [how he famously pronounced the word, Savannah young lady tutors notwithstanding] doing in a taxi business anyway?"

My mother took eighteen-year-old Minna as her special project. We all knew that my mother kept some savings from her grocery money in an old Crisco can on a shelf, but we had never seen her use any, and it appeared that now she would. She would send Minna to a commercial school to learn typing and shorthand so that she would have some skills and not have to take a job in a downtown factory, as she herself had done when her schooling had ended at the third grade. College for Minna was not a consideration. Despite that Miss Bookie Caldwell had gone to college, my mother had put this bit of information in the imaginary drawer labeled "Miss Bookie's Foolish Ideas" and had clung to her own opinion that college was for boys and not girls.

It didn't matter to Minna. She was not interested in college; she was interested in boys and dates. "I 'clare," she would say, sounding to me just like her Union City girlfriends as they played auction bridge on Saturdays and talked endlessly about boys, Minna usually about her crush, Campbell Garth. "Boys don't care for college girls," Minna would say to us. "They like girls who don't entertain things of a serious nature." So Minna accepted without protest being taught a skill instead of a profession. Still, we all knew that Minna's finding a job—with a skill *or* a profession—would not be easy. The papers were saying that the out-of-work rate was now one in four, and it didn't seem to us that Minna's office skills would count for much if all the offices were closing down.

NEW YORK'S DEPRESSION "ENTERTAINMENTS"

Will tried to introduce us to the New York pleasures he himself had been introduced to when he had first come to New York, but the Depression kept getting in the way. Except for a few city-sponsored attractions, they cost money, and we had to settle on Depression-style entertainments, meaning things that didn't cost a dime. You could even make money on some of the entertainments, and Ruth and I felt sure we could make a bit in the talent competitions for tap dancing and singing and recitations. And dance marathons.

Our Union City successes looming large—the ones when, to great applause, Ruth and I floated about the front room in the piano shawl—we wanted to enter some of the competitions, and we assessed our talents. We didn't think much of our tap dancing. In Union City, Hortense Mabry's black patent leather shoes with taps on the bottom and a big black bow on top were so daunting as to have discouraged us from learning more than a basic tap dance shuffle, so we crossed tap dancing off the list.

We had high hopes, however, for our singing and recitation talents. In P.S. 86, everybody (speech clinician an exception) seemed to be moved in some deep way by Ruth's and my southern accents, and we were constantly being asked to "say" things and to tell (the same) jokes over and over. So wouldn't recitations be well received? My brother Will was not so sure: he thought our singing might pass muster, but he thought maybe "recitation" was just a Tennessee thing. "I don't think New York people are going to pay to watch you two ninnies stand up there and fling your arms about," he would say to us, "while you quote things you don't even understand." What? Didn't he know our southern accents were intriguing to others? Didn't he know we were celebrities? In the end, we ignored Will and convinced ourselves that our accents were irresistible.

We turned out to be right. Ruth and I used our accents in any possible capacity, drawing out words until they begged for mercy, and, in an added feature, infused our songs with what we thought was a proper mood. We sang "Yes, sir, that's my baby; no, sir, I don't mean maybe . . ." with such pep we quickly ran out of breath, and we cupped our hands behind our ears to listen for the "ting-a-ling" when we sang "All alone by the telephone, waiting for a ting-a-ling," doing all this with such a melancholy air we might be suffering from a bad case of lumbago. Recitations consisted of excerpts from Longfellow's "The Song of Hiawatha" ("On the Mountains of the Prairie / On the great Red Pipe-stone Quarry / Itche Manito, the mighty / He the Master of Life, descending . . ."). We sang and we recited, and we almost always took home the prize, more often than not a dollar bill.

We passed on the dance marathons. Although this event required no talent, just an ability to keep your feet moving, we suspected that my mother would not approve, and she didn't. We were at any rate too young to qualify, so we didn't argue with her, just settled in to nag her to allow us to watch one. We had heard that our next door neighbor, Max Needleman, an "out-of-work vet," which was a phrase very much in use, had entered, and though my mother was distressed and said, "Such a nice man. And he's going to have to dance 'til he goes crazy," she parted with two nickels and let us attend the thing.

What we saw was Max looking nothing like the Max we knew, the teasing, joking Max who lived next door. Was that our Max shuffling and stumbling around? Was that our Max holding his partner up so the judges wouldn't come over and tap them on the shoulder and motion to them to get off the floor because they had failed to stay upright? Was that our Max looking at us but showing no sign that he recognized us? After a very short while there was no fun in it at all, and Ruth and I were very glad when Mrs. Needleman came to take her son home.

The marathon had been an excruciating sight, so awful that when we described it to my mother, she burst into tears. It's true that my mother cried easily, but crying over Max Needleman was, to my father, completely appropriate. He did not himself burst into tears over Max, but he had plenty to say. "It's an insult," he cried out to us in one of his outrages. "It's an insult a veteran should go through such a thing. And so what happens if we should have another war? Is this what the veterans will have to do after *that* war?" When somebody might remind him that the last war was being called "the war to end all wars," my father would say, "Don't count on it."

SOME VERY DEPRESSING DEPRESSION STORIES

During our first semester in school, our need for heavier winter coats became plain. In New York as in Union City once the Depression had taken over, any purchase of new clothes had first to submit itself to a family discussion. So after we agreed that we Kaufman children absolutely, positively had to have winter coats heavier than the ones we had brought from Union City, my mother took Ruth and me downtown, to Fourteenth Street, to S. Klein on the Square, which we had learned was the go-to emporium for bargains. As the savant of all things wearable, my father went with us.

Immediately after we got off the subway, a picture of big-city–style Depression came to life. It was in the little realities, and the little realities were not only everywhere, they were startling. One of the realities was that it was a Saturday and children were on the streets, but were they skipping rope or hopping around on a chalked sidewalk? No, they were not: they were intent on serious matters, like bringing home some money. Paper bags in hand, they were running from one passerby to the other, proffering the bag and pleading for a handout. "I haven't eaten today," one might say. Or, "I need it for my little brother. Mama says he needs some milk."

My mother was stopped in her tracks. I pulled at her hand, urging her onward—toward S. Klein and my new coat. She remained motionless, her face caught in a look of surprise as if she were trying to make sense of something that defied making sense. How could this be? How could children be out on the street *begging?* That children should have to plead—"to go on living," she would say—was to her inconceivable, the most dreadful sight the Depression had yet visited on her, worse even than Max Needleman and the dance marathon.

In a moment my mother was overwhelmed, and she struggled to stay on her feet. I had seen her sad, angry, frustrated, but I had never seen her like this. It was as if she didn't know what to feel or what to think. She was just standing, letting my father hold her, and her head was in her hands. Was she going to cry? Oh, Mama, please don't cry in the street! While I tried to look away, my father was saying to her, "Cry, Rebecca. Cry if you want to."

It turned out that she was now beyond crying. She was seeking an answer. And I had no doubt what she was seeking an answer *to*—how to help these children. But what did she have to help them with? Well, she had the money my father had given her to buy our coats. And weren't we on our way to S. Klein to buy them? Well, yes, we were, but that was before these children had come into her day. What to do? My father said nothing to her, letting her know in this way that it was her decision. And finally, I saw that my mother had made up her mind. She knew exactly what she had to do.

What she had to do was march us to the used clothing store she had noticed near S. Klein. There, at that store, she said, were perfectly good coats and there we would buy them. My father, she explained to us, would look them over to make sure they were of good quality and had been cleaned, and we would buy one for Ruth and one for me. Oh, Mama, from the used clothing store? Yes, from the used clothing store. "You'll see," my mother said. "You'll be glad later what you did." In our despair, Ruth and I turned to my father, but he gave no indication that he was going to get involved. It was my mother's decision, and we all knew it. In a moment, we had walked to the store, and in another moment, we had bought two coats.

My mother then set to figuring: she would have paid approximately that much at S. Klein and she had paid this much at the used clothing store, and having arrived at a differential, she asked the clerk to convert the differential into an assortment of change, which she then divided, putting some of the money in Ruth's pocket and some in mine. Ruth and I may not have liked having used coats instead of new ones, may even have *despised* it, but we knew that at this moment we could not nag, argue, or plead. And so it was that when we left the store and went into the street, every paper bag held out to us received a nickel, sometimes a dime, and occasionally a quarter.

It was also around S. Klein that I saw the men. There they were, in clusters on the street corners looking aimlessly around, or standing behind wooden crates selling apples at five cents each. There they were seeking food on the "breadlines," as they were called, which stretched not just down the street but around the block. There was also the lone man at the corner yelling at passersby, and when I made us stop so I could listen, what I heard was, "I fought for you. Why didn't you fight for me?"

This man was obviously a doughboy. Even if he had said nothing, I could have spotted him as a vet from the overcoat he was wearing—one of those service-issued garments we all knew so well and made such fun of. The coats were not only of a particularly cheerless olive drab but also so ponderous that the jokes wrote themselves. "Put one on and you got your tent right there," the veterans said.

I knew the coats because my father had a few in our Tennessee store, come to him by way of veterans bartering for something more useful. My father had agreed to the barter, even though he knew he couldn't sell the coats. Tennessee's winters were cold but not severe, and even though my father had put the price down to the ground, nobody wanted the ungainly things. "Maybe some farmer needs an extra barn," my father would joke. In the end, he and I and the overcoats went out in our wagon to where the black people lived, our horse Willy leading the way, and we handed them out to anybody who would take them. I noticed that our cook, Willie Arnold, whose house I visited often, had laid one out—sleeves removed, buttons dispensed with—to serve as the rug in her little front room.

On the New York street as I watched the men on the breadline, I fantasized who they might have been before the Depression had hit us. In the main, they were not wearing old service uniforms: they were wearing the typical suit, coat, tie, and fedora of the businessman. According to my father, many of the men in their now shapeless suits, unsmiling under their rumpled brimmed hats, had been Wall Street "big shots" or at least had held jobs in some big business or corporation. To me they were celebrities; they were the businessmen we had read so much about, the ones whose fall in fortune had signaled the arrival of the Depression.

As the men moved up to the distribution table, I wondered what was being handed out. Their queue may have been called a breadline, but were the men actually getting just bread, and could they get by on just bread? Furthermore, who was feeding the family at home? When I asked my mother, she explained that they were getting a baloney sandwich and a bowl of soup. "And then tomorrow they look for work, and they don't find it, and they come back," she said, her dark eyes moistening. "They don't know from nothing but breadlines."

How, I wondered, did the men manage it? Did they drink the soup and then bring the sandwich home and divide it up among the wife and children? Surely they would have liked to bring the soup home too. It was something to think about on the subway back to the Bronx, and I concluded that however the men on the breadline worked this out, it was not going to make them happy.

THE DEPRESSION SHOWS ITS OTHER NEW YORK SIDE

As I found out, however, New York was not all Great Depression and poverty. In particular midtown neighborhoods, I saw few signs of bad times. Those tall mansions that lined the streets, "brownstones" I learned they were called, often had long black limousines at the curb, along with a uniformed chauffeur leaning on a fender. When my mother expressed shock that these private homes had no backyards and therefore no gardens, my father said, "Don't be silly, Rebecca. They want nature, they call out the chauffeur and he takes them to their second home in the country." Chauffeur? Second home in the country? During the Depression such things still existed? It was a revelation. I could only think that in New York, the Great Depression had occasionally pulled its punches.

Well, I thought, channeling my inner need to find a silver lining, at least all this high living was providing jobs for chauffeurs. Chauffeuring was in fact, as my father informed me, a profession much in demand because there were so few New Yorkers who could qualify. "Up here, they don't drive," he would say. "Why should they drive when they got all these subways and buses?" Could this be true? In Union City after cars and trucks came to us, every man, and every boy able to see over the steering wheel, drove trucks to market; and when Will at the age of twelve drove my father to the wholesale houses in St. Louis, nobody in town thought it was anything to get hot and bothered about. So when my father asked me, "You know anybody in New York who drives?" I had to admit that I knew only one, an uncle whose junk business demanded a truck. At this point, my father was no doubt having memories of our Studebaker, the Big Six Tourer model that had been the talk of the town. He had told often the story of our local banker, Charley Miles, who stood observing it as it sat in front of the store, and who finally said, "I swan, M.A., if Union City 'twas on the Mississip', you could sail this thing clear down to Orleens."

And so, ever concerned about Will's future in that snobby field of engineering and even though Will was now working in the taxi repair shop, I asked my father if all else failed, couldn't Will maybe become a chauffeur? To which my father gave no real answer, just a sigh.

4

World War I Redux

THE DOUGHBOYS ARE IN WASHINGTON

It was 1932, and we had been in New York just over a year when the veterans of World War I came in great numbers to Washington, D.C., for a big event the newspapers were calling the Bonus March, and whose purpose was to petition for promised bonuses. Though it was true that the bonuses had not been promised for delivery until 1945, these men, out of work like everyone else, desperate like everyone else, had concluded that those bonuses would never be more needed than they were now, so now was when they wanted them. As my father explained to ten-year-old me, the situation was like my weekly nickel allowance, which was awarded to me on Saturdays: "Let's say you're dying of thirst on a Wednesday," he explained, "and you could be saved by a dope [what in Union City we called a Coca-Cola when we weren't calling it a "Co-cola"], wouldn't I be mean not to advance your allowance?" And when I agreed that he would be *very* mean, he said, "So what these men need is an advance on their bonus. They need a lifesaver."

My father was not a veteran, having been given a deferment like all other fathers with children under twelve, but he was as ardent a patriot as could be found. And on Hoover and his response to the Bonus Marchers—Hoover's response was, largely, to ignore them—my father was unusually outdone and outspoken, and he would say, "The man's the boss, for crying out loud. What boss don't look out for his customers?"

To this ardent patriot, the reception in Washington was a slap in the face to America's noblest. What the veterans were demanding seemed to my father fair enough, and he would ask, "Since when is petitioning for a bill to advance their bonuses such a terrible thing?"

My mother too felt that the "doughboys," or as she called them in her way, the "dogboys," were being treated badly, and she offered "*Oy*, that terrible man," meaning Herbert Hoover. It had none of my father's zing, but we had long accepted that minimal comments, softly articulated, were the best she could do. It really didn't matter, because her sentiments, however stated, always echoed my father's, except, notably, the times when her two imperatives came charging out.

Newsreels now led off with the story of the veterans and their takeover of Washington and how more than seventeen thousand veterans of the Great War had marched into the capital. Newspapers were full of the story as well, and we were shown scenes of veterans setting up housing as near to the Capitol building as possible—in the Mall, in the parks, and along the river. At the movies, as Ruth and I sat looking at their shelters—tents, abandoned automobiles, flimsy wood constructions laid over with thatch and scrap tin rescued from nearby junk piles—I would think that Peaches, the horse owned by my friend Doris, lived better than these veterans did.

Some of the veterans brought along their wives and children, and while Congress carried on its deliberations, the wives tried to create a semblance of a home by hanging up rags of some sort over holes in the "walls" and putting up men's pants to act as a front door. And they grew things. Newsreels showed women planting seeds right there in the Mall sward, the children helping in a sort of listless way, as if they would rather be anywhere than in Washington, D.C. We wondered if the veterans would be there long enough for the plants to mature, and we definitely hoped they wouldn't. We wanted their bonuses to be awarded, and soon.

Because of the strong focus of the newsreels and newspapers, we felt we were watching the very lives of the Bonus Marchers. We saw the men standing around in clusters as they waited, and we saw them impatiently moving around the city, talking among themselves, no doubt reinforcing each other in the hope that the march—in effect, an occupation of Washington, D.C.—would pay off. And as they waited, we waited with them.

Hip, hip, hooray! The House passed it—passed the bill! Newspapers gave the news their biggest, blackest headlines; newsreels showed men laughing and patting each other on the back. But wait. Hold on. Were we jumping the gun? Didn't the Senate have to confirm? I recalled the first lessons in government given to me by my father when he advised me to put my faith in the House of Representatives and not in the Senate because the House, my father said, rather vaguely, was "more dependable." And in the end just as he—and I—had feared, the Senate said no, it didn't think so. The bill was dead and, as far as my father and I were concerned, it was a most ignoble death.

THE DEATH MARCH

If it was a hard blow to those who had followed it all, it was a terrible one to the veterans, and we wondered what they would do now. Would they fold up their tents—um, their scruffy dwellings—and silently slip away? No, it appeared they would not. The newsreels now began to show us the veterans of the Great War raising their fists and vowing to fight on. The battleground for the continuing fight would be the one they had already staked out—Washington, D.C.

The papers called this newest development a "death march," and Ruth and I shivered when we heard the term. March 'til they died? Just go 'round and 'round Washington 'til there was no breath left in them at all? "No," my father said, "they won't die. They'll do what they did in France— just keep fighting until they win."

Reality, however, trumped my father's optimism. The veterans may have kept fighting, but there was no winning: great umbrage was taken by President Herbert Hoover—"Mister High and Mightyness," Willie Arnold would have called him, as she called all important people who thought they were just *so* important—and he ordered the veterans to go home. Go home? It was a puzzler. I knew from my exchanges with the men who came to our back door that many had no homes to return to—at least no homes where they could find a job. So where would they go? To improvised camps along railroad tracks? To a tent in a park in some other town?

While talking about all this with Jack, I was surprised to learn that his Uncle Frank had been among the marchers. His uncle had a very sad, but undoubtedly not unique, story: he had served in France and though he came home unscathed, he had later died of the influenza he had contracted in the mud of the trenches. So why submit himself to this new ordeal? "He was used to battles," Jack explained to me, "and he didn't want to be left out of this one."

The march in Washington went on, and the newsreels recorded as much as they could. We saw reporters asking the marchers what their response was to the get-out-of-town order, and we saw how the men cupped their hands to their ears as if they were hard of hearing and couldn't be expected to have heard what Hoover had said. To which my father said, "A good time for the boys to go deaf."

The implication clearly was that they would go on with the march. It was an implication that apparently did not sit well with President Hoover, and pretty soon Mister High and Mightyness had ordered the military to physically evict the marchers. And now the newsreels showed military troops, guns drawn, herding marchers out of town and smashing the shelters into rubble. And, my father reported in one of his outrages, some of his acquaintances had said, "What can you expect? After all, they were just looking for a handout."

My father clearly had quite a different take on things. Troops called out to harass and punish the veterans? "Can you beat it?" he would cry when the papers showed the pictures. "These boys fought over there, and their buddies died over there, and now the generals are running after them with sticks." My mother would hold her head and say, "It's a *shonda!*" It was a shame beyond all other shames. And for me, it was hard to believe that these soldiers who had been so hailed and so respected were now so dishonored.

MACARTHUR, EISENHOWER, AND PATTON

Then would come the invoking by my father of the names of officers charged with the task of running the veterans out, which, as I understood it, were a general named MacArthur and two officers my father called "his henchmen" named Eisenhower and Patton. "What kind of guys are these?" my father would shout at us from behind his rattling newspaper as he sat at the breakfast table. "Big shots on their horses showing off their fancy uniforms." Shoving the paper at the rest of us at the table (not at my mother; my mother didn't sit, only hovered), he would say, "Look at this, children. Look what's happening. Who could believe this?"

If I didn't understand the issues down to the last comma, I understood the pictures. What I saw were smartly dressed military men looking impatient and eager as they went about their jobs. And the look of the men in shapeless, years-old clothes? No longer was there the anger we had seen as they roamed around Washington. Now, faced as they were with a rearing horse and a thrusting baton, the look was one of surrender.

I was not the only one perplexed about Hoover's directives. Mixed opinions filled the newspapers. Some editorials shouted my mother's "For shame!" at the administration, while others thought the veterans were at fault and should have packed up and gone home, thus saving themselves the indignity of being chased out. "Not the way for Americans to ask for things," was the gist of what those editorials said. To which my father would respond, his voice at its most aggrieved, "No, they should have written the president a letter on fancy stationery."

If the Bonus March had brought a new and painful dimension to our national nightmare, it also brought a new and painful dimension to my father's rage at the current Republican administration. He had one comfort: the Democratic Party convention was coming up in a few weeks, and he clung to the hope that the Democratic nominee would boot Republicans back to where they came from, which in his view was three-story mansions on four-acre properties.

My father did not relent in his attacks on President Hoover. If some argued that there was good in Hoover, that he had been a respected engineer who had contributed much in the Great War, that he was trying his best, my father would say, "Well, his best's not good enough. Don't we have somebody who knows his beans from his turnips?" To which he would add, in a spluttering of outrage, "That Hoover. What did we do to deserve him?"

5

Roosevelt Is in, and So Are the New Deal and Fireside Chats

When, in 1932, Franklin Delano Roosevelt was chosen as the Democratic candidate for president, when at the convention he said, "I pledge you, I pledge myself, to a new deal for the American people," my father fairly leaped into his corner. And then, with no RomanCatholics to muddy the waters, the South returned to its traditional Democratic place and Roosevelt defeated Hoover in the November general election, the family grew ecstatic, and in our apartment in the Bronx, Roosevelt's campaign song, "Happy Days Are Here Again," rang out loudly and often. Although we all, including ten-year-old me, sang it knowing that "happy days" were *not* here again, could not magically be here again in the instant after an election, we were optimistic. "Now that we got Roosevelt," my father would say, "you'll see some action," always adding, "Now that's a President. Now that's a *mensch,*" which meant that Roosevelt was a man who knew his duty and would do it. And in those Depression days, a man in high position doing his duty meant a man who would do his level best to lift the economy out of its deep hole.

Roosevelt apparently knew his duty so well that on the day after he took office in March 1933, on the day after his inaugural address in which he said "the only thing we have to fear is fear itself," he declared what the papers were calling a bank holiday. For four days the nation's banks were closed, and all financial transactions were stopped. Even as I was disappointed that it was not a usual "holiday" when my school would not be open, my father was delighted. "So what did I tell you?" he said to us. "He's doing what needs to be done." And indeed, even I understood that the bank holiday not only stopped the run on banks but it also gave Roosevelt time to get Congress to give him some control of them. And only three short days later, nearly a thousand banks were up and running again.

FIRESIDE CHATS

A week or so afterward, Jack and his family were, as I learned, gathering in his Bronx apartment at the exact same moment that we were gathering in *our* Bronx apartment. I don't exactly know what kind of radio the Subermans were gathering around, but we were around our Atwater Kent. Both families, however, were listening to the same thing—what our president was calling a "fireside chat." And so simple was Roosevelt's language that we not only listened, we learned. Roosevelt talked about how well everybody had accepted the bank holiday, explained its necessity, and we nodded in understanding.

After the "chat" was over, my mother said, "What do I know from banks? What did I know from the innies and outies of banks? But Roosevelt knows, and so now I know." Jack said that after the "chat," even his father, a victim emotionally and physically of the Depression, felt a sense of comfort. "A very little sense," Jack said to me. "Like he made a foul shot with his opponent twenty-five points ahead."

Through the coming years, we would hear thirty fireside chats, and they would range from such specific issues as drought conditions, loan drives, and judiciary reorganization, and—after December 7, 1941—to such sweeping ones as the rationale for the declaration of war on Japan and the responsibilities on the home front. We always listened and we always learned. My father would say as we gathered before the Atwater Kent, "Let's hear, children. He's not talking just to hear himself talk."

Soon after the first fireside chat, a second one brought us to the Atwater Kent, and it was on that night that we heard the outline of what Roosevelt called his "new deal," a term capitalized in the papers as a more formidable "New Deal," and we heard some details of his plans for putting it into place. Roosevelt had earlier said he was going to keep us informed of what he was doing, and these fireside chats were apparently his way of doing it. When we heard the one specifically about the Civilian Conservation Corps, a project charged with maintaining and restoring forests, beaches, and parks, my mother, ever like my father a strong Roosevelt booster, and ever the loving gardener, afterward said, "It's good for the men, and it's good for the nature."

We hoped, hoped, hoped that there would be more projects to come. We hoped that this man with the confident grin, the one with the hat brim turned up to expose a demeanor cheerful and optimistic, the one with the cigarette holder pointing jauntily to the sky—we hoped that this man could find us a way back to who we used to be. But in the early Roosevelt period, in the time before World War II, in the darkest days of the Depression, what we wanted to hear him say, *longed* to hear him say, was that the Depression was over and that on the morrow we would look in the mirror and there would be our old selves, our summer of 1929 selves. But it was a long time before it was said. And it was not actually he who said it; it was quite another man.

THE VETERANS MAKE NOISES AGAIN

We heard again about the veterans in March 1933 as we were preparing to leave New York. What we heard was that they were again threatening a march on Washington. Once more a Bonus March? No, President Roosevelt defused the march by supporting the men in their protest and by promising that he would never direct military action against them. It sounded good, as if Roosevelt was ready to make things right. I felt sure that the man who so understood America's woes, the man who was striving in every way to put the chicken in every pot that Hoover had promised (and never delivered) would finally approve the bonuses. "Just a swipe of your pen, Mr. President," I pleaded in my head, feeling confident that we would soon hear that the swipe had been made.

The swipe never came. The president may have been Franklin Roosevelt, and Franklin Roosevelt may have been a Democrat, and Franklin Roosevelt may have been compassion itself, but he did not give in to the veterans' wishes. In his statement of refusal, he said that all of the Depression's victims, not just the veterans, had to be considered. My father, still showing confidence, would say, "Don't worry; he'll find something." And down the road, after we had left New York, Roosevelt did find something, and it seemed to be the perfect answer. Well, it seemed that way at first.

A VERY SPECIAL MOVIE

In New York, we followed our old custom of going to the movies once a week, and they were still offering the same Depression fare, though going to the movies in New York offered something extra: when you bought a ticket, they gave you things. You got free dishes, free picture frames, sometimes free loaves of bread. We forked over our dimes, however, only when the "something extra" was something we couldn't live without, like a package of cupcakes or a shiny bracelet acting like it was silver, a bracelet decidedly puttin' on.

Movies were now extending their escapist fare to elaborate musicals, usually brought to us by Busby Berkeley, and we knew what to expect— movies light as a balloon, frothy as a vanilla flip, and teeming with girls, girls, girls. The girls didn't so much dance as perform, usually in large-writ geometric and kaleidoscopic configurations, or they cartwheeled around as spokes on mammoth bicycles, or, dressed in black or white, they acted as keys on an outsized piano. And oh, that time when they were giant jigsaw puzzle pieces arranging themselves into the face of Ruby Keeler! Oh, Doris, I vow and declare it was the best thing ever!

If the Busby Berkeley movies were spectacular, they were also, as Miss Bookie might have said, spectacularly mindless. Still, mindless or not, they served a purpose beyond providing the drabness with a flash of glamour. In some important way these rigidly designed spectacles spoke to our need for order in our world of chaos. This had to be the case. Otherwise, why were we so eager, nay *compelled*, to see them?

Well, one reason might have been that they were providing jobs and we felt the need to support the effort. I for one definitely took to heart that the girls had paychecks. Still, as this thought comforted, I had the counter- thought—that for every hundred or so employed Berkeley girls a sole man might be so lucky. Men in a Busby Berkeley movie were a postscript. I had to believe that even in Hollywood, veterans were out of luck.

Considering that movies exploited any possibility, it was only a mat- ter of time before they would get to the story of the Bonus March and the Bonus Army. We had many a reminder in song and story of the plight of the World War I veterans, and most families, including my own, had the record in which Bing Crosby was a doughboy singing to the world that he and his buddies were "once in khaki suits, full of that Yankee doodle-dee-dum" and were now on the streets with their hands out, asking, "Brother, can you spare a dime?" Still, movies seemed to have avoided this very dreary story. Movies about the Great War itself, yes. Movies about our luckless veterans, no.

And then all at once the movies took a stab at it. The way they did it, however—the way they handled the bonus story—confounded us: could it be that a Busby Berkeley musical was going dark, was being serious? It turned out that it was. The serious moment was in a Busby Berkeley movie called *Gold Diggers of 1933*, and it was serious as all get out.

Of course, we kids couldn't wait for Saturday so we could put our dimes on the marble slab of the box office window and settle in to watch the latest offering from this master of "forget your troubles and just be happy." Another Busby Berkeley movie, another escape into dazzling lights and breathtaking spectacle, another moment to sit back in our seats in happy anticipation. We relaxed as the opening sequences of *Gold Diggers of 1933* ran true to Busby Berkeley form. Ginger Rogers sang "We're in the Money" in pig latin, and girls costumed as huge golden discs representing dollars moved around her. I for one was dutifully mesmerized by the Ginger Rogers number even though, young as I was, I was hard-times savvy and knew that we were not in the "oney-may," and I knew that the "epression-day" was still very much with us.

A little more dancing and frothy chatter, and then—*what?*—the Busby Berkeley girls were no more and the light on the screen had dimmed. It was a new look, a new mood, and I was startled by the change. It seemed that *Gold Diggers of 1933* had something different in mind, and Ginger Rogers and her fluency in pig latin were not it. The new look was still built around a musical number, but how different it was: no flashy ladies at all. Just men in their Great War uniforms marching across a fitfully shadowed screen, and down-on-their luck veterans on a sidewalk passed out from drink. And all the while Joan Blondell (not the sassy Joan Blondell we were used to, but a forlorn, somber one) was singing "Remember My Forgotten Man."

At first, seeing what appeared to be hundreds of men on the screen, I wanted to be thrilled that men were finally getting their share of Hollywood jobs. And that indeed was the small message. But the larger one was that these marching men represented all the veterans who had come home from fighting a war and who, once home, had been obliged to fight another. It was a war, my father would have said, that they were fighting not with their blood but with their souls. "Their blood they left in France," he would have said, "and now this is what's happened to their souls."

When Ruth and I went home after the movie, after we tried out a little pig latin, we put on overseas caps from Will's collection of war mementoes and pulled broomsticks out of the closet to act as rifles, and we marched around. As we marched, we sang as much as we could remember of the "forgotten man" song, and I wondered if Doris and the other kids in Union City had been stirred to do what we were doing. What I could not know was that at that moment most every kid in the country was engaged in imitating that marching, singing platoon of men.

Although we had all sung the Bing Crosby song, it had been hard to work in "Brother, can you spare a dime?" into everyday conversation. But "forgotten man"? That was easy. So easy was it that it soon became shorthand for the entire concept of a veteran who had returned home to a country of short memory. No more fumbling and fiddling for a full description. We all knew what "forgotten man" implied. When Jack and I talked it over, he said, "It was a movie that gave us an easy way to say something hard."

6

So Long, Sidewalks of New York; Hello, Moon over Miami

From the moment we arrived in New York, my father had begun plotting an escape. After investing in the taxi repair company, he had almost immediately *di*-vested, and though the venture didn't lose him any money, it didn't make him any either. Was Will, I wondered, now going to be a chauffeur? No, he was going to take a job with an uncle in the construction business and get paid five dollars a week.

My father spoke often—sometimes only in mutterings to himself—of how much he missed the courtly air of the South. "I'll be derned if I can find anything good about New York," he would say, to nobody's surprise. "It's just a bunch of noise and insults." Nothing was to his liking. He would never get used to New York, he would say, even if he lived longer than his grandfather, who, we had all been told, died at the age of ninety-six. Of course no one could ever be sure of his grandfather's age because births were seldom recorded, certainly not in Russia on behalf of Jews, but everybody agreed that past ninety and near one hundred was about right.

I worried. If we left New York, where would we go? And when we got there, what would my father do for a business? I soon learned that my father wouldn't answer our questions, that he would just go on with what he was doing, which was studying up on United States geography. To my surprise, I noticed that Florida—not Tennessee—had suddenly begun to shine a light his way. His thought apparently was that he knew all about Tennessee and its opportunities and what he knew was discouraging, so maybe Florida had something up its sleeve? The truth was that my father had never gotten Florida out of his mind. Though he knew that the land boom had finally gone bust, he didn't forget what knowledgeable people had said about Florida—that it was the place of the future, the place to put your money. It was something he liked the sound of.

If my father was ready to pull up stakes, my mother had yet to be convinced. Her second imperative—that her daughters marry Jewish boys—had not been fulfilled. Ruth and I were not yet of marriageable age, but Minna was, and my mother's imperative was kicking up a storm. Minna had gotten a lot of attention from New York Jewish boys and had, like Ruth and me, been asked to "say" things in her southern accent, and the boys had flirted with her. Moreover, having perfected the art in the way of all Union City girls, she had flirted right back. But flirting was not proposing marriage, and proposing marriage was off the table with these boys because proposing marriage meant you could afford a wife and none of them could. And because this was how Minna's prospects for marriage seemed to be playing out, my mother finally agreed to listen to my father's plea to leave New York. But only if he listened first to *her*.

My mother didn't want to go to a town where Jews "stuck out like sore thumbs," she told my father. "Didn't I have to teach them," she asked, "that we didn't have horns or humps on our backs?" And she might have added, "or Christian babies on our tables?" She agreed that she had eventually been happy in Union City, but "eventually" was her operative word, for she remembered that she had experienced a lot of discouraging moments before happiness had been achieved. "I don't want to start out like I did then," she said to my father. "I don't want to have to teach nobody not to be afraid of us."

To convince my mother that Florida was a Jew-friendly place, my father brought to her attention the fact that Florida's governor at the time was named Dave Sholtz, and wasn't "Sholtz" a Jewish name, Rebecca? And, "Rebecca, listen to this: Dave Sholtz is from Brooklyn!" Okay, Governor Sholtz never said he was Jewish and he had been living not in the Jewish mother lode in Miami / Miami Beach but in Daytona Beach, and he was married to an obvious *shiksa* named Alice May Agee, but did that make him not Jewish? Whatever the truth, Governor Sholtz was definitely a Democrat and a governor who busied himself putting Roosevelt's New Deal programs to work, so wasn't he "aces"? It was an incidental plus, but a plus nevertheless.

Because my father knew he needed all the plusses he could get, he kept trying. From what he had heard, he told my mother, Miami Beach was not only full of Jews, it had only one industry—tourism, and "Listen to this, Rebecca," my father said to her, pausing for a triumphant revelation. "The tourists are all Jews!" Well, this was not quite true; as we found out, the tourists were not *all* Jews, but there was, as we would have said in Union City, "a gracious plenty" of them. And so, my father wanted to know, couldn't my mother see herself in such a place?

My mother finally decided that yes, she could see herself in such a place. Even when her sister Molly—the one my father called "the shop boss"—told her she was *meshuggeh* to go back to the South, crazy to go back to living with "yokels," my mother had a different view. She thought that although my father might have exaggerated the number of Jews in the town, surely there would be enough of them that she wouldn't have to teach them what was what about Jewish people.

And so very soon it was goodbye to the sidewalks of New York (where, despite my best efforts, I had never learned to trip that "light fantastic" because I could never find out what it was), and hello to the moon over Miami. And hello down the road to meeting Jack and that instant spark that stayed lit forever.

Of course leaving New York before the apartment lease was up presented a problem, but so great was my father's need to flee that he was willing to sacrifice the deposit. My mother did a "tch-tch" over the idea of handing money to a landlord who hadn't earned it, and she would say, "You don't give away money in times like these." Never mind. My father said a business deal was a business deal and off we went, leaving the deposit behind us.

CROSSING THE MASON-DIXON LINE

We had left Will in New York at his five dollar a week job, so he was not with us on the train that took us from New York to Miami, a trip that was tiresome and dusty but not without its interesting moments. Unlike in Tennessee, blacks had been on the train with us, but as I was now schooled in New York City transport ways, I knew that you did not call the cops if a black person sat down next to you.

When we crossed into Washington, D.C., however, I felt I was back in Tennessee. Black people were suddenly being singled out by the conductor and being issued orders. And no-nonsense orders they were: all Negro passengers were to get up from their seats, gather their suitcases and packages, and proceed immediately to a back car. Looking around at the questioning faces of the passengers—if they were questioning, there were no doubt northerners—the conductor explained, unhelpfully, "We're in Washington," and went on his way. What the conductor had left out, of course, was that when we got to Washington, we had crossed the Mason-Dixon Line and were into that part of the South where blacks and whites were required to be segregated under the so-called Jim Crow laws that had been in force since they were enacted late in the nineteenth century. In Union City, we had no need for such laws: we knew that blacks and whites weren't supposed to mix, and no one had to quote laws to tell us that. Actually, the only question I had about the incident was whether Washington was really in the South. Nothing else about it bothered me. Obviously, my RSB (Reformed Southern Bigot) credentials had not yet arrived.

* * *

Miami immediately showed us its tropical (well, subtropical) side in its stuccoed train station the color of the pink sweet william in my mother's garden. Despite that we were as tired as our old horse Willie after a trek to the Obion County fair, my father was ecstatic. And full of instructions. "Breathe in!" he cried out to us. "Deep breaths all around! Feel the air! Oy, like silk!" When my mother let herself "breathe in," she said it was like a baby's kiss, and I set myself to remembering "my" baby across the street in Union City, whose mother had insisted he was partly mine because I had attended his christening—his sprinkling—at the First Methodist Church. And yes, after the often acrid air of New York City, Miami's air was a definite improvement.

While we milled around the station, my father found us a jitney, a sort of taxi that limited its runs to the causeway between Miami and Miami Beach. Because jitneys had jumpseats, they were meant for seven passengers, but we were five people with a lot of stuff, so my father hired it exclusively for us, and though this was not normally what jitneys did, the driver took us directly to our destination, which was a rented apartment on the ocean. "You're getting special service," the driver said to us. "I want your first day should be nice, should be *gemutlich.*" And my father nudged my mother with an elbow as if to say, "What did I tell you? Didn't I tell you to expect Jewish people?"

My father arranged with the driver to pick us up the next day to show us the town. Sight-unseen, Miami Beach was already to my father a "tropical paradise," a phrase he had no doubt picked up from one of his brochures. The next day, however, we were introduced to a city that may have been tropical (er, subtropical) but definitely not a paradise.

The driver was not only Jewish but an old-timer who liked to talk Florida history, and the sightseeing started well. We had a lot to learn, and the driver had a lot of material. About the presence of Jews, he assured us that Miami Beach would not disappoint us. "You can forget about Jacksonville," he said, as if we had been stubbornly remembering that city, and he went on to inform us that Jacksonville had been home to the early settlements of whatever Florida Jews there were—and, we were told, Jews had been in Florida since the eighteenth century—but now, he insisted, Miami/Miami Beach had all other towns beat and we should forget about Jacksonville. Okay, we forgot about Jacksonville. But forget about the beauties of Miami Beach? Not my father. Indeed, as we drove up Ocean Drive, he grew more and more ebullient. The ocean! The palm trees! The grass thick like a rug! "Did I lie?" he kept saying. "Didn't I tell you to expect beautiful?"

OH, THOSE SIGNS

Well, yes, he had told us. But he hadn't told us everything. He hadn't told us about the signs. And when we switched over to Collins Avenue and got north of Lincoln Road, there they were—signs big and little, signs in black, signs in color. Signs that said "Jews Not Welcome," signs that said "No Jews Allowed," signs that said "No Dogs or Jews Allowed."

My mother was as if struck by a lightning bolt. "Whoever heard?" she cried, grabbing at my father. "You said a Jewish town! What kind of a Jewish town is this?" As more and more signs came into view, her cries grew ever more frantic. "Even in Union City you wouldn't see nothing like this!" And it was true: in Union City, you wouldn't see nothing like this.

My father was nonplussed, but he kept his head. "Wait," he kept saying. "Wait. It's just some of the hotels, not all." And, as the driver rushed us back down to South Beach, it was true that the signs disappeared, even if the shock of them had not. My father was confused not only by the messages of the signs but by the utter lack of business savvy they revealed. They went against every business principle he had ever understood, and he asked himself, "With such a big interest in Jewish tourism, the town allows such signs?"

When he thought about it later, he understood that a business principle was indeed operating. If some Miami Beach tourists wanted Jew-free hotels, someone would provide them. So even if the practice confounded a moral principle, it fitted nicely into the principle of the niche market. My father tried to understand this: that in the Depression, no matter how small the market, no matter how distasteful, it was to be nurtured. In those hard times, in other words, allowances were made: it was understood that "business is business" and you did what it took. He may have understood this principle, but as he would say, "It sits with me like a piece of bad fish."

STRANGERS IN A STRANGE LAND

When we arrived in Miami Beach in late 1933, my father realized almost immediately that he had made a mistake in thinking that south Florida was the South, and we were soon aware that we were country people set down in a place of sophistication and glamour. In Miami Beach we would not be interacting with farmers and seed merchants, but as Minna tried to explain to us, we would know very different people—"snowbirds," she had heard them called, meaning they came only in the winters. And when I wondered how they lived their lives as part-time residents, Minna said they did a lot of shopping, which cheered me up considerably. But when I expressed the thought that if they did so much shopping, my father might consider opening a store, Minna said to me, "You silly thing, do you think these people shop in a Jew store? Shoot, they only buy their clothes in swanky shops, don't you know anything?" Well, I didn't know the word "swanky." And I wondered if all these people doing all this shopping meant that the Depression didn't come to resort towns. As I was to find out, it most certainly did.

Having detected nothing in my father's behavior to suggest that he was planning another escape, my mother soon said, "Enough with the beach already," and we bought a house. My father did not have a business yet, but we had a house. Whether my mother wanted one because she was longing for a garden or because she wanted to be free of tracked-in sand, she didn't say, but the fact was that she liked that little cottage on Michigan Avenue just shy of Flamingo Park, the city park. The house was between Ninth and Tenth Streets, in the central section of Miami Beach, and it cost $4,000—$400 down, and $35 a month. As for a garden, it was definitely in my mother's plans even if she would have to eschew her temperate zone Tennessee gardenias and camellias in favor of subtropical-zone Florida mangoes and avocadoes and papayas. Actually, she didn't mind too much. "It works out perfect," she said to us. "So nice it is to eat what I grow." Her Depression thrift itch had apparently thus been nicely scratched.

I missed the apartment. Well, I missed its location. From the apartment, Ruth and I could go to the beach every day, and for two girls who had never seen an ocean, having one just outside the door was the stuff of dreams. We learned to swim there, how to swim with and against the waves, and I wrote to Doris, "We go in the ocean every day and it doesn't cost anything. Do you still wade in Irene's pond?" Gosh, was I puttin' on, or what? And then, not wanting to be mean, I'm sure I wrote, "Y'all come on down soon, you hear?"

Because Ruth and I both had my mother's fair skin, she issued warnings about all that beachgoing we were doing. "Stay out of the sun," she would say. "Do you want to have freckles like me?"—freckles being to her the first thing you didn't want to have. Stay out of the sun? She might as well have said, Don't breathe. And to prove the point, Ruth and I went to bed each night in scorched skin festooned with blisters, and awash in calamine lotion.

I missed the apartment also because of the park on nearby Second Street, where I had made friends with the granddaughter of a Communist family, and, no, she didn't teach me the *Communist Manifesto*, she taught me to play tennis on the public asphalt court situated in the park. The family owned the bakery that produced the breads and pastries for the whole town, and as this seemed to be an unthreatening line of work, the town did not judge their politics, only their *challahs* and their *rugelachs*, although I had yet to become a judge of such breads and little cakes. And I didn't care what the family was as long as they weren't Republicans.

Still, a house and garden made my mother happy, and she was made happier still by the fact that the location of the house enabled her to walk to the little synagogue down on Washington Avenue every Saturday morning. Religion—any religion—not being in the air in the Miami Beach of the 1930s, she didn't try to make us go with her. She had gotten the family to live among Jewish people, and that was good enough.

BUSINESSES

After we bought the house, I wanted the next thing we bought to be a business for my father. What I was hoping for, despite Minna's doubt on the subject, was another dry goods store like the one we had on First Street where we had been among Union City's business elite. Sadly for me, it didn't work out that way. When my father decided that yes, he would buy something, it turned out to be Florida real estate. He found a promising strip of property on Twenty-third Street, talked a bank into lending him the down payment, and we suddenly owned a little piece of Florida.

My father planned to build retail stores on the strip, but if I thought he was planning to open a Jew store in one of them, it was my thought, not his. What he was going to do was to rent out all the stores, though he would discover that finding renters during the Depression was not easy. Few prospective renters had capital of their own, and banks were not lending. "Nobody wants to risk anything," my father said, as I listened to every word. Well, I thought, wasn't my father risking something? Wasn't he risking the little sum in the bank and the "play money," as my father called it, that the shoe factory was paying back, and his "carfare" from the sale of the store? I pictured the sums clinging to each other in my father's pocket in the hope of appearing more formidable.

A retail store of his own was never far from my father's thoughts, however, and pretty soon he talked a bank into a loan and bought a drugstore. It had been offered Depression cheap, and my father, trying to convince us that it wasn't much of a risk, said that in hard times a drugstore had advantages over a dry goods one. "Drugstores don't depend on styles sometimes in and sometimes out," he said to us. "And," he added, no doubt remembering the ad in the Union City paper that had left out the "r" in the "Big Shirt Sale" banner, "no advertising in the paper." He reminded us furthermore that a drugstore was more indispensable than a store that sold what was called "soft goods," meaning wearables and domestics. "You can get by without those things in hard times," my father would say, "but who can do without iodine?" Calling our new store a "drugstore," however, was actually a misnomer. It was more of a luncheonette than anything else, and it did not dispense prescription drugs, only patent medicines.

The store was located on Fifth Street, which, depending on your point of reference, either began at the Fifth Street Causeway or ended there, and the area flanking it abounded in cheap hotels. My father took this as a good sign. Hotels meant that those who stayed in them had their meals out, and *cheap* hotels meant that those who stayed in them were not particular about where they ate. "So they eat in a drugstore? So what?" my father said to us. "What do they care who says what about what they do?"

We of course immediately set to talking about what kind of business we could expect in these times in this specific store and in this specific resort town, and we thought that during "the season"—the height of which we had been told was December 15 to March 15—we might expect decent trade. "But don't compare now to then," my father cautioned us. "It stands to reason that the season is not what it used to be." But if this was true, what about *after* the season, during the summer, when tourists thought that if you went to south Florida, so hot would you get, you might burst into flames. So what did we do then for business? What about what we had heard—that during summer months, hotels and shops that catered to the ritzy class were in fact shuttered? We took a little comfort in knowing that as a store of no claim whatsoever to ritziness, in the summers ours would stay open.

My father had discovered that the mainstay of the business was race-track touts who dwelled in the hotels around us, and this was the good news, for there were a lot of these men. Many were veterans of World War I, older men who had given up on finding jobs and had settled on trying for a win at the track. But also among the ranks were men too young to have participated in the guns-and-tanks war but even so were battle-weary veterans of another kind of war, the one called the Depression.

The bad news was that our bread and butter customers were in Miami for the racing season—at Hialeah and Tropical tracks—and would not be around in the summer when the tracks were closed. And when I asked my father (with some feeling of not wanting to hear the answer) who would be trading with us then, he would say, "We'll find customers, don't worry. The rich tourists don't trade with us much anyway." Was that an answer? If it was, I didn't quite get it.

Some employees came with the store, and if we needed to replace them, finding new ones was easy. Men with no special skills and looking for work, usually veterans, roamed Miami Beach streets at all hours, ever on the lookout for a way to earn some cash. My father had immediately put in the window one of those National Recovery Act signs with the blue eagle that said "We Do Our Part," which meant that the store was following Roosevelt's suggestion of limiting work hours to enable hiring more workers, and the result was that we had two shifts of three men each. Still, the veterans' disgust with life showing up in everything they did— some simply drank themselves out their jobs, and I would see them at the beach, or even on the streets, sleeping one off, and although at first I tried to greet them—"Hey, Jimmie. Can I get you a Co-Cola?"—after a while I just walked around them. Business-wise, my father wasn't bothered. If a worker didn't show up, he would shrug and say, "So what? There are plenty, plenty others." But veteran-wise, it was another story.

Despite all the issues pertaining to our new businesses, our interest in the veterans of the Great War had not wavered. When an election—any election—was coming up, my father tried to prevail on anybody within earshot to elect those who had at heart the welfare of veterans, and he directed Ruth and me to send letters to Washington and to the newspapers. In the store, he had displayed small metal collection boxes in which customers could put their change, and he flanked them with tiny American flags and little signs that read, "Give to our boys."

I hoped that veterans themselves would somehow know about our little boxes. To me, they meant something important: they meant that despite how it might appear, some of us remembered. And it was true that though the well-being of veterans stayed on the minds of my family, the subject seemed to have disappeared from the national conversation. We read nothing about veterans; we saw nothing of them in the newsreels.

THE CONSTRUCTION MEN AND THE GARMENT WORKERS

A surprising number of substantial jobs calling for skilled labor were also to be had in Miami Beach. The Miami Beach hotel industry was not going strong, but it was going. Hotels—those aqua, pink, and lemon yellow art deco palaces—seemed ever under construction on Ocean Drive or on Collins Avenue, and tourists, at least those who had resources that could withstand a financial hit, were still coming down and driving over to the racetracks in their Auburns and Cords. So there were construction jobs, and some of the veterans who had worked at them before World War I were working at them again.

Still, the wages of construction workers kept descending, and they were having a tough time. Ours was one of the post-work hangouts the men patronized, and they often pulled up to our store after work in their decades-old Fords and Chevrolets rattling and backfiring away, to settle in for a few beers. After a bit of joshing about the sights available from the beachside hotel in which they were laboring—"Did you see that looker today? The one with the bathing suit painted on? Wow!"—they fell to talking about the usual, about how they could just about "put food on the table," which was, I was learning, an expression in common currency among the Depression-afflicted. Speaking to their frustration, somebody might say, "I've got a good boy coming along. He wants to go to college, and I want to send him. But how do I do that?" And somebody would answer, "You don't."

I knew some things about these men. I knew where they lived and I knew their families. As I had been finding out, Miami Beach was loosely comprised of three groups—people with money; people who directly served people with money; and people like the hotel construction workers who *indirectly* served people with money. The people with money lived in beach-front mansions or in opulent hotels, and a lot of the others, including the construction men, lived in a jam-up of humble rental houses called Smith Cottages way down on South Beach.

Down there also—in Smith Cottages or elsewhere in South Beach—lived retired workers. These were chiefly New York garment industry workers—mostly women and mostly Jewish—who had traditionally inhabited modest apartments below Fifth Street, and the Depression did not keep them from continuing to do so. They paid their rents with their union pensions, and though the pensions had shrunk considerably, so had their apartment rents.

When the construction men came in for their post-work beers, the retired garment workers would often engage them, like it or not, in conversation. The retirees called the men "fellow workers," and they always found a way to steer the conversation around to unions. Like the rest of the South, Miami Beach had no unions to speak of, and the construction workers had no union, and the retirees made it their business to tell them what they were missing. "It's the answer," they would say to the men, and the men would respond with, "Answer to what? We can't even ask the question." The men would then look incredulous and say, "How are you going to argue with the guy who owns you? If you ask for a union, you think he's going to say, 'Go to it, boys'? No, he's going to fire your butt." Still, the former garment workers always had an answer. "So what are you telling us?" they would say. "That you don't have no voice where you work?" After a while the men would leave, some to Smith Cottages, some to a room in a South Beach side-street hotel that, with the coming of the Depression, was nothing but a flophouse.

Despite that the construction workers were not particularly overjoyed to be engaged in conversation by the garment worker retirees, the retirees were always welcome in the store, especially if my mother was there. My mother and they spoke to each other in the *mamalushen,* the old tongue, and they shared stories about working in the factories. When my mother was a factory worker, she had not belonged to a union—factories had not yet been uniformly unionized—but she and the garment workers remembered it all and together they talked about it all: they remembered the camaraderie among the girls, and they remembered how you couldn't let it be known you were Jewish if you wanted to get along with the Polish or German or Czech shift manager. And they remembered the Triangle Shirtwaist Factory fire in 1911 when almost 150 young women workers—mostly Italian and Jewish—had died, among them two fourteen-year-old girls. And they remembered why it had happened, and when they remembered, someone— or all of them—would cry out, "Because the doors were locked!" And they would say, "Can you imagine?! They locked the doors because some poor *shnook* might want to sneak out for some fresh air!" After each telling, my mother and the other women would moisten up a bit, and the retirees would say, "Thank God for unions. No more locked doors."

We needed the garment workers for things other than for conversing with my mother. The family venture needed them as customers. We had not expected the store to set any new records for sales, but we had been too cavalier about summer business. In the summers, business slowed to a crawl, and only those who lived permanently in the town could be counted on—like the garment worker retirees.

THE NON-TOURIST MIAMI BEACH LIFE

In time I—and the family—learned the ways of Miami Beach and learned to live as year-rounders. Ruth and I were in school and Minna was work-ing in an office. Yes. Minna had found a use for her skills in a real estate office, for which she was paid seven dollars a week. My father had arranged it. He had said to the real estate agent who negotiated the Twenty-third Street deal, "You got a job for my daughter?" and the agent, not wanting to jeopardize the sale, said he did. Thus a barter was struck—a sale in ex-change for a job.

Ruth and I got to school on our boy-style bicycle, the kind with a bar across, and while I sat on the bar and cried "Ow! Ow!" Ruth did the pedal-ing. Our school was Ida M. Fisher, which was named after the mother of Florida's premier promoter, Carl Fisher, who was well known for flooding the country with signs that proclaimed, "It's June in Miami!" Ida M. Fisher was a junior high school pretty much equally divided between Jews and non-Jews, and between the rich and the poor.

Our family had come to Miami three years before Jack's family had come, and I always felt I knew more about the place than he did—I had gone to school there, and he had gone to school in New York—but I couldn't answer his question as to why the offspring of the rich tourists weren't sent to expensive prep schools, which might seem to be their more natural habitat. It did seem strange that some kids came to school in chauffeur-driven limousines and sat next to kids who arrived in their father's truck. Could they too have been watching their pennies?

This hardly seemed likely when I knew how they lived: I knew that rich tourists went to the races, shopped at the exclusive little Lincoln Road shops, and ate in the most expensive restaurants south of New York. I knew all of this because I did a lot of babysitting for the people who did these things.

Ruth was also babysitting, and though my father said we were "running nice little businesses," Ruth was going to need more than babysitting money to go to New York to study art, which was her plan. And so, when my father rented one of the empty stores in the Twenty-third Street lineup to a shoe business (which meant three of the seven were still empty), Ruth decided to try for a job in that store and further decided that my father should teach her the basics of shoe leather, my father having convinced us all that he was the world's leading leather expert. "In my *shtetl* who did the Russian landowners come to for their boots?" he would say to us. "To me, that's to who." So, even as my father was telling Ruth that in her target store, it didn't matter if she knew anything about leather because nobody in that store "knows calfskin from linoleum," he taught Ruth a few things, and in the end she managed to dazzle the owner into hiring her for Saturdays. So Ruth was making some money and she was saving to go to New York.

I wasn't saving for anything. What I made at babysitting, I pretty much spent. I had no thought of saving for higher education, not of any kind.

ENTERTAINING OURSELVES MIAMI BEACH–STYLE

Fun for us kids began or ended with the beach. It was free and it was near, so we met there, had picnics there, carried on our romances there. We went to high school football games, which were also free, and we went to movies, which, if not a nickel a ticket as in Union City, were at least the semi-affordable New York dime.

We still went to the movies a lot, and at this moment in time the movies had something new to help us escape our Depression blues. Actually it was *someone* new, and the someone new was a little girl named Shirley Temple. We took joy in the sweetness of that little person, in those dimples and those curls, and as we watched her, no Depression thoughts were allowed in. It was as if her *Good Ship Lollipop* was taking us far away, to silly thoughts and happy adventures.

Sometimes we babysitters would splurge. We might go see an Ellsworth Vines exhibition tennis match at Flamingo Park or we might go across the causeway to town (Miami proper) to see a personal appearance by the newest screen idol, Gene Raymond, or the movie's funny girl, Una Merkel. Sometimes, but not often, we took ourselves to Greynolds Park in town and, for fifty cents an hour, rode horses.

Going around to the Al Capone house on Palm Island was also a diversion. Although Capone lived in Miami Beach, he was presently making his home in a prison cell somewhere, but we could peek through his iron gate and see everything still in place—his limousines, his docked boat, his huge swimming pool. It was clear from the general conversation that a kind of folk hero aura had formed around Capone. Sure, people said, sure, he was a gangland boss and a ruthless killer, but after the stock market crash, hadn't he opened soup kitchens in Chicago for the needy? Even my mother weighed in. "Didn't he give to the poor?" she said to us. "Didn't he do what was right?" I was convinced: shouldn't we be grateful to anyone who showed Depression compassion, even one who got his "Scarface" nickname from a gun battle with the police?

We danced a lot, in the school patio and in living rooms—the Manhattan, the Lindy Hop—and we learned Cuban dances from the expatriates who went to St. Pat's High School. I told Jack that the ex-generalissimo Gerardo Machado and his entourage had arrived practically the same day we had, and "Big deal," Jack said, meaning, who needs an ex-generalissimo? Well, we didn't, but we took a proprietary interest in him because although other exiled generalissimos had "retired" to Miami Beach before him, he was ours. And we knew all about him. We knew that having been deposed (read: chased out), he had been flown over from Cuba in his private plane, and at present he and his very large clique were occupying an impressive baronial mansion called a "safe house."

Minna was very impressed with the Cubans. "Can't you just see them dancin' to all those rumbas and cha-chas? And don't those Cuban boys look better'n pie?" "Better'n pie" they might have looked, but Minna knew to keep her distance. "So what's wrong with the Jewish boys around here?" my mother would say to her. "Some have very good prospects, if you notice."

I learned many things from the Cubans, and not just their dances. My new Cuban friends being mostly Catholics made me understand that my

Klan-inspired fear of Roman Catholics was nonsense. And I learned that among the Cuban kids were a few Jewish ones and that they called themselves "Jewbans," something that delighted my father even as it puzzled my mother. I also learned that if these rich, not to say super-rich, émigrés were affected by the Depression, you certainly couldn't tell by how they lived their lives.

* * *

If the Cubans were welcome to live in Miami Beach, black people were not. Indeed, they were forbidden to live in Miami Beach, except in servants' quarters. A city ordinance saw to this. Because I hadn't as yet unloaded my Union City racial baggage, I didn't pay much attention. Actually I didn't unload that baggage until wartime, when Johnny Bulla, a good friend and Jack's fellow cadet, described for me the discrimination he had experienced as a Mexican American. Johnny had made me see that I was nothing but a bigot, and when this lovely boy died in a training accident, I promised in his memory never to go down that road again. But at this point, all that was poised to happen, and in Miami Beach I was still serene in my beliefs.

THE ALPHABET SOUP

Miami Beach was as talkative a community as Union City. People often came into the store to talk, and you wouldn't want to be caught dead not being informed. If residents like the garment industry retirees couldn't afford much of anything else, they could afford nickel newspapers, and dozens of newsstands lined both Fifth Street and Washington Avenue. Our own store carried both the *Miami Herald* and the *Miami Daily News* and even the *Miami Beach Sun*, which tried to be relevant by carrying the racing news and even supplying a handicapper called a "seer." Because the *New York Times* and the *New York Herald-Tribune* came in a couple of days late, we didn't think to carry them, but when the garment workers complained— not about the *Herald-Tribune*, as it had a Republican editorial ideology—we took them on, along with the daily racing form. Even the racing touts gave a thorough reading to the newspapers, after, of course, applying themselves to the racing news.

Depression items always led off, and we knew all the recent developments. Acronymic programs continued to come down from Washington in a seemingly endless stream until we were inundated with a Rooseveltian combinations of letters, which everybody called "Roosevelt's alphabet soup."

We knew most of the programs that made up the alphabet soup, and we knew which program was supposed to get us out of what hole. One tackled the lack of jobs, another the loss of homes, yet another the need for health care. Some looked into the way banks operated, one banned child labor, another set a minimum wage. The pace was feverish, the decrees falling all over themselves in their determination to be relevant.

The federal program that provided old-age pensions for workers, which was so big, so far-reaching that it did not seem appropriate to simply list it as an ingredient in the alphabet soup. Rolled out in 1935, passed by the House on a 372 to 33 vote, passed by the Senate 77 to 6, signed instantly by Roosevelt, it was the program of programs—the Social Security Act— which provided benefits for thousands of workers in commerce and in- dustry. My father could scarcely get his head around it. "Never in my life would I expect such a thing," he said to us. "Something that helps so many people. Even from Roosevelt, who would have thought?" How popular was it with others beside my father? Popular enough that when, two years later, a subsequent act required workers to pay taxes of 2 percent to support the program, few uttered a peep.

We were beginning to see evidence of Roosevelt's efforts and of the cooperation with them. Construction sites displayed signs reading "USA Work Program" and, like ours, stores proclaimed that they were comply- ing with the National Recovery Act with window signs saying "We Do Our Part." We were surprised to learn that the Works Progress Administra- tion—the WPA, as everybody referred to it, the umbrella administration for the job-seeking part of the New Deal—even had a program for artists. For a stipend, painters painted, and sculptors sculpted, and a number of the artists—especially the painters—saw their work go up in post offices and other public buildings. If Roosevelt was physically crippled, as some hinted he was, we wondered at his stamina. As Jack said, "If he used a crutch, he used it to knock things out of his way."

In the summer of 1937 I myself did a little two-step with a Roosevelt program—the NYA, the National Youth Administration. The NYA was set up to teach skills and to find jobs for young people, and though I already had a skill—I had learned to type in high school—the local NYA office needed a typist "yesterday," as the office manager said, to prepare their directory, and that would be me. Jack always thought I was nothing less than a wonder to be able to type. "And you put together a directory!" he marveled to me. "That really takes talent." I had observed through the years that only people who couldn't type were in awe of those who could, so I didn't take it as much of a compliment. Typing to me was a process that anybody could learn. Would-be typists had only to follow the word of choice of Miss Anita Sternberg, our assistant office manager, which was "patience," and which she often delivered to work seekers. This was how I felt about learning to type. It only required patience. I did, however, agree with Jack that putting together a directory for the whole of Dade County was pretty darned tricky.

Every Saturday I took a jitney across the causeway to the NYA office in town. I looked forward to those Saturdays. The job paid fifty cents an hour, and the activity in the office was exciting. Kids—those who had graduated high school and those who had already dropped out—came in all day long. The majority of them were looking for jobs, and because we had a list of places that had jobs, we would send job seekers over, usually as unskilled laborers. But sometimes, after a talk with Miss Sternberg, they opted for learning a skill. "If you have the *patience* to learn a skill," she would say, emphasizing her word of choice, "it will pay off in the end. You'll see." And if they agreed, she would send them at government expense to train for positions as airplane mechanics or typists or nurses.

In the late afternoon, Miss Sternberg, who also lived in Miami Beach, delivered me home in her car, and in the car she would run down the list of social programs innovated by the Roosevelt administration and lecture me on the glories of the New Deal, though I felt I had already been pretty well apprised of its glories from an assortment of believers—my father, the garment workers, indeed all the Democrats I knew, young and old. Miss Sternberg, however, had another New Deal glory for me, and that was its gender blindness. "The New Deal is about putting all Americans to work who want to work, emphasis on the 'all,' " Miss Sternberg might say to me. And when I dared to argue that the Depression was still not putting everybody to work, Miss Sternberg would erupt with her usual "Patience! Show a little patience!"

Unfortunately, Miss Sternberg was not issuing an advisory just to hear herself talk, as my father would say. Yes, the New Deal programs sounded promising and doable, and Congress and the Supreme Court were (at first) mostly cooperating. But we all knew that we had not yet awakened from our national nightmare. Paved with good intentions though the road might have been, the depth of the problems Roosevelt had inherited made the road back unnervingly stubborn and a smooth, quick recovery impossible. Despite our president's being a Democrat, despite all the letters of the al-phabet that he had showered over us, the Depression was not going away. Yes, patience was required. I could only listen to Miss Sternberg and hope that if we had patience, we could once again be our real selves.

VETERANS AND THE FLORIDA KEYS

I took a cue from my father and tried not to blame Roosevelt for the fact that the Depression was still with us. Even my teenage understanding accepted that the Depression had plunged us into a depth so profound that breaking to the surface would require stamina and endurance. But I did hold out hope that an improvement in one particular area could happen soon: I wanted Roosevelt to review his thinking and decide to do something for the veterans of World War I. So far he had not budged, and it seemed that our "forgotten man" was still forgotten. But then—ring bells and blow trumpets—it was rumored that Roosevelt had something on the drawing board, and it had to do with the Florida Keys. It was a moment of elation, but as it turned out, it was, sadly, only a moment.

On a map the Florida Keys might look to be within spitting distance of Miami, but I had never been there, Ruth had never been there, my parents had never been there, nor had the majority of the people I knew ever been there. The only person I knew who had been there was my classmate Sally Pinder, and she had been there because she was born there, and she would say that she almost never went back because it was so hard to get there. And it was true that the only way through the Keys was by what was called the Overseas Railway, which had been built all the way back in 1908, and those who had traveled on it said it acted its age. It apparently stopped and started every few miles, ran completely out of energy at the village of Marathon, and then, totally exhausted, just plain called it quits.

If you were going all the way to Key West, you might take a trip by a ferry, but it was reported to go aground on a regular basis in the Keys' shallow waters. It wasn't surprising, therefore, that newspaper editorials—especially the *Miami Herald*—kept up a steady drumbeat for a decent road to the Keys, arguing that a road would spark a regionwide economic upturn; in other words, if people could drive down to the Keys, the Keys could become a destination target and a tourist economy would follow.

As if he had been reading the *Miami Herald* editorials, President Roosevelt suddenly came up with a plan to build that road. What he had conjectured was obviously not just a tourist amenity but a project that would provide jobs—jobs that were, happily, specifically aimed at veterans.

You would have thought that such a plan would spark triumphant handshakes all around, but such was not the case. There was a hitch, and it came—*what?*—from the veterans. They were refusing to sign up. Was I reading right? Jobs were being offered specifically to veterans and veterans were turning them down? What were they thinking? Whatever it was, if

Roosevelt had, as everyone claimed, profound powers of persuasion, when he tried to persuade the veterans, they pretty much stayed unpersuaded.

The newspapers told us the reasons, and there were a lot of them: the vets didn't want to leave their families to go to another state; they rejected mosquito-infested swamplands and heat that registered over one hundred degrees. They compared Florida, unfavorably, to their experiences in France. Letters to the editor said things like, "Worse than the trenches at Chateau-Thierry," and "Any veteran who remembers the dysentery and body lice of the battlefield does not want a repeat in Florida." Or they said, "Give me a trench rat over mosquitoes any day." I didn't know which way to go; I didn't want the veterans to live in a hellhole, but we're talking JOBS, you forgotten man you, JOBS.

So now what was Roosevelt going to do? Well, he was going to call on his wife, and I was going to sit back and relax, for I knew that the problem was now in good hands. We had all become familiar with Mrs. Roosevelt's method of getting her way, and her way was to hold meetings. And we knew that when Mrs. Roosevelt held meetings, pretty soon there would be promises and after the promises, there would be an agreement.

When Mrs. Roosevelt called meetings with the veterans, the results were what we had predicted: promises were made, and agreement was reached. Housing would be available for veterans' families; screens and mosquito netting for doors and windows would be hung; showers would be provided with disinfectant soap to discourage body lice. The result of all this negotiation was that pretty soon the grousing had stopped, and pretty soon almost a thousand veterans had signed up to build the bridge that would link the upper Keys to Key West. If President Roosevelt's powers of persuasion had failed, Mrs. Roosevelt's had not.

Florida newspapers were full of it. "Road to the Keys to Start," the headlines read, and my father would again be rattling his paper in front of me, and this time it would be rattling in triumph. My father, like other Miami Beach merchants, was interested in the road for a lot of reasons, not just as jobs for veterans but as a business plus: he figured that when the road was in place, people driving from the North might stop over in Miami Beach, and since he still had a few empty stores, he figured that, if the tourists came down Twenty-third Street, they might get some ideas; and if nothing else, they could stop in at the drugstore for a refreshing ice cream soda or a replenishment of their sundries.

Considering I was one for whom the Keys had been terra incognita, I not only cheered the building of the road, I fantasized the trips I would make. It seemed a win-win situation, and I was among the winners. With a road to Key West, I would finally see a sunset over Mallory Square and that sudden flare of color, the famous "green flash" when the sun melted into the blue of the sea. And when my brother Will came down to visit, I would take him to Ernest Hemingway's house and we would take a look at where the writer lived and worked and we would discuss its influences on Hemingway's work, and we would marvel at Hemingway's famous extra-toed cats.

I was now thirteen years old and of an age to have a crush, and I knew that my fourteen-year-old crushee would not be interested in Ernest Hemingway, but he would definitely be interested in the vaunted Keys fishing, and I knew that *his* particular fantasy was getting in on the bonefishing unique to the Keys. Or, as he said, he might get a weekend job as a crew member on boats going out for tarpon and sailfish. So he too would have a win.

This latter was a win that I decided not to mention to my mother, for I knew how she felt about my crushee. He was a gentile of the most stereotypical kind—blond and blue-eyed—and when she talked about him, there was a shadow to her voice. And when I would say, "But, Mama, I'm only thirteen and I'm not going to marry him," she would say, "But wasn't I only seventeen when I got married?" Of course I and my crushee parted ways in the usual number of weeks, but it was too bad that my mother—always worried that we would be bewitched by a gentile boy—couldn't know that Jack Suberman was out there waiting to be met.

I found another, and more serious, reason for cheering the road to the Keys. My father's boosterish ways had been passed on to me—he was invariably a booster for wherever he landed, with the exception of New York—and I had in some sense become a Florida booster. It in no way detracted from my abiding Tennessee boosterism, and in fact Florida ran a rather poor second. Nevertheless, I was pleased that south Florida now had a project of a substantial nature, one that would counter its reputation for trivial pursuits. But boosters or not, whoever we were in Miami Beach— Jews, New York garment worker retirees, Cubans, Communists, maybe even ex-gangsters—we wanted that road to the Keys. And we kept up with every moment of the building of it.

We talked about it endlessly. The men had started coming down! Shelters were going up! Some of the veterans were said to have their families with them, and though the shelters were in reality nothing more than flimsy shacks, we envisioned the wives fixing them up, and we saw the camps turning into little communities. We pictured the veterans going off to work, jumping joyfully onto the trucks that carried them to their work sites, and after a hard day's work, we heard their banter on the trucks that carried them home. When I told Jack about the interest being generated by the prospect of a road to the Keys, he said although it had happened a year before his family had gotten to Miami, he had certainly been aware of it. But not as much as I was, of that I was sure.

We read that three camps for the road builders had been set up and that more than seven hundred veterans of the Great War were now housed at the camps and working on the road. Newspapers reported how morale at the camps was good, that the veterans were working hard, and that they were making progress. Did you hear? Bridge piers are up!

Because the morale of the veterans was good, so was ours. We all smiled and said, "Good. Good for the veterans, good for us." It seemed that veterans had finally gotten their share of luck. It was luck, however, that lasted only until Labor Day, because ironically enough, it was on that day that the veterans' luck ran out. Bad timing, bad weather, and bad planning had conspired against the veterans and struck them down.

The causal event was supposed to have been just another of those weather extremes typical to Florida—one of those signature Florida hurricanes. This one had been well predicted, and we had set about with our usual pre-hurricane preparations. We stocked canned goods, put up the shutters, tied things down, filled the bathtub with water. We knew the electricity would fail, and before it did, we listened nonstop to the radio to learn what we could about the progress of the storm. We also wanted to know what was being done about the veterans down there in the work camps.

What we learned put us at ease. Plans, we were told, were in place for the veterans' evacuation. We were informed of a ten-car train proceeding southward from Homestead to pick up the veterans and their families, who were lining up along the route. Good, my parents and Minna and Ruth and I said to each other; good, the veterans are being looked after. And then the electricity shut down, and we settled in to await the winds and the rains.

With the radio mute, we learned nothing more that day. The hurricane came to us, blew hard, smacked the shutters around, tore up the screens, leveled a few trees, and left town. The next day we went around on the streets, took note of what things were no longer there, talked with others. On that morning, there was no electricity and no newspaper.

Somehow, however, by word of mouth from some who-knows-what source came news of the veterans, and it was news nobody wanted to hear.

The veterans had not boarded the train because there was no train to board. In Upper Matecumbe Key the storm had pushed the train off its track, and the planned rescue, seemingly so well planned, so comforting, had become a hopeless debacle. So while we had been sitting out the storm in our house, an assault of powerful winds and a seventeen-foot water surge had overwhelmed the waiting veterans and their families, and lives had been lost.

The *Herald* presses were up and running on the second day, and we could now learn the casualty count, and what we learned was that more than two hundred veterans and their families had perished. Bodies were recovered as far away as the southwestern tip of the mainland. Horrors were reported: two-by-fours driven through bodies, skin sandblasted off by the wind. Adding insult to injury, as my father would say, only a few of the concrete highway bridge piers built by the veterans remained as evidence that the veterans had ever been there. And when my mother cried out, "How can God be so hard on such good people?" though my father usually laughed at my mother's persistence in giving plusses and minuses to God, this time there was no laugh in him.

So again doughboys were big news. Once again the veterans had become victims. We in Miami Beach could talk of nothing else—not the usual post-hurricane talk of how we had lost, variously, roofs, garages, screen porches—but how the veterans had lost everything.

It was a time for national mourning, and after the mourning came the blame. My Communist friends, subscribers to the Communist periodical *The New Masses,* wanted me to read an Ernest Hemingway piece that was in it. Its title was "Who Murdered the Vets? A First-Hand Report on the Florida Hurricane," and Hemingway had written, "You're dead now, brother, but who left you there in the hurricane months on the Keys where a thousand men died before you when they were building the road that's washed out now? Who left you there?" When I later told Jack this story, he said it was what he expected from Hemingway. "He knows he's got the public's ear," he said to me. "And he was sending a message as only he could do it."

National newspapers took up the battle and carried picture after picture of the disaster. The editorials said things that implied that the veterans had given up their lives for a country that had consistently ignored them. And then Congress apparently remembered some things—maybe what had gone on in Washington in 1933?—and they finally took action. The bonus bill was passed, and when Roosevelt, citing budget constraints and the need for more general assistance, vetoed it, Congress got itself together and overrode the veto.

So World War I veterans at last received what for so long they had been fighting. But did any of us ever forget their struggle to get it? Or the cost? I'd have to say we did not. Still, my father, in his elation, might say, "What it proves is that you could count our boys down, but you couldn't count them out," and I would wonder if we could look at the Depression that way. We were down, but were we out? At that point we might not have been out, but we were certainly not in.

THE ZIMMERMANS

In 1938, while Ruth was setting out to go to New York, her boyfriend Jack Simon was setting out for Spain. Why he was going to Spain was something of a mystery to me. I was still trying to keep up with all the news, but between playing on the high school tennis team and maintaining grades and helping out in the store occasionally, I was not as diligent as I might have been. I knew there was a war going on in Spain, but so?

It was at a going-away party for Jack Simon that I learned more about that war. I learned first of all that Jack Simon was joining something called the Abraham Lincoln Brigade, and he was going to Spain to fight alongside "the Loyalists" against "the Fascists." But who in the world were *they?*

I was not the only one at the party who didn't know one from the other. None of us knew much about the political entities that had sprung up in Europe, though I did know more than a little about the German Nazis. What I knew had come from a few items in the *Miami Herald,* though its coverage of the news had been pretty puny. The stories were chiefly of the Nazi leaders and their rise to power, as if the *Herald* was merely offering its readers a political overview.

The concentration camps were not mentioned. Indeed, the newspaper was so *sotto voce* on the subject of the Jews in Germany that events there were scarcely mentioned at all, and the *New York Times* and the other national newspapers were not very forthcoming either. Still, it was easy to see that my parents, and all Miami Beach Jews for that matter, were getting more than a little anxious on the subject, and whenever the word "Nazis" was invoked, it was usually followed by a disdainful "pooie" and a forceful spit.

If the Miami Beach Jewish community was nervous about what they already knew concerning the Jews of Europe, it was about to get a lot more nervous when sometime in 1938, a German refugee family came to town with some unsettling stories. These were the Zimmermans, and I first knew of them when Mr. Zimmerman came into the store. And when we

met him, we knew that we had an eyewitness, and we said, "So tell us, Mr.
Zimmerman, tell us."

Mr. Zimmerman was intriguing: he had German ways and a German accent, and he was Jewish. We found out at once that he was not a reluctant
storyteller, and he opened his narrative by explaining a few personal
things, including why the Zimmermans—he, his wife, and his son—had
left Germany. It was because, he said in his English/German way of speaking, that they had "schmelled a schmell, and it was *farstunkeneh.*" The smell
they smelled, that putrid smell was, I took it, what we would call the handwriting on the wall.

They had most strongly smelled the smell after *Kristallnacht,* the 1938
night when throughout Germany and Austria, Jewish homes had been ran-
sacked and Jewish businesses destroyed. The Zimmermans had smelled
it even earlier, however, following the 1935 Nuremberg laws, when Jews
were required to wear the yellow armband, and when Jews were denied
entrance to museums and movie houses. And the smell was everywhere
when other prohibitions were announced—Jewish children not allowed
in schools; Jewish teachers not allowed to teach; Jewish doctors not allowed to practice; Jewish people not allowed, not allowed, not allowed. It
seemed to me very like Jim Crow laws in the Deep South, the ones that
were put into practice on the train coming to Miami, and I wondered if
German Jewish people had to ride in separate train cars. It was still a time
when I could not know that train cars would figure very prominently in
the European Jewish experience, and at this moment in time not even Mr.
Zimmerman could know.

The smell was overpowering when the Zimmermans had looked out
the window of their Berlin apartment and had seen Jewish neighbors being
led off by the Gestapo. But the smell that sent the Zimmermans to America was one that so assaulted their nostrils that they could no longer tolerate
it. And this happened when the Zimmerman son Gottfried, a star professor
of physics at a German university, had become there suddenly, and om-
inously, persona non grata. Previously treated with respect, Gottfried was
all at once, as he himself said, treated like "the guy who makes go the lawn-
mower," and he knew, despite that he had not as yet been fired, that his
days were numbered.

Gottfried had then done something "schmatt," Mr. Zimmerman said.
The smart thing he had done was to realize that his name in the field would
make him sought after in other countries, and when he wrote to a couple
of prestigious universities in the United States, he discovered just how right

he had been. And so he took one of the proffered jobs and, when he went, he took his parents with him. Gottfried's departure was, as we were to find out, part of the flow of elite professionals, artists, and others who exiled themselves from Germany and came to the United States.

And now, during their summer vacation, the Zimmermans were down from Gottfried's new university and spending time in Miami Beach. The Zimmermans called Miami Beach "a spa maybe not so nice like Baden-Baden but nice." I had no way of knowing if Miami Beach was nice or not so nice like Baden-Baden, but the booster in me asked: Did Baden-Baden have a beach like ours? Or a gangster? Or an ex-generalissimo? No, it did not.

The Zimmermans lived two doors down from us, and Ruth and I, at my mother's prodding, visited them often. "So be nice to them," my mother might say. "They're so far from what they know." When we visited, the Zimmermans were quick to bring out tea and cake and quicker still to settle in for a talk about their lives in Germany before the "troubles" set in, meaning before Hitler came to power. When they referred to Hitler, they did not use the phrase I was accustomed to hearing, which was "that Nazi piece of *dreck.*" That Hitler was a piece of excrement was something that everybody, Democrats and Republicans alike, could agree on, but the Zimmermans did not call him that: they called him "the little Austrian."

It was obvious that the Zimmermans had lived well in Germany and obvious also that they had many a soft spot in their hearts for their home-land. They talked about the big house they had lived in, the skiing in Switzerland, the fine schools they had attended. And they told us about the few treasured pieces of furniture they had been able to bring over, among them, they said, a Biedermeier cabinet, which held the Meissen china we were drinking our tea from. The cabinet was too big to transport from their new home, but they had insisted on bringing the cups and saucers. When they talked about the Biedermeier cabinet, they confided in a somewhat embarrassed way that it was Austrian, and Austrians, Ruth and I were be-ginning to gather, were not considered on the same level—intellectually, culturally, or socially—with Germans.

As they knew about furniture, the Zimmermans knew about art and music. They talked with nostalgia about the enriching experiences Berlin offered, about the glories of the Weimar Republic, and they said that though it was true—"tch-tch"—that unemployment and inflation were rampant then, it was also a period of high culture. And when they talked about the Bauhaus school of art, which had been in ascendancy until the Bauhaus artists fled the country with Hitler's rise to power, they knew what had happened to the artists. "Did they go to the cities, to New York?" they asked, no doubt knowing their question to be rhetorical in an audience consisting of the ignorant twosome of Ruth and me. "No," they said darkly, "there might be German spies there." So what did the artists do? As the Zimmermans explained it, when the artists had fled Germany and had come to America, in their determination to pursue their art, they had taken places in Black Mountain College in Black Mountain, North Carolina. This bit of information confirmed for Ruth that true artists pursued their life in art despite the challenges.

Mr. Zimmerman also had things to say about Miami Beach mores—the freedom given the children, the absence of the afternoon rite of tea and pastry—but, more emphatically, the hotel signs. He would say to my father, "The Jewish people here don't care that they're insulted?" And my father would answer that yes, they did care, but he would say to Mr. Zimmerman that the Jews had learned from long experience not to make waves. And Mr. Zimmerman would say to this, "Did we make waves in Germany? No, we did not? So why is what's happening in Germany happening?"

We were surprised that we had found the Zimmermans so fascinating. They were different from the Jewish immigrants we knew: the Jewish immigrants we knew in the places we had lived—Tennessee and New York and now Miami Beach—were eastern Europeans, chiefly Russian, Polish, Hungarian, Romanian, and occasionally Czech—and though they had much to offer, they could not offer what this German Jewish family did. Here was our first real insight into the diversity of Jewish culture, and though we had expected our visits to the Zimmermans to be in the nature of a duty, we found out they were a treat. We were grateful to the Zimmermans for another reason as well: they were in Miami Beach in the summer and so swelled by three our thin summer crowd of customers. Despite my father's hopeful words, summers in the store were invariably dead as a beached flounder. And winters were not much better. Business-wise, we were not doing very well.

7

The New York Depression Kid

Whenever Jack talked about how it had been with him in those Depression days, he laid the groundwork by telling tales of his life before the Depression as the son of a prosperous businessman. "Until the Depression came," he would say, in his eyes-wide-open way, "I was spoiled rotten. We all were." I assumed that the "we" referred to his New York friends, the ones in what his parents called their "crowd." As I listened to Jack, I came to understand that he remembered his young pre-Depression life as a life filled with only good things, and that he had taken for granted that his adult life would be the same, that it would be pleasure filled and worry free like his father's. Wasn't his father a peerless businessman and a wise and caring mentor? And his mother? Wasn't she a fierce protector and—as Jack would say with a laugh—an easy mark?

When I pictured Jack's early life, it was hard not to picture his possessions, which seemed to me breathtaking in number and quality. I saw a bedroom overflowing with everything a boy might want—a movie projector, a sleek electric train with all the appendages it could support, a two-wheeled sidewalk bicycle, a violin, and bookcases full of books, including full sets of both the *Book of Knowledge* and the *Encyclopedia Britannica*.

I had to agree that Jack was indeed spoiled rotten if that meant he had all the playthings and equipment he wanted, if he had a substantial allowance, if he was given lessons in everything he cared to take lessons in, and if he was sent to the best summer camp money could buy. When I would say this, Jack would answer, "Sure, we were spoiled, but you'd have to say we got our comeuppance." And I would say yes, we were all spoiled, and we all got our comeuppance.

I never saw myself, however, spoiled in the same way as Jack. Still, though my collection of toys and games were not so much "the latest" as were Jack's, they even so could have filled a barn. I guess I was spoiled in a more simple Union City way, not the New York one of keeping up with your "crowd." As for pleasantness and abundance, however, our lives matched: during those pre-Depression years, we knew nothing else.

If you asked Jack what he had liked most about growing up as he did, he would not have said his sidewalk bike or his Lou Gehrig baseball glove or his shelves of books, he would have said it was no contest, that it was, hands-down, going to summer camp. Jack—and later his brother and sister—went annually to camp, one run by Jews and for Jews. It was called Camp Roosevelt and named for President Theodore Roosevelt, which the owners no doubt hoped would suggest that the camp was dedicated to the natural life.

Despite its emphasis on living freely among the trees and under the sun and with any wildlife that might be around, living free with nature did not come free—nor even cheap—at Camp Roosevelt. Indeed, Camp Roosevelt was extremely pricey, and the owners might have said it was pricey for good reason, what with a one-to-five ratio of counselors to campers, expansive grounds, equipment the latest, food ample to the level of "too much already." Jack's father, according to Jack, didn't balk, just sat down at the Chinese black lacquered desk in the living room and wrote out the hefty check. Jack's father had heard that Camp Roosevelt was "the best," and because "the best" was what he strove for, Camp Roosevelt was where his children would go.

For Jack, going to camp meant a summer of pleasure and excitement. His father drove him up to Camp Roosevelt in the big black Buick, and Jack would say that as soon as he had opened the car door and jumped out, he never looked back. "Camp" was sports and books, and friends, and girls at the adjoining camp—all in all, a summer of bliss. Although Jack didn't usually sound as if he had just come from reading all the books in the New York Public Library, he would say, "I thought I was living the empyrean life." And when I asked Jack what the heck *empyrean* meant, it was to Jack another teachable moment, and he suggested I look it up, and when I did, I understood that when Jack was in camp he was in his own paradise.

I met Jack's parents soon after I met Jack, and when I had dinner at their house, we sat together afterward, and out came a lot of life stories. I liked listening to the Subermans. It was a way for me to learn about their—and Jack's—New York lives. Both Mr. Suberman and Mrs. Suberman liked to talk, to tell "how it was," and still chock-full of those southern manners—I even "ma'am-ed" and "sir-ed" them—I knew that I must be attentive. Actually, I didn't mind: perhaps unbeknownst to my storytellers, most everything I heard told me something I didn't know about New York lives, particularly Jewish ones. Indeed, the Subermans' lives seemed fantastical ones, of a sort hitherto unknown to me.

Listening to the Subermans was a way for me to get to know New York, period. Most of what I knew about New York when we still lived in Union City came from listening to my mother singing songs invoking New York. Yes, after we left Union City, we had taken up residence in New York, but it had been so short a stay that we considered it just a layover on our way to Miami Beach.

Moreover, the people I knew up there—my parent's relatives—didn't live as the Subermans did. The social lives of my relatives centered around the family and not around a "crowd"; and my New York relatives did not lead economically unrestrained lives. So to me, learning about the Subermans and New York was simultaneously serendipitous. I therefore listened, never pulled back, never made excuses. And I didn't need to put my "interviewing" skills to work: getting Mr. and Mrs. Suberman to talk was not a problem. Not to be underestimated was that if one of them forgot an incident, couldn't remember a detail, ignored something relevant, Jack was with us and very happy to step in.

When we talked, we usually sat on the front porch of their Miami home, with Jack's father in the rattan chaise longue that he invariably commandeered whenever the need for explication or pontification was upon him. Mr. Suberman was modest in build, not as tall as either of his sons but not short either, and he was thin, something that Mrs. Suberman liked to comment on. "He's so thin now, like a rail," she would say. And then she would add, with some pride, "Before the Depression, he wore Portly. You know, he was prosperous-looking." What she meant by this, I took it, was that in the old days she fed him so well that he had a lot of girth to show for it. As the daughter of a dry goods store owner, I knew that "Portly" was a euphemistically labeled suit size, which naturally meant that the would-be wearer was . . . um . . . fat. But if Mrs. Suberman preferred "prosperous looking," it was all right with me.

Mr. Suberman could talk about many things, but when he talked to me, any need to explicate or pontificate had to do with the economy in general and his lost business in particular. Prior to the Depression, having been the beneficiary of a booming economy, and having later been a casualty of a crashing one, Mr. Suberman thought of himself as an expert on the economy's vagaries.

What was clear to me from the moment I first plunked myself down on a cushion on the porch floor and looked up at Mr. Suberman was that he longed to be back in New York living his old life. His conversation was studded with stories of the glory days when he had made it, when he had made his crowd's version of "a fortune." He would stop to ask me questions—rhetorically, as was his habit—such as, "What's a life in Miami compared to a life in New York?" And when I would suggest that he seemed to enjoy his newfound hobby—playing bridge at a bridge club downtown—he would say, "How can you compare shuffling cards to doing business in the world's 'commercial center'?" "Commercial center" was no doubt a phrase he had picked up from the *Times* or from his broker's office, where, as I was learning, he had been a steady visitor. Still, even as his face grew dark at the memories, even as he sighed deep sighs, Mr. Suberman would admit that although he had "made it" in New York, he had also lost it there.

Mr. Suberman, like my father, had come to America as an immigrant from eastern Europe. He would say he had come as "a penniless urchin," another phrase I assumed he had picked up, this one perhaps from Jack, and he had, by means of his energy and a little luck—a little *mazel*, he would say—established himself. Mr. Suberman spoke what his crowd would call "a very good English," though with an accent, but whether the accent was Yiddish, Russian, or Polish (any of which were possible) I had no clue; nor, I suspect, did Mr. Suberman. His little *shtetl* of Pinsk was a town, he explained, that couldn't make up its mind whether it was in Russia or in Poland, since both countries periodically staked a claim to it. "Not that it made any difference to the Jews there," he would say. "Russian or Polish, even the horses were anti-Semites."

Anti-Semitism in America seemed to Mr. Suberman to bear only a faint resemblance to the way it played out in Pinsk. He had come to know it in America, but compared with what he had endured in Europe, American anti-Semitism was a joke. "Over there with the pogroms, they either kill you on the spot or leave you to die later, take your choice," Mr. Suberman said to me. "Here the best they got is insults." This wasn't quite true, for as Jack had told me, incidents of violence against Jews were daily occurrences in certain parts of the city. But Mr. Suberman, now in Miami and removed from that tumultuous metropolis, chose to remember through the rosiest of spectacles.

Despite the anti-Semitism, Mr. Suberman's father had had a pretty good job in Pinsk as a bookkeeper for a man who owned a lumberyard, and Mr. Suberman's father actually owned a piece of it himself. But, as Mr. Suberman would declare often, he wouldn't have exchanged America for all the stands of fir trees in all of Pinsk.

I kept thinking about those fir trees. If Mr. Suberman's father had owned a piece of a lumber business, in what way was Mr. Suberman "a penniless urchin"? Jack explained that there was a competition among Mr. Suberman's associates—"the boys"—in which each strived to be declared the most penniless immigrant. All "the boys" having come from eastern Europe, a part of the world famous for its penniless emigrants, they knew that to win, they had to come up with some pretty sad stories "to take the *kuchl*" (to take the cake).

Jack recounted for me some of the stories as the men vied to take the *kuchl*. "You came with two kopecks in your pocket?" one of the boys might ask. "In my pocket I had only a big hole." Or, "You knew a cousin when you came? Me, the only thing I was acquainted with was the roach in my suitcase." Still, the boys would have agreed that though their possessions were few, their expectations were huge.

MR. SUBERMAN AND HIS FUR BUSINESS

Mr. Suberman's New York business week started on Monday morning when he entered the subway that would take him downtown to the fur district, though if the weather was inclement or if he was in a particular hurry, he took a "cab," which was one of the few things I had learned in New York—that a "taxi" was called a "cab"—though I kept in mind that if I used the term in my letters to Doris, it would have confirmed for her that I was puttin' on more and more. At any rate, although it was a long way from his apartment in the west Bronx to his downtown place of business on Twenty-seventh Street in the fur district, Mr. Suberman did not question the expense of a cab ride, perhaps because he knew that more often than not a good day awaited him, one that would add to the profit side of his balance sheet.

Mr. Suberman's place in the New York business world had its genesis around 1910 when he first arrived, found a job as a fur skin "trimmer," and picked up the particulars of the fur trade. He worked hard, with the goal of moving up from "trimmer" to "nailer" because nailing paid more and nailers were more respected. The nailer's job was to dry the skins by nailing them to the wall after finding the "sweet spot," that special place where a hole could be made without affecting the value of the skin. This could only be entrusted to expert nailers, and Mr. Suberman admired their skills. "The best ones don't lose an inch," he would say. "Only the hole they throw away."

In time Mr. Suberman learned the business and joined with some entrepreneur-minded acquaintances to open a small factory for the manufacture of fur garments. It fell to Mr. Suberman to be salesman and designer, and when he landed an account with Macy's Department Store, it was *mazeltov* time. Congratulations! Break out the Champagne! The boys did indeed open a bottle of Champagne and drank to the new account, though most of the Champagne was left in the bottle considering that none of the boys were what you would call "drinkers," or *schickers*. A man serious about his business wasn't a *schicker*, they would have said. A little *schnapps* maybe, but no more than that.

The *mazeltov* moment was over quickly. It was over on the day Macy's buyers asked for something Mr. Suberman couldn't provide, which was the Holy Grail of the fur industry, the zippered jacket. It was a request that left Mr. Suberman stunned: *They want jackets with zippers?* Some problem Macy's had given him.

Mr. Suberman set himself to work on the problem, but if no one had yet solved it, Mr. Suberman didn't solve it either. "It was like trying to make the zippers stop doing what they're invented for," Mr. Suberman said. And although he worked on the problem "'til today was tomorrow," he said, the zippers continued to grab at the jacket's fur, and Macy's in the end canceled. "Big business goes by its own rules," was one of Mr. Suberman's enduring mottoes, and something he would repeat to anybody who might be in hearing distance. "And if they have to break your heart, they go right ahead and do it."

When Macy's canceled, the mood in the shop turned bad, and harsh words passed among the partners. And when later that year—1926—thousands of fur trade workers went on strike, Mr. Suberman remembered his first job and his admiration for his fellow workers, and he was disgusted that his associates could not make up their minds about supporting the strikers. Indeed there was talk of calling in professional thugs to stop the strikes. Mr. Suberman said that these would be Jewish thugs—Jewish mobsters who made their living "helping out" in such situations.

Mr. Suberman himself had thought unions were good for workers and good for business and good for the country, and to his associates who grumbled about union shops, he would say, "How can you turn your back on the workers? Did you boys ever think you would live so well? That you could send your sons to college and give your daughters a wedding soup to nuts?" It was one of Mr. Suberman's stories that Jack knew very well, and, as he listened to it once more out there on the porch, I understood that he had learned something and it was not about fur skins. It was about social values.

After the quarrel with his associates, a young Alex Suberman decided to leave the manufacturing side of the fur trade and take on the skin importing side. Now he was "supply" and not "demand," and as one of only two bosses, he had only one partner to convince to have a union shop.

Still, fur importing was even more risky than fur manufacturing. It was a business that was hostage to many things, one of which was the weather, and the other was fashion taste, both of which depended on predictions. Mr. Suberman would say, "Such a thing with the weather. This year snow up to your *pipick;* next year you can't buy a snowflake," which I translated as some years there was snow up to your belly button, and some years no snow at all. Furthermore, taste in fashion was always fickle at best, and Mr. Suberman said, "This year the women go for fox collars with a silver patch just right, next year they go for purple dogs." *Dogs?* I was glad to learn that no skins—purple or otherwise—actually came from "dogs." The term was only the in-trade name for Siberian wolves.

With all the risks, Mr. Suberman decided to up his life insurance policy, and he took out the most expensive one his finances could tolerate. It was one that paid a handsome lump sum upon the signatory's natural death and a much less handsome monthly stipend if the signatory was disabled and couldn't work. The handsome amount impressed Mr. Suberman; the less handsome one was just an extra line in the policy, one he scarcely read. So you couldn't exactly call Mr. Suberman "prescient" when the extra line came to mean a great deal in his life.

Mr. Suberman's new importing business started well, and he found pleasures that his last business did not offer, one of which was traveling to far-off places. If you're going to sell fur skins, he would say, you first have to buy them—as, in Union City, my father would have said that if you want to sell pants you first have to buy them. But Mr. Suberman's buying trips were a bit more exotic than my father's: Mr. Suberman's took him to eastern Europe and Asia, where he dealt with animal trappers and skin traders; my father's took him to St. Louis, where he dealt with Mr. Landsman's wholesale house on Washington Street.

Such were the times that when Mr. Suberman came home from a buying trip, his skins sold very well, and he would say, "Like they were what nobody could live without." Shoppers were, pre-Depression, both fur-conscious and fur-consuming, never mind the weather. And if the suppliers had previously worried about style changes, they now hired scouts skilled in trend-spotting. The scouts were called "sniffers," and they "knew their onions," Mr. Suberman would say. "You have to say they sniffed us into a very good living."

If most of the Jewish entrepreneurs of Mr. Suberman's acquaintance expected their sons to enter their businesses, Mr. Suberman did not. He knew Jack wasn't interested in the fur business, and he had reluctantly accepted that Jack was not cut out for business life. In explaining the relationship of his son—my Jack—to his business, Mr. Suberman would start off with a little laugh and tell about taking young Jack to his warehouse, where Jack had performed, Mr. Suberman said, "at a level just above no good." He had given Jack the job of counting skins recently arrived at the Port of New York, and as the furs still showed the blood from the skinning process, I could imagine that Jack was not terribly taken with the job. I didn't argue when Mr. Suberman said that his oldest son had absolutely "no *kopf* for business," let alone *hislawes*—enthusiasm—for it. I just kept to my fantasy that Jack had a *kopf*—a head—for teaching literature.

It was clear that Mr. Suberman had not actually worried about Jack's disinclination toward business: Jack was definitely going to college. In their crowd, sons went to college, and Mr. Suberman took for granted that Jack would follow the convention. In the years before the Depression, he had full confidence that Jack would be going to a very good college, one of Jack's own choosing, never mind the coy quota system whereby, the colleges proclaimed, Jews were admitted on the basis of their percentage in the general population. Jack made very good grades, and Mr. Suberman had felt that no quota system could deny him. And, he projected, there in that good college, maybe in an Ivy League one, Jack would find a real interest. So if Jack didn't feel inclined toward the fur business, Mr. Suberman was not going to argue. A doctor or lawyer in the family would be very nice. Well, that was Mr. Suberman's thinking back then, back in those sublime days.

It seemed odd to me that even boys in their crowd who planned to enter the family business were slated for college. Manufacturing men's pants or ladies' hats did not require a college degree, so why college? The fathers would have answered that there was something about a diploma. A college diploma had a magic about it. There were doubters, of course—those who said that a college diploma was for boys with "their heads stuck in the clouds"—but the majority of fathers felt that it didn't hurt to have a son's college diploma hanging on the wall. It said something to the customers.

* * *

Mr. Suberman had lunch every day, Monday through Friday, with the boys, and they ate at one of the several fur district delicatessens, though sometimes they took a cab down to the Lower East Side to treat themselves to a meal at Ratner's on Delancey Street, which, as I learned, was the pinnacle of kosher dairy cuisine, and never mind how much their lunches cost and never mind the calories. When Mr. Suberman spoke of Ratner's, it was as if he was speaking of the pleasure dome of Kublai Khan. "The *kugel!*" he would say speaking in exclamation points of the noodle pudding. "Enough sour cream to take a swim in!" Could that man be the same spare man I came to know in Miami, the one who, I had noticed, weighed his food on a scale so he could know down to the ounce what he was ingesting? Could the man I knew have once made a practice of dining wherever and on whatever calorie-laden dish took his fancy, perhaps matzo ball soup thickly filmed o'er with chicken fat? And had he *noshed* in the afternoon on a couple of nice buttery rugelachs and a cup of tea gentled with copious amounts of sugar? Could they be the same man? Yes, they were indeed one and the same, and in a short while I would find out why this was so.

On Friday afternoons Mr. Suberman went from his office to his stockbroker. It was a visit he looked forward to. His broker was ever cheerful, or as Mr. Suberman would say, "always all smiles," and he would add, "So why not? What was not to be all smiles about?" Well, what *was* not to be "all smiles" about? Mr. Suberman's stocks were faring well, the broker was making money for Mr. Suberman and for his other clients, and the broker, as Mr. Suberman said, kept for himself "not a small piece." And so before Mr. Suberman went home for Friday night dinner with the family, it was his habit to spend a happy hour or two in his broker's office, talking and joking, and watching the stock ticker rolling out the tape with quotations good enough to ensure all smiles all around.

MRS. SUBERMAN AND THE APARTMENT

Mr. Suberman, comfortable in his business life, went uptown to a comfortable home life. Home was his wife and his three children, but home was also the family apartment in the Bronx, which was, at least in the family's mind, an apartment of distinction, one that was a character in its own right. And it was clear that in Miami, as Mr. Suberman missed his business, so Mrs. Suberman missed her apartment. In Miami, they had bought a modest house in town, one that apparently had little of the cachet of that New York apartment.

In their west Bronx apartment house, Mrs. Suberman was well served: a doorman helped her through the door with her packages, and an elevator man carried the packages down the hall to her door. "Such nice men they were, Joseph and Karl," Mrs. Suberman would say. "I know they were working for tips, but they treated me like a queen."

When I first met Jack's mother, I at last knew where Jack and his brother Irwin had gotten their height, for Mrs. Suberman was unusually tall among the Jewish women I knew. She was different in other ways as well: she was blue-eyed, blondish, straight-featured, and straight-haired. All in all, she looked nothing like my own mother nor any of my aunts, nor for that matter like anybody in the whole extended family, the *mishpoucha*, as it was known.

Mrs. Suberman appeared to me more like Union City women. When I mentioned this to Jack, he said that his mother's looks came no doubt from Cossack presence in the Russian *shtetls*. "For sure," Jack joked, "the Cossacks went into the *shtetls*, and like it or not, they sprinkled their genes." And he brought in the diaspora—the Jews who left ancient Israel and went out into the world. "The Jews in Europe started looking like everybody else in Europe," he said to me. "That's why you have fair skin and I have blue eyes." So, I figured, Jack had the combination—eyes of Cossack blue, and hair Middle East dark brown.

Mrs. Suberman held sway in their apartment, and I gathered that Mr. Suberman was happy to let her do it. It was obvious to me that he was proud of her, and he would say, "Some *ballabusta*, my wife." I knew what this meant: it meant that she kept the apartment organized, she was a good cook, and she saw to it that the children were well fed and well clothed.

Mr. Suberman took pleasure in the fact that his wife had been born in America. What it suggested to him was that she knew better than he how to live in this new country, how to fall in with the American lifestyle—well, the middle-class Jewish lifestyle—how to "keep up." It was important to him, this conforming to the American way. He was in love with America, and he longed to be a "real American," as he might say. To him, America was everything Pinsk was not: in America everything was up to the minute, everything there for the buying, schools a must, firemen who could sometimes put out a fire. And if police did not always follow faithfully the rule to protect any and all regardless of race, color, or creed, in Pinsk the rule was not even in the handbook.

As the designated *ballabusta,* Mrs. Suberman prepared the work directives and schedules for the maid Millie, who came in every day Monday
through Friday. Millie did no cooking, and though in the South her title
would even so have been "the cook," in New York she was called "the girl."
Though many of the New York "girls" were Polish or German immigrants,
Millie followed in the southern servant tradition of being black and of living in a one-race section of town. Millie lived in Harlem, however, and as
I was beginning to understand, Harlem was like our black section of town
only because it was a black-only community; in other ways, it was very unlike it. Not all who lived in Harlem worked at low-level jobs, and Harlem
was in fact so economically diverse that many of its inhabitants lived in
mansions. Millie did not live in a mansion, but unlike our Willie Arnold,
she had gone to school, and Millie could not only read and write, she could
play chess, and when called upon to babysit, she and the boys settled right
into a game. I tried to picture Willie Arnold playing chess. If offered the
chance, she would have said, "I got enough to do without messin' with that
fool thing."

The apartment Mrs. Suberman described for me seemed truly lavish.
Although Jack had been born in uptown Manhattan, the Subermans had
moved to a flat in the upper reaches of an apartment house in a choice section of the west Bronx when Mrs. Suberman wanted to be closer to her
family. The apartment was comprised of three bedrooms and two baths,
the two-bath feature being the feature that Mrs. Suberman liked to dwell
on. "You should have seen the women when they heard," Mrs. Suberman
would say, with a quick little laugh. "Nobody had two bathrooms like us." It
was also apparently impressive to her friends that the apartment was across
the street from the public school, which meant that the Suberman children
got to school by braving only minimum street traffic. It was a choice location, and Mrs. Suberman said, "Of course we had to pay more, but who
counts money when your children are crossing streets?"

Mrs. Suberman described the décor of the apartment as "up-to-the-
minute," the "minute" at that time being Chinese modern. "Oh, it was
really something," Mrs. Suberman said, her blue eyes bright with remembering black lacquered tables and bamboo carvings on the cabinets. She
apparently spent as she wished, and when I—trained by a mother whose
words to live by was said in the family to be "Don't spend too much"—
might offer that it all sounded pretty expensive, Mrs. Suberman would say
to me, "So why not? In those days, money came and went like water from
the tap."

There was no violence against Jews where the Subermans lived. The building was almost uniformly tenanted by Jewish families, and perhaps because the Jewish tenants handed out generous Christmas bonuses, the staff treated them with more than a modicum of respect. The only hint of anti-Semitism, Mr. Suberman would say, was from the Polish janitor, who was sometimes heard to mutter "little kikes" under his breath when the children of the building ran wildly through the lobby. This seemed to Mr. Suberman relatively harmless, however, and he did not feel that it rated a confrontation.

THE BAR MITZVAH QUESTION

Mrs. Suberman had no luck in keeping up with her friends about lessons. The children of her friends apparently took lessons in things thought good for their souls or their futures, but the Subermans didn't fully comply. That the lessons were "very dear," the term in use by Mrs. Suberman for my mother's "costs too much," did not enter into it. What entered into it was Jack's lack of cooperation. Jack apparently refused to go to his violin lessons, and "How can you make a boy take lessons when he uses his violin for a hockey stick?" Mrs. Suberman would ask. And forget the Hebrew lessons at the Cheder, where Hebrew was learned for the bar mitzvah. On this, Mr. Suberman himself had put his foot down, and he had put it down hard.

Jack's father was a nonbeliever like my own father—both of them having been through things in Europe that made God persona non grata, maybe *persona non existente* is the better phrase—and the pleas from Jack's mother had not swayed him. When she had tried to shame him by suggesting that their crowd would disapprove, when she said, "They'll think you're depriving Jack of something," Mr. Suberman had thundered, "So if the *schoites* want to have their bar mitzvahs, who's stopping them?" He wasn't going to stop dunces from having bar mitzvahs, but his own family was his own family and that was a different story. Putting his foot down may have been a rare thing for Mr. Suberman, but when it came to religious rites and ceremonies, he put his foot down so hard that Mrs. Suberman could only put up a hand and say, "So stop with the yelling already." In the end Jack had no bar mitzvah, and neither he nor his father cared that he was the only son in their crowd who hadn't.

NOT VERY HIGH SOCIETY BUT HIGH ENOUGH

The Suberman family, minus Mr. Suberman, went to *shul* only on the High Holidays and only to please Mrs. Suberman. She would say, "It's an occasion for getting all dolled up," leaving me to guess at her true religious feelings. So, as I learned, most ordinary Friday nights in New York were spent by the family at somebody's apartment, with "the boys" playing pinochle or poker in the dining room, the wives playing mah-jongg with real ivory tiles in the living room, and the kids playing with whatever new toy or game had just been acquired.

Mrs. Suberman shopped a lot. She shopped downtown on Thirty-fourth Street and on Fifth Avenue. As Mr. Suberman had his "boys," Mrs. Suberman had her "girls," and while the boys might be lunching at Ratner's or gathering to congratulate each other at their broker's office, the girls might be shopping at B. Altman or Saks Fifth Avenue, or sometimes "having a little splurge" at Bergdorf Goodman. Lunch was a two-hour affair at the Russian Tea Room.

On Saturday nights the husbands took their wives to dinner at some upscale Midtown restaurant, where they ate very well. They had all the courses, and there was no looking at the right side of the menu, and no dieting. There was only "enjoying," as Mrs. Suberman said. And when the check came, there was no "divvying it up," no "Let's see—you had soup *and* a salad, and Lester had the Hungarian steak"; there was just a show of argument over the check—"No, I've got it . . . No, I've got it"—and when one of the men finally "got it," the others would say, "Okay, this time, but next time it's mine."

These restaurant dinners were only a minor break for the wives. The major break came in the summers, when the men sent the family to the Catskill Mountains. With the kids in camps, the wives played cards or mah-jongg every day, ate foods crammed with whatever might be made even better with "just another bitty-bit" of cream or butter, and they slept in the cool of the Catskill nights. The men drove up in their cars on weekends, and they went with their wives to the hotel shows and laughed at the comics whose routines were more often than not built around the Yiddish immigrant experience, and they danced to the orchestra that offered mostly foxtrots. They played outdoor and indoor games arranged by the social activities director, the *tummeler,* and they said, "Such a hot summer in the city. What a *broche* to be up here." They enjoyed this blessing summer after summer, taking unto themselves pleasure upon pleasure, until it all came crashing down.

THE CRASH

When the crash came that October in 1929, Mr. Suberman's first worry was about his stocks. And when he ran to his broker's office to gather some facts, his broker was not "all smiles"; he was now "all gray," as Mr. Suberman described him. In the office Mr. Suberman found dozens of the broker's other clients trying to make sense of things. The only thing they knew was that stocks had taken not only a plunge, they had disappeared from view.

He left the office thinking, okay, my stocks are worthless. Okay, those stock certificates in my safety deposit box can be thrown out. Okay, pull up your socks and get busy with your business. And then he thought, Business? What business? A stock market crash—wouldn't it knock the business for a loop? Mr. Suberman had no experience with such a thing as a stock market crash, so how could he know what would happen? He felt he was in a state of suspended animation. One shoe had fallen—his stocks—and he was waiting for all the other shoes that might be teetering.

He worried about the skins still in the basement; he worried about his investments—the shipment of skins just due to arrive. He worried about his customers. He had heard nothing from them, and he interpreted this as a sign that they were getting ready to default on what they owed him. He read and reread the *Times* hoping for a bit of solace, but it was chockablock with stories of gloom and doom. And the pictures! Photos of the hullabaloo in the financial district and of Wall Street money men gathering in clusters with cutlines that read, in a wrong-headed attempt at a jaunty pun, "Wall Street Brokers Tied Up in Knots."

Mr. Suberman was not amused; he was in fact frantic. He listened to the radio until one or two in the morning. He went to business, came home early, went back the same day. He went to his broker's office only to find his broker not there and nobody knowing where he was. "Nobody knew from anything," he said.

It went on this way. By the spring of the next year, the nation's unemployment had tripled, and though President Hoover had said it was "foolish" to think that all was not well with American business, Mr. Suberman was frightened as he had never been in his life—"not even on my first day over," he said—meaning the day he had gotten off the boat. He began to hate the business he had chosen for himself. He was in a luxury business, and in times like these, he felt he was being punished for playing fast and loose with the really important things of life. And when, by the next year—1930—business nationwide was reported to be not only flat but "laid out in the cemetery," as Mr. Suberman described it, he began to believe that the other shoes had fallen and that they had fallen on *him*.

It turned out in fact that he still had a business, but such a negligible one that he had no need for workers, and he laid off his last two. "I was in a wholesale business," he told me, "so I had to lay off wholesale." Pretty soon, nobody was left but him and his partner, and Jack was pressed into service on the weekends to count and recount the skins. Anything sold? Well, maybe one or two.

After a couple of years, Mr. Suberman and his partner decided to sell all the skins for whatever they could get, and then they just closed their doors. "Women were not only not buying furs, they were hocking them," Mr. Suberman said, and I pictured women bundling their furs under their arms and trying to slip unnoticed into pawn shops. Mr. Suberman understood the plight of the fur-loving and fur-owning women. "Why should they keep their furs?" he would ask me, in his usual rhetorical way. "Where are they going to wear them? To the pushcarts on Hester Street?" I knew what he meant—that women like Jack's mother were no longer dressing up to go shopping on Fifth Avenue.

So what means had he left? As the astute businessman, Mr. Suberman had habitually put some money away in a small account, and he had to depend on that: "It wasn't much," Mr. Suberman said, "but it kept us in noodles." Still, as the Depression bore in, despite the rent on the wonderful apartment being lowered, the Subermans could no longer pay even that, and they moved out.

SACRIFICING, BUT NOT SUFFERING

No more a six-room, two-bath apartment on the top floor; now a four-room, one-bath one on ground level. No more views of the great yonder but a glimpse of passersby, who returned the favor by peering into the windows. Millie was no more, nor were Joseph and Karl. That no one was in the elevator to greet them now meant little: on the ground floor, what use had they for an elevator? The massive living room Chinese modern furniture? It couldn't find a place for itself, and a man came in and offered something for the black lacquered tables and the cabinets with the bamboo etchings and the dining room set—the dining venue was now the kitchen—and though Jack's mother said the man offered her *bupkis*— whose real translation is "goat excrement," though usually interpreted as "precious little"—she could only look on with *umet*, with sadness, as she let him take it all away. "We sacrificed everything," Mrs. Suberman said. "We were left with nothing. *Oy*, how we suffered." Well, not really, Jack would say.

Jack never thought of his family as "suffering." He saw his family's new lifestyle as simply an adjustment. Was anybody in the family going without food or shelter? No? So where was the suffering? Disappointments, sure, even deprivations. Sacrifices, maybe; but *suffering?*

Jack was a student at Townsend Harris, a downtown prep school for the then well-respected City College of New York, and he had been aware at school of the sacrifices the Depression had demanded. There was now little after-school "klatching" among the boys; they had to get to their after-school jobs if they had one, or go look for one if they hadn't. Some boys were leaving school. The Japanese boy who was on track to be valedictorian had left for a job in his uncle's restaurant, and the tall black boy Jack had played basketball with was now working all day as a delivery boy in his own neighborhood. In New York City, if you were over fourteen, compulsory school attendance did not apply, and for many the tenth grade was the last of their schooling.

It was when Jack got off the subway that took him to his school that he saw not just the sacrificing but the suffering, for in the streets he had a close-up of Depression-inflicted misery. Men and women down on their luck were on every block, and they did not hesitate to approach him for a handout, even if he was obviously a teenager with perhaps only lunch money in his pocket. It didn't matter: the men called him "buddy" and asked for whatever he could spare. Women were on the street as well, and with a baby in one arm, they might come up to Jack and reach out to him with the other. No, his family's disappointments did not seem to him to count for much in the way of suffering.

Jack joked that he soon thereafter had a reality check. Into his new lifestyle had come a deprivation that he laughingly called "suffering": he was told that he would not be going to camp. Not go to his dearly loved Camp Roosevelt? Not have his empyrean summer? His mother, trying to ease his disappointment, said that he could go if he got a job at the camp. Jack may have been squeamish about handling blood-tinged fur skins, but if going to camp depended on a job in which, as he said, he had to "wipe the behinds of little kids," he would gratefully take it.

Jobs at Camp Roosevelt, however, were not easy to get: the majority of campers were in the same boat as Jack. Their fathers, like Jack's, had fallen on hard times, and they too wanted their empyrean summer. In the end, Jack and some of the boys got hired, he as a waiter, and Mr. Suberman harrumphed that it was the least the bosses could do after all the money he had given them through the years. Still, as Jack admitted, waiting tables, even wiping little kids' behinds, was not suffering.

MR. SUBERMAN'S "DISLOYAL" HEART

Before I met Jack's father, Jack had already told me about his father's heart attack. I knew that a couple of years after the crash, Mr. Suberman had been walking home from the subway station on a rainy day—I took it that rain or no rain, there were no more taxis in Mr. Suberman's life—and on this day while walking up a slight incline, he had suddenly felt a pain in his arm, in the next moment he was on the ground, and then an ambulance was taking him to the hospital. Jack and his mother had rushed there, and when Jack had seen his father lying ashen and mute, it was a sight he never could have imagined. "I couldn't believe what I was seeing," Jack told me. "It never occurred to me that my father could ever be struck down." The all-wise man lying helpless in a hospital bed? The peerless businessman a victim?

Mr. Suberman might say that he was a victim of a disloyal heart, but Jack said that his father was a victim of the Depression—that the tyrant had seized his father's heart and squeezed the life out of it. "And my father was not the only one," Jack said. "There was an epidemic of heart attacks upon the land." And Mrs. Suberman would nod and say, "There were some that died from it. I can only thank God it didn't happen to us."

At this, Mr. Suberman would smile ruefully and after the usual "God had nothing to do with it," would say, well, if it *had* happened to them, the family would have collected a lot of money on his insurance policy. Not if he had been a suicide, of course, because policies did not pay off for suicides, and even I knew from reading the papers that Depression suicides had also constituted an epidemic.

This brought Mr. Suberman to the subject of insurance companies. Even if the deaths had not been suicides, Mr. Suberman said, insurance companies tried their best to turn them into ones, claiming an overdose of medication, and in court their lawyers would hold up the dead man's prescribed medication to show that the bottle held fewer pills than it should, or that the man had purposely ignored his medication and, according to the insurance lawyer, "thereby had set the stage for his death." At any rate, the issue was moot in Mr. Suberman's case, for he had neither committed suicide nor died of natural causes. He had simply become physically unfit to work. "If there had been any work," Mr. Suberman would say.

But wait: that insurance policy Mr. Suberman had signed up for? What was happening with the disability clause, the one he had paid no attention to? Suddenly that underrated, trivialized addendum was heard from. When Mr. Suberman was declared disabled—several doctors had affirmed it—the insurance company was forced to honor the disability obligation, "forced" apparently being the operative word. "Give in without a fight?" Mr. Suberman said. "Not those *goniffs.*" Those thieves, according to Mr. Suberman, "tried to give us the works, and wiggled the words around so much, I didn't know what language I was hearing." In the end, however, the insurance company paid off, but in monthly amounts so meager, Mr. Suberman said, that in the old days he would have thrown the check in the drawer and forgotten about it. But not now. Not now.

I took it that Mr. Suberman's story was a typical insurance story of the times, and it had an interesting coda: insurance companies suddenly ceased offering these "double indemnity" policies. "These insurance companies are looking at their bottom line," he said, "and their bottom line says you're giving people too many breaks."

MIAMI

At the time of his father's heart attack, Jack was about to graduate from Townsend Harris, and Mr. Suberman's little insurance allowance and that small reserve of his was enough for Jack to go to college. But what college? The ability to beat the quota system was now irrelevant, for there was no money for a private university. The only logical college was the tuitionless CCNY, to which Townsend Harris students were admitted automatically, and this was all right with Jack. Didn't he have an abiding fantasy of playing basketball for their iconic coach, Nat Holman? Didn't he have idols on the team? Jack assured me that all this being true, going to CCNY was okay with him.

CCNY, however, was about to be ruled out. Just as Jack was graduating, the family was making plans that did not include CCNY. Mr. Suberman's doctor had some advice for his patient, and the Subermans were anxious to do whatever the doctor said—in their crowd a doctor's words were words to embroider on a pillow—and the first thing he said was that Mr. Suberman should watch his diet, and now I understood about the presence of the little scale that weighed Mr. Suberman's food. What else did the all-knowing doctor say? The doctor said that Mr. Suberman should live in a milder climate.

The Subermans did not question this, and when the doctor said, "Why not go to Miami?" they didn't question that either. If he had said, "Why not go to Tahiti?" they might also have said, "Yes, of course." But he had said Miami, and so they would relocate to Miami. Well, it wasn't all because of the doctor's directive: it was also that the Subermans had vacationed a bit in Miami, and they remembered the city's climate, and they, like the doctor, said, "Why not Miami?"

They established themselves in Miami in 1936, in a little house that the small amount of insurance money enabled them to buy, and like most college-bound Florida boys, Jack would go to the University of Florida, the all-boys state school. Actually, for Jack and, as he found out, for most financially strapped Florida boys who had college in their plans, the state-run, practically tuition-free University of Florida (for those who had established state residency) was not so much a choice as a foregone conclusion.

8

1939 and 1940

In the summer of 1939, there was bad news and good news. If my mother—and I—had early on voiced concerns that summer business would be hard to come by, we were proven right year after year, and the year 1939 was no exception. Even the winter season had only "huffed and puffed," as my father would say, but our summer business in 1939 did not huff and it did not puff. It just lay there. That was the bad news.

I started off the summer of 1939 by graduating from high school, and I didn't know if graduation would bring me good news or not. Ruth had already had taken off for school in New York with her shoe store money, so there was good news there. Minna was married, so good news there as well. She had married Mike Langer, whose family operated a wholesale fish business in the Catskill Mountains, a place well known for Jewish summering—the place where the Subermans had spent their summers—just as Miami Beach was known for Jewish wintering. And because Mike would be joining his well-established family business, my mother figured that even with the Depression, it wasn't going bust tomorrow. So Mike was deemed an eligible candidate, and my mother gave her blessings.

On the national stage that summer, big things were happening. In August the Nazis and the Soviets signed a non-aggression pact—the Molotov-Ribbentrop Pact—and as everybody seemed to be making a fuss, I charged over to my Communist friends to hear the news behind the news, and I found them in a state of bewilderment and outrage. "Double-crossed," they cried to me. "We've been had." As Americans, they felt deceived by the Soviets, and they said, "How could they? How could they shake hands with our enemy?" Of course they were not "our" enemy yet, but the sympathy of most Americans was not with the Nazis. Furthermore, my Communist friends also felt a sense of betrayal as Jews: they were incensed that the party in which they had placed such hope had buddied up to "that piece of anti-Semitic *dreck.*" Still, as we read in the papers, Communists and non-Communists were protesting on behalf of the Soviet Union, saying in essence that maybe the Soviet Union knew something we didn't know, which implied a method to the Soviets' madness. As it turned out, this was indeed the case, for the pact protected them for some months against the German assault that the Soviet Union most certainly knew was coming their way.

The truly bad news was yet to come. In the late summer of 1939 we woke up one morning to discover that the troubles in Europe had turned truly scary. Germany had invaded Poland, and "Uh oh," my father said, "we're in for it now."

THE CARDBOARD COLLEGE

And what about the personal front in the summer of 1939? I had graduated from high school, but I was already convinced that I was not going to college. I had known that despite the words to my mother—"Rebecca, now don't get your britches in an uproar about girls going to college"—from her intimidator, Miss Bookie Caldwell of Union City, Tennessee, my mother remained uninterested in the proposition.

In the end, however, I did go to college. It was not because my parents had a burning desire to see me there but because Miss Anita Sternberg of the NYA had delivered them a persuasive lecture. She had informed them with her usual certainty that being a girl did not disqualify me for college and that girls could have careers as well as boys. Still, it was not Miss Sternberg's message that caused the change of mind; it was Miss Sternberg's job: my parents had never wavered in the belief they had acquired as immigrants—that those who worked for the government did important work and what they advised should be heeded.

The University of Miami was the logical choice: I could live at home and save on dormitory expenses. Another no surprise. The university seemed to me the logical choice for another reason. Did I plan a career as a professional? No, I did not. If anything, I was going to spend my life in a store, in a retail business. And as an institution of no educational distinction whatsoever, what better place not to plan for a professional career than at the University of Miami? Its physical plant was primitive, comprised as it was of a single building surrounding a patio, and wasn't it a bit of a stretch to even call it a "university"? Could this one partitioned building inspire serious learning? Could something nicknamed "Cardboard College" motivate students? I didn't think it could—inspire and motivate, that is—and I didn't care that it couldn't.

At the university I played a lot—a *lot*—of tennis. I was on the tennis team, which was coached by the nationally ranked tennis player Gardnar Mulloy, and we went around the state playing other tennis teams. Gardnar had also enticed Bobby Riggs—who everybody following tennis knew was headed for the number-one tennis ranking in the coming years—to enter the university, though Bobby wasn't interested in being on the men's team; he was interested in using the nearby Biltmore Hotel courts as a gambling venue where he could "take the guests for a few," as he would say, no doubt thinking that desperate times called for desperate measures.

Okay, I was at the university, and I had to have a major, so I decided on one in English literature. With this in mind, I volunteered to work for the student newspaper. I liked the idea of it—of being that savvy-sounding thing, a "news-hen." The paper's advisor had a mature view of the role of newspapers, and he had a word for us "journalists." Our role, he said, was to keep the student body informed, and he advised us to adapt items in national newspapers to do this. "There are historical events taking place out there," he told us. "So get off your duffs. Tell your reader things they ought to know." The university had at last inspired me, and I felt a noble purpose descending. I felt further that this professor and I understood each other, that he knew as well as I just how trivia-filled were the heads of University of Miami students and how it was our duty to inform them.

Thus challenged, I thought of something to write about. I had seen a ship carrying Jewish refugees, the SS *St. Louis,* anchored off the Miami Beach shore, and using my father's binoculars I had seen passengers lined up against the rail. I didn't know much about its fate, only what the *Miami Herald* had reported—that the ship had been denied entry and had returned to Nazi-held Germany.

Still, I had been an eyewitness to the ship's hopes of entry, and I thought to inform my readers of what I knew. And because it would be a feature story, I indulged in a little editorializing. I wrote, "Even if the passengers could not see me as I trained my binoculars on them, they could see the gleaming white hotels that line the Miami Beach shore." I wrote of the pain that the sight of the hotels must have caused them, and I ended, grandly I must say, with "It was a particularly poignant case of so near and yet so far."

When my piece was duly published, I thought it was pretty good, and I thought it might raise consciousness among University of Miami students. But when I asked my advisor if he agreed, he laughed and said, "The Nazis took over Poland, but neither the Nazis or the Poles have taken over the interest of the students." I remembered my father's "Uh oh, we're in for it now," and I had to think that the interest would come.

In reality, things were changing. Suddenly at the university, young men in uniform were all at once walking around the halls looking earnest and carrying themselves with an altogether different demeanor from typical University of Miami male students. They were imposing, not lax; they moved with alacrity, not apathy. The new guys were in class with you if you took math or engineering courses, and you noticed that they took their studies seriously. They ate with you in the cafeteria, in their uniforms, at tables assigned exclusively to them, as if their missions required isolation. As we found out, they were military men stationed in Miami and assigned by the military to take courses at the university.

The campus now indeed began to buzz with talk of war. And when France fell to the Nazis, talk exploded into disbelief. And then, in what seemed instant fallout, Washington announced what was called "Selective Service," which it described merely as a "peacetime" draft in an attempt, no doubt, to tamp down panic. I wondered if World War I had started like this and if this new draft was the modern version of the World War I one.

On behalf of the school paper, I went around taking a poll about what students thought. One of my questions was, "What do you think of Hitler?" And another was, "What could you do in the army?" The questions were inane, I was inane, and to judge by their answers, so were the students. Maybe I'm being too hard on us. Maybe we were just in denial.

After the Selective Service announcement, however, University of Miami students, like students no doubt across the country, little-jack-little came out of their denial: it was hard to dismiss that the war in Europe was on track to becoming our war, and my male classmates suddenly woke up to the fact that it might be only a matter of months, maybe days, before they would be tapped by Uncle Sam. They joked and they joshed and, perhaps dreaming of the German actress Marlene Dietrich, she of the most talked-about legs since legs were invented, they said, "Let me at those frauleins." So despite its alternate, and equally disparaging, nickname of "Suntan U.," which implied that any serious thinking on the campus involved whether butter or Vaseline produced a deeper tan, the University of Miami was becoming fully engaged.

And now the campus (read: the patio) became alive with war talk and petitions. Small groups gathered to exchange views on things other than Saturday's football game in the new Roddy Burdine Stadium (which we would later know as the Orange Bowl) or the latest shipment of Brigance sportswear to Saks Fifth Avenue. And the patio was now the scene of petition tables.

I liked the idea of petition tables. They were more than ads; they expressed a viewpoint, and when I spotted one with a placard reading JOIN THE ABRAHAM LINCOLN BRIGADE, I felt instant kinship because of Jack Simon, Ruth's old boyfriend, the one who had gone to Spain as a member of the brigade, and I asked to be at the table. I waited for signatures, or at least for questions, and then I waited some more. No takers. When I looked over at the one protesting the Molotov-Ribbentrop Pact, however, I saw lines of students waiting to sign. It seemed that fighting the Fascists in Spain was old news. The new news was Germany and the Nazis.

GAME, SET, AND MATCH

World news may have made us doubtful, but in my little personal world, in the winter of 1940 I was on track to win the biggest match ever—the one with a prize so meaningful that I could not imagine my life without it. It happened at the moment when Jack Suberman appeared, and all at once I had the game, the set, and the match. I have to believe that it happened this way because Jack Suberman had all the right answers. For me, Was he smart? Yes. Was he an athlete? Yes. For my mother, Was he Jewish? Oh, yes, Mama, yes, he's Jewish! And for my father, Was he a good Democrat? Yes, Dad, of course he is! The only answer Jack didn't have was the answer to a question I didn't ask, and that was, Did he have prospects? And the reason I didn't ask was that I already knew the answer. And the answer of course was, No, he didn't.

* * *

After Jack and I met, he came down from Gainesville on weekends to see me. With no money for buses or trains, he hitchhiked, and as a city boy born and bred, he had to learn the rules. They were rules I already knew. In Tennessee, hitching rides was a way of life. You walked along the road, and somebody came by, usually in a wagon and later maybe a truck, and you got picked up. It seemed to be different in Florida, however, and Jack had to learn. He had to learn how to stand prominently out on the highway outside Gainesville and hold up his thumb, and he had to learn not to be choosy. He had to learn that whoever came by and in whatever vehicle, he had to accept the hitch so long as the vehicle was going in his general direction. If the wait was long, if cars were few and far between, or when talk between him and his driver was in fits and starts and sometimes in no starts at all, he had to learn to carry a book in his pocket.

Jack had many memorable rides, one of which began when he was hoping to get as far as Melbourne, had made his way to Kissimmee, and had been picked up by a rural mailman. "Have you in Melbourne in a minute," the mailman had said as he zipped off to Lakeland, which lay fifty or so miles away in another direction. Still, there was a nice bit of serendipity: while in Lakeland Jack talked the mailman into taking a break, and Jack walked around the Florida Southern College campus for a look at the buildings under construction designed by the country's leading architect, Frank Lloyd Wright.

We in Florida had sat up and taken notice when Frank Lloyd Wright and his architecture came into the state. We didn't often get in on the best that American culture had to offer—as my university professors often pointed out—and here we were welcoming the world's greatest architect, if, as one of my professors noted, Wright said so himself. At the time of Jack's visit the chapel was going up, and it was said that Wright envisioned it as a building moving from the earth up to the light, as if to say that the darkness of the Depression—the earth—would be pierced by the sunlight of recovery. And the story was also told that when the woman who had provided the money for the chapel came to dedicate it, she glanced around at the spare construction and at the sunlight freely pouring in, and she said, "They tell me it's finished, but you sure can't tell by lookin' at it."

Jack got to know a lot about Florida by hitching rides. Every ride showed him something he didn't know about the state, and he found himself riding through the hitherto unknown green pastures of the Ocala horse spreads— where horses were still stabled in luxury, as if the Depression had been beaten back with a riding crop—and the catfish camp country around Lake Okeechobee, where commercial fishermen sold their catches to restaurants at prices that scarcely paid for their bait.

He already knew about the orange groves—the whole country knew about them—but what he did not know was how vast they were, how they reached out almost county line to county line. Or how beautiful they were. Jack was smitten, so smitten, in fact, that in trying to describe for me his feelings, he took to reciting poetry, and he quoted lines from Wilfrid Wilson Gibson that went, "By the lamplit stall I loitered, Feasting my eyes, On colours ripe and rich for the heart's desire. . . . Oranges like old sunsets over Tyre." Jack reciting poetry! Oh, my Mr. Chips! O, my fantasy!

Like everybody else, orange growers were having a hard time, but according to one orange grower with whom Jack had hitched a ride, there was light at the end of the tunnel, and it was frozen orange juice concentrate. The grower was enthusiastic. "Put all your money into frozen orange juice," he advised this impecunious college boy. "And remember who told you." Jack remembered the man, but did he put his money into frozen orange juice concentrate? Well, no. Almost all of Jack's money was at this moment in his pocket, and just enough, he said, to spring for a hamburger.

Other interesting items were to be learned. Sometimes, to make conversation, the man at the wheel might ask Jack about the book he had been holding as he waited alongside the road, and on the occasion that Jack informed his farmer/driver that he was carrying a copy of *The Yearling*, he and the farmer/driver suddenly were flying off toward the book's setting of Cross Creek. Pointing out a little nondescript cottage where its author, Marjorie Kinnan Rawlings, lived and from which many of her novels went out the door to her New York publisher, the man said, "You bein' such a reader of Miz Rawlins's, I figured I could hep you out." When Jack told this story, did he delight in saying "hep" for "help"? Of course he did, and you couldn't miss that he did.

Jack discovered that riding the country roads presented other items of interest. Railroad crossings, for example, had no guardrails because Depression-hit farmers had prevailed upon the state legislature to outlaw fences, and the result was that stock roamed at will in search of scrub. On one occasion Jack's driver hit a goat and a farmer appeared out of nowhere and said, "Hold it one derned minute," and demanded remuneration. After the driver paid up, he told Jack it was a setup. "They can't get anything for their crops, so they station themselves by the side of the road. And when they see you hit something, they pounce."

When home on summer vacations, the Gainesville boys no longer hung out on the beach and played volleyball; they tried to find some kind of gainful employment. Jack's gainful employment was at hotel construction sites, where, having no construction skills at all, he was usually hired as a timekeeper. The job was easy, but it had its down moments. "How would you like to keep tabs on men who make only a little more per hour," he would say to me, "than you were making as a baby sitter?" Jack liked the men, even if, after Jack and I had met, they ragged him endlessly about having a girlfriend. After work, the men went for a beer—often at our store—and when Jack had to cut the time short to rush home to get to our date, they would say, "Jack's girlfriend won't let him drink," and then they'd say, "Probably won't let him do anything else either. No wonder he's so jumpy." All followed by a big guffaw.

*   *   *

If on that first date I had discovered Jack's love of books, on date after date afterward we spent a lot of time talking about them, and it was not unusual for us to sit in the car for a few extra minutes with the interior light on (batteries be damned, despite every Depression advisory) reading a book passage to each other before we said goodnight. We had both been reading *For Whom the Bell Tolls*, the recently published Hemingway novel based on the Loyalist-Fascist conflict in Spain, and though we were both Hemingway fans, I had a special reason for liking him: he continued to be, even after the awful 1935 hurricane had stopped being talked about, a staunch defender of veterans' rights.

Book talk Jack and I may have engaged in, but serious Depression talk always came in somewhere. What did we know? In 1940, among the things we knew was that more than ten thousand banks had already failed and had taken their depositors' funds with them; and we knew that more than eight million Americans were out of work. We couldn't not talk about the Depression: the Depression clung to Jack and me like a burdensome ruck-sack, as it did with most Americans.

JACK AT THE UNIVERSITY OF FLORIDA

Responding to the strictures of the Depression, Jack had his own way of going to college. He was scheduled to graduate in June 1942, and during his three-and-a-half years at the University of Florida, he had been an outstanding athlete, an active member of a social fraternity, but only a passing resemblance to a student. It had been no different at Townsend Harris in New York, for even there, though he had made good grades, he felt himself a non-student. "Why study more than you have to?" Jack would ask me. "When the Depression laid its hand on me, I knew I couldn't get out from under that cold, dead thing." How then to explain his good grades? Probably, I thought, because of that passion for books.

At the University of Florida, with the Depression pressing ever more heavily, Jack had continued to show little enthusiasm for studying, and any-hopes he might have entertained for the future ("Future? What future?" he would have said) had gradually disappeared. When asked what he was studying, Jack would laugh and say, "I'm not studying anything. I'm indulging a hobby." If pressed to name a major, he would have said, "English," and not because he had any confidence that an English major would get him a job. In reality, he didn't feel he was majoring in anything; he felt he was just larking around.

While larking around, he took a variety of courses. On the advice of a professor who had seen this Jewish kid from New York sitting in front of him and this professor apparently thinking that this kid could benefit from some rural exposure, had advised Jack to take courses in the agriculture school. When explaining these curious choices, Jack would say, "I'm furthering my education. You never know when I might have to castrate a pig." What he was actually saying was that it was all an exercise in futility anyway.

Jack would tell me that the majority of boys in his fraternity had that "exercise in futility" sensibility. Jack was a member of Pi Lambda Phi, one of the two Jewish fraternities at the University of Florida, and when we met, Jack was its president (of course!). The "exercise in futility" attitude had an extra dimension for these boys: the job market was very tight, and for Jews, even tighter.

I learned about the boys. The majority of them came from families who owned retail stores in Florida towns, and most of them had already failed or were in the process of failing. Hello, Kaufman's Low-Price Store. At any rate, these boys now had no guaranteed futures. Guaranteed futures, Jack said, were for those very few whose fathers were lawyers or accountants, and upon graduation they would enter those practices, even though their fathers' client lists might be down to a precious few. Still, no similar track existed for Jack and most of the others, and these boys saw nothing out there but frustration.

According to Jack, in the fraternity house they talked about this a lot, about financial predicaments and career uncertainties. They told stories about being in college "on a dime so thin you can see through it," and about observing little economies being practiced. There was the one about the student who was seen in the dining hall putting ketchup into a cup, filling it with hot water from the coffee bar, and calling it tomato soup, and when Jack said, "Pretty ingenious," I remembered the hard joking of the black people in Union City and the similar hard joking of any of the Depression-afflicted. And there were stories about students who shared the cost of books and spent time setting up elaborate study schedules. Many a room around Gainesville housed four or five occupants; and the rooming house owner apparently went along with the scheme because it meant the room was—praise the lord—bringing in some rent.

Jack told me how the boys questioned each other about job prospects. Someone might ask, "Any chance of a job when you get through?" and someone might answer, "Are you kidding? There's not a decent job in all of Jacksonville." Or somebody might say, "I'm going to finish school, but don't ask me why."

Jack's brother Irwin was also at the University of Florida, studying engineering, apparently determined like my brother Will to be an engineer despite the bias. Paradoxically, when the fraternity boys sought a Jewish faculty member to act as advisor, one of the few faculty Jews was Joseph Weil, the dean of the engineering school. And it was perhaps in the spirit of lessons learned that when Irwin (or any other engineer wannabe) informed Dean Weil that he was hoping for an engineering degree, the dean would say, according to the story, "The engineering profession will welcome you like an orange grove owner welcomes thirty-two degrees."

"Exercise in futility" thus became a campus cry, and Jack would say that if you walked down a dormitory hall and peeked into a room and asked the occupant what he was doing, the answer came back often as not, "Just doing my exercises in futility."

FLORIDA STATE COLLEGE FOR WOMEN

Soon Jack and I were telling each other that having only weekends together was not enough, and when I sighed about this around the house, my mother said, unhelpfully, "So you'll see him when you see him." And when I said I wanted to transfer to Florida State College for Women in Tallahassee, which was closer to Gainesville—300 miles to Miami, 150 to Tallahassee—she said, "Why are you getting so serious about a boy with no prospects?" Despite this, my mother really liked Jack, perhaps because he was Jewish and she could stop worrying about *shagetz* boyfriends. My father liked Jack for other reasons. "A good man to have on your team," he would say. Whether this meant in sports or in life I didn't know, but I thought it could apply to both.

At this point Ruth was at Pratt Institute in New York studying interior design. She was living in the Bronx, sharing a room with two cousins in the apartment of our aunt, my mother's sister, to whom my mother was sending compensation of five dollars a month. Ruth traveled downtown to school by subway, and tried to manage on the two dollars a week she got from home, which, she wrote me, covered her subway fare (two nickels for the round-trip), her school supplies, and her peanut butter cracker lunch.

When I joked in a letter to Ruth that she might want to enter a dance marathon like our old friend Max Needleman, she wrote back that dance marathons had gone out of style and had been supplanted by hot dog eating competitions. Ruth wrote me her thoughts about his new development, and I noticed that she had also picked up some New York lingo. "The people who enter these things are just plain hungry," Ruth wrote. "There are plenty of hungry people in New York. I see them all the time when I look out the El window." *The El?* I knew that "The El" was New York lingo for the elevated train, the train that the subway turned into when it went from subterranean to above ground (although I was aware that some trains were elevated for their whole route), but I never said it out loud. It seemed too much like puttin' on.

Had Ruth gone New York? Did she now say the Met, the Village, the Lower East Side? Had she forgotten our little town in Tennessee? As if to reassure me, in one of her later letters she recalled a few things from our days in Union City. "Do you remember," she wrote, "when we played skip rope in front of our house, how the mayor, Mr. Joe Prieto down at the end of our road, would wave to us to join him when the need for a game of catch came over him?" Yes, I remembered, and I remembered that Ruth and I agreed that playing catch was Mr. Prieto's way of relaxing after a tough day mayoring a town of five thousand in his office on Second Street and Church. "Do you remember?" Ruth wrote. And yes, Ruth, of course I did.

* * *

I had some lobbying to do if I was to convince my mother to let me make the transfer from the University of Miami to FSCW, and I was glad to be able to report that tuition at FSCW was free and that room and board came to just over three hundred dollars a semester. So my mother finally said okay, despite Jack's lack of prospects.

As for giving up significant learning opportunities, learning opportunities were the least of it, the most of it being my spot on the University of Miami tennis team, though Bobby Riggs and his entertaining ways had already moved on. Where I went to school meant nothing to me. I just wanted to be nearer to my "darling," as we called each other, trying hard to imitate the lovers in the novels of the much-admired English writer Evelyn Waugh.

I had no trouble settling into Tallahassee, chiefly because it was southern, very southern. Signs everywhere all but said, "We do separation of the races." If you read between the lines, the signs were saying, "This is a southern city, and this is our custom, so get used to it."

FSCW was southern down to its "Floridy" and "Georgy," and I was definitely pleased to be interacting once more with the southern language. When the girls gossiped and chattered, especially about their boyfriends, I was back in Union City, on our front porch, listening to Minna and her friends saying, "Listen, y'all," and nattering on about boys who were "dead attractive" or boys who drank too much white lightnin' or Purple Jesus punch and were "just so dissipated." Much of the talk, however, was devoted to marriage matters, for no doubt about it, the girls of Union City saw themselves in the future as married women.

So did the girls at FSCW, and the FSCW curriculum was ideal for that. The faculty knew with whom they were dealing—girls like me who kept to the marriage track—and this gave them freedom to devise courses that educated without equipping for careers. It was a curriculum that departed from the one at the University of Florida, where the boys were given hard-nosed courses to prepare them for jobs—in the seemingly unlikely event that jobs ever turned up.

A few FSCW girls were actually hoping to "be" something, and those who were in this mode studied to be teachers and took education courses, though even they did not stray from the marriage track. They kept their eyes open for possibilities, and with Gainesville so close, possibilities were abundant, even if they seldom resulted in anything to call the newspapers about.

There were some Jewish students at FSCW, and if they were from one of the small towns, chances were they were the daughters of Jew store owners. Some few were from Miami Beach, and if they were Jewish as well—of which a handful of us were—you not only got a lot of attention, you occasionally sensed you were being looked over for one of the features thought unique to Jews. The Tallahassee girls had various ideas on the subject, depending on whose insights they were following, but they generally agreed on horns. Some thought (yes!) a vestigial tail was involved, and occasionally a "lump" on the back of the neck. The lump was puzzling. When I asked Jack, he offered a simple explanation: the word "lump," he said, was simply being confused with "hump," and a "hump" was a feature that old-time writers chose to portray the obsequiousness of their Jewish characters.

Well, I knew that when I first met Doris and the others in Union City, they talked about horns, but not, as I recalled, about tails and lumps. If they did so early on, they didn't as the years went by. They knew all six of us Jewish Kaufmans, and they knew that none of us had any of those features. As to their hope that Will would develop his horns when he grew up, the girls grew up right alongside him, and they finally gave up on it. "I 'clare, Willie," they would say. "You're just never goin' to grow horns, are you? Tell the truth now." After a while, disappointed though everyone might have been, horns, tails, and lumps disappeared from the conversation.

It was obvious that when I got my dormitory assignment, thought had been given to appropriate roommates, and I was informed that I would be sharing a room with a Jewish girl, Myra Rubin from Daytona Beach. Myra had spent two years at FSCW and was wise to its ways, and we talked and laughed about the tails and the lumps. And the room assignments. "Jewish girls rooming with gentile ones?" she would joke. "It's agin' nature." And she would say, "When you get a package from home, who you gonna share your matzo balls with? With Sally Lou Bynum from the family farm in LaBelle?"

On weekdays, when we "Tallahassee lassies," as we called ourselves, were dateless, as I was when Jack couldn't come over from Gainesville, we danced. We brought our records to the rec room, and somebody brought her record player, and we danced to Benny Goodman and Les Brown and Artie Shaw and whoever else put us into a faint. Miami Beach girls were thought to be adventurous and therefore knowledgeable about the latest, and we taught girls from Pahokee and Eustis to do the Lindy Hop and the Manhattan, not to mention the rumba and the samba, which we had learned from the fleeing Cubans. While in the rec room, the Jewish girls who taught the dances were no longer Jews but mentors, though it's probably true that when we left the rec rooms, we were once again Jews.

WAKULLA SPRINGS AND THE SILVER SLIPPER

Jack and I were seeing each other most every weekend, either in Tallahassee or in Gainesville. Jack came over on hitched rides, and on one occasion he borrowed a car. "Be my guest," Jack said to me, as he opened the car door, "and let me take you to glamorous places," as I wondered what glamorous places were to be visited in Tallahassee. As it happened, it had several glamorous places.

One of them was Wakulla Springs, which turned out to be a wildlife refuge full of anhingas and ospreys and more than the occasional alligator. For a New York boy and a Union City/Miami Beach girl, Wakulla was a sensation. And because it didn't cost anything, you could call it Florida's gift to the Depression-afflicted.

Actually, we already had subliminal knowledge of Wakulla. Like all moviegoers—in America, in the world, in the universe perhaps—we knew the Tarzan movies, and we now discovered that when Johnny Weissmuller went swinging and yodeling through a profusion of trees, he had swung and yodeled in Wakulla Springs. Still, we somehow learned that Tarzan never swam in the waters of Wakulla; he did his swimming down the state in the translucent waters of Silver Springs, where, unlike at Wakulla where the alligators bellowed and snapped, any alligators were products of the workshop.

On the more usual weekends, the ones when we didn't have a car—which was all the other weekends—Jack and I had a regular routine: the movies and then dinner at the Dutch Kitchen near the state government buildings. It was a routine pretty much followed by all the FSCW girls and their boyfriends, with the optional feature of a half-hour or so behind a tree on the hill above campus or in the bushes brushing up against the dorms.

Jack and I did, however, depart from routine on one weekend by having dinner at the Silver Slipper, a very expensive dine and dance place that we could afford only because Jack had won five dollars in a fraternity poker game. The Silver Slipper was done out in turn-of-the-century red velvet and gilt chandeliers, and when we came in, Jack looked around and said to me, "I'm looking for Marcel Proust. He's gotta be here." I had to agree that if the French master had subjected his frail body to a trip across the Atlantic to the Florida state capital of Tallahassee, he would have felt instantly at home in one of the curtained-off dining nooks—the "snugs," as they were called—of the Silver Slipper. But he would not find in the next nook the Count d'Alexandre with his little friend from the Folies Bergère; he would find the representative from Possum County with his little friend from the steno pool.

I was not surprised that Jack had been playing cards. I knew that playing cards was something he did, and I knew that he bore the genes of a family who played. Apparently these genes were very active and kicked in at the very mention of bridge, gin rummy, poker, or any card game that involved shuffling and an exchange of money. They were very different from my family: we played Casino for hard candies.

Jack's gambling was a practice I was sometimes tolerant of and sometimes not, depending on the circumstance. I was tolerant of it later when Jack was in combat and played cards between missions. And on this Tallahassee occasion, how could I be less than tolerant when it had brought me to the Silver Slipper of the red velvet and the gilt ornaments and the western steaks? The Silver Slipper was a far cry from the campus dining hall, a bastion of southern cooking, whose menu shouted "Depression" down to its chicken gizzards and rice. "One more chicken gizzard," Myra would say, "and those clucking sounds you hear will be coming from me."

THE DRAFT

As the draft began making its demands, the University of Florida boys were plucked out one by one. The plucked-out ones were apparently draft-eligible, which meant that they were between the ages of twenty-one and twenty-six, and Jack, only twenty, was not draft-eligible, at least not yet. Some of these draftees were now at Camp Blanding near Jacksonville or at Ft. Benning in Georgia, and in letters to their FSCW girlfriends, they referred to things like "boot camp" and they complained of "snafus," which, as we found out, stood for "Situation Normal, All Fouled Up," though in the boys' natural habitat the "F" stood for a different word. It was a new language, though one that we would all be fluent in before too long. The boys wrote about how much they missed their girlfriends, and they said, "See you soon. Don't forget, the army said I'd be here for only a year." Well, as it turned out, good luck with that.

The draft was now evident also on the FSCW campus. We now saw platoons of GIs—short for "Government Issue," a term applied to all things military, including the military men—and the girls found themselves looking with enthusiasm at toned men in sharply creased uniforms and jaunty overseas caps. This made their draftee boyfriends very unsettled, and they took to writing cautions about having "too much fun," as one letter-writer called it. This particular draftee went on to advise that his girlfriend take steps to avoid having too much fun by ingesting heavy doses of saltpeter, a chemical widely believed to discourage sexual arousal and thought to be injected into dining hall food. "Honey pot, you make sure to eat all your meals in the dining hall," the draftee instructed, "and stay out of the Silver Slipper, you hear?"

Those still on the Gainesville campus apparently were also beginning to take seriously their military-related programs, so jokes were out. The jokes were usually aimed at the ROTC (the Reserve Officer Training Corps) program, which featured a cavalry unit with horses pulling French "75" caissons, and all of it already out of the date in the last war. "Can you believe we still have a cavalry?" Jack would say to me. "It's horse and buggy time. I guess it's because those old guys like their traditions, and they're going to keep to them through hell and high water."

Although Jack had taken the minimum of ROTC, he now signed up for a government-sponsored program, this one for pilot training. Unlike the cavalry, the air corps was thought to be in for a glorious role in the coming war, and Jack decided he wanted to get in on it. If he completed the course, he would have a pilot's license and, he figured, when he got into service, having a pilot's license would put him in a prime position for getting his wings.

FALL FROLICS

Although the war was now right over our shoulders, I was looking forward to going over from Tallahassee to Gainesville for the annual University of Florida festival called Fall Frolics. I was to stay at the Thomas Hotel with an FSCW girl who was going over and wanted to share expenses, and because my mother always slipped a dollar bill into her letters, and the hotel rate was a nightly three dollars, between Jack and me and my FSCW friend, we cobbled together the three bucks to put us into the Thomas Hotel for one night.

Fall Frolics was an annual campuswide party, and many a Florida girl had its date marked in red on her calendar. It was such a bright event in those drab days and an invitation so sought-after that it was conceivable that every girl in the state from thirteen to thirty was daily checking her mailbox for that magic summons. Some of the girls saved all year: going to Fall Frolics was not cheap, not when you figured new dresses and beauty parlors and bus tickets.

Fall Frolics invariably featured big-name bands and big-name singers, and this one topped them all—Tommy Dorsey's orchestra and Frank Sinatra! The very thought of dancing to these two icons of swing, swing, swing had us swooning: Tommy Dorsey and "I'm Getting Sentimental Over You"! Frank Sinatra and his turn-your-knees-to-jelly "I'll Never Smile Again"! We could scarcely think about it without going into a deep fog, as we said in Union City.

That was before. That was before the say-it's-not-so moment when reality showed up. Tommy Dorsey and Frank Sinatra would not be coming. They had sent their regrets, and the event committee said they had been forced to cancel.

Forced to cancel? *Forced to cancel?* Oh say not so. We searched for reasons: maybe the university couldn't in the end scrape up enough money; maybe Frank Sinatra's delicate voice had given out; maybe the orchestra had gone on a drunk from which they had not yet recovered. But no, the reason, as we later learned, was that Tommy Dorsey and company had a commitment to play at an army recruiting event.

The explanation soothed us. After all, the band had answered not a "request" but a "command," and we were beginning to hear a lot about military commands. We even began to feel good about our role in the cancellation. We liked that we had been asked to participate in a "military commitment." We liked when the administration thanked us for our "sacrifice," and we liked that we were being asked to play a part, small though it might have been, in what was as big an event as the world had ever seen. In the end we made do with a local band, and if there was no swooning, there was still dancing, and though we didn't swoon, we dreamed.

If the cancellation of Tommy Dorsey and Frank Sinatra had been a shocker, and if we thought it would take us a long time to forget it, it didn't turn out that way. The fact was that it was suddenly December 7, 1941, and Tommy Dorsey and Frank Sinatra flew out of our heads, if only to return in a new—wartime—incarnation.

Ruth, *in rear,* author, *on left,* and best friend Doris Johnson, *on right,* "puttin' on," around 1928.

Author's father is at the wheel, and Will is in the backseat of the Studebaker. Around 1926.

The author, *on left,* the "young 'un," and Ruth, the "knee baby," in 1928.

In 1928, Minna looks out at the wider world.

The polite southerner, sitting in a classroom at P.S. 86 in 1931 in New York.

The Suberman family (Jack's parents, the two boys and daughter) in Miami Beach in 1937.

The *Miami Herald*'s 1942 wedding picture of Ruth and Lt. Philip Heckerling.

Lt. Jack Suberman in 1942, stationed at Davis-Monthan Field in Tucson, Arizona, one of his last assignments before going overseas.

Capt. Jack Suberman in 1944 (with a fellow crewman) in India, in front of his plane. Camels on the plane represent missions over the hump and bombs represent combat missions.

Rick and the author in Miami in 1944.

1944, Miami Beach: author's father, mother, Rick, and mango tree.

Ruth and son Dale in 1944.

Birthday party in Gainesville for Rick's third birthday (second party following the one given by the fraternity boys).

George showing Rick how to play Missouri marbles in front of the Harpers' Victory Village domicile in Chapel Hill in 1949; Bobby on steps.

Jack, having just graduated from the University of North Carolina with his Ph.D., and showing signs of having celebrated the occasion quite well. He is flanked by his mother and the author.

Dean Jack Suberman, in Boca Raton on the campus of Florida Atlantic University in 1967.

Jack Rubin, he of the German prisoner-of-war ordeal, visiting in Boca Raton in 1975.

Jack and the author, sixty-nine years after their wedding day of January 31, 1942.

9

World War II

Jack and I learned of the Japanese attack on our naval base at Pearl Harbor in Hawaii as we were coming out of the Tallahassee picture show on the late Sunday afternoon of December 7, 1941, and saw a newsboy hawking newspapers. A hawking newsboy was an unusual sight in Tallahassee, and Jack walked over to see what the fuss was about. He got a paper, and when he had stared at the headline for a few seconds, he passed the paper over to me, and as I read the headline—JAPANESE BOMB PEARL HARBOR—my only reaction was, So? So what? Where was Pearl Harbor and why had the Japanese bombed it? Did Jack know? Well, he knew enough to understand it was a big story.

We found out afterward just how big it was. When President Roosevelt spoke the next day, when he said, "I ask that the Congress declare that since the unprovoked and dastardly attack by Japan on Sunday, December 7th, 1941, a state of war has existed between the United States and the Japanese empire," I knew that something profoundly big had entered our lives, that Jack was to be a part of it, and that our lives would be changing. What we didn't know was that our lives would be changed forever.

Yes, we were at war, and not only with Japan. Since Germany and Italy were allied with Japan, in what was known as the Axis, to show in what affection they held their Japanese friends, Germany and Italy lickety split declared war on us.

* * *

After Pearl Harbor, life on campus, strange to say, took a turn toward the optimistic. Suddenly the boys had a desirable option, and it was military service. When I next saw Jack, he had already volunteered for the army air corps and seemed euphoric about it. "Somebody's asking for me," he said. "Somebody wants me." And it was true that for college boys, the exercises in futility were dropped like the useless things they were and replaced with something meaningful, the chance to take an active role in a war.

JACK AND I MAKE THE *MIAMI HERALD*

We took for granted that the moment had come for all Americans to do their part. Jack wanted to do his, but there were a couple of other reasons for his being so—to use the military expression—gung ho. It was certainly true that Jack hoped for his chance against the Nazis, but there was another compelling reason: he—we—could get married. The air corps promised a seventy-five-dollar monthly stipend, and Jack could finally tell my mother that he had "prospects." He had achieved a two-fer: in one fell swoop he had landed himself a job and a wife. And I was at last going to be at Jack's side, to "square [his] blunders and share [his] dreams," as our song went. We had only to finish our fall semesters, go home, do the deed, and await Jack's first assignment.

When I brought the news to my parents that I was getting married, I found that something new had been added to the family list of rights and wrongs. Was it right, my mother wondered, that her third daughter should get married before her second? I left it to my father to take care of it, to say things like, "There's a war on, Rebecca. And you're going to worry about who gets married first?"

Jack and I prepared for marriage chiefly by getting our pictures taken for the *Miami Herald,* and the *Herald* did its job by running the picture with the whole story underneath: "Mr. and Mrs. Morris A. Kaufman, formerly of Union City, Tennessee, announce the marriage of their daughter Stella (known to her Miami Beach Senior High School friends as Marcella) to Jack Suberman, son of Mr. and Mrs. Alexander Suberman, formerly of New York City. . . ." What the item confirmed, among other things, was that everybody in Miami Beach was from somewhere else and that Jack and I owned almost identical V-necked sweaters.

Despite the flurry of getting married, at that moment we had more imminent issues: Jack's being assigned, Jack's being trained, Jack's eventual—yes, it must be considered—going into combat. And that other unvoiced question: what if Jack didn't come back? And what about the future?

We could only allow ourselves to think of the *foreseeable* future. We did not think beyond that; we spent no time on how we would proceed *after* the war. How could we think about that? No, we were consumed by the present; to focus on anything beyond the here and now would have required a mind of the most awesome discipline. Moreover, we had no control over anything; the ball was definitely in somebody else's court. Jack was in the army now—well, in the army air corps—and he was waiting to be summoned.

When he got the call, however, did the possession of a pilot's license get him into pilot training? No, it did not. Nor did it for a lot of other already pilot-licensed volunteers. The line for those wanting to be pilots was so long, and boys so eager to get going, that they swallowed hard and said, okay, send me to wherever the line is shorter, just make sure it's the air corps.

Why such a yen for the air corps? Maybe a lot of the boys liked the idea of being one with the wild blue yonder, maybe some of them thought the air corps was the defense/offense wave of the future. Or maybe they were taken with the flying officer's hat, called "raunchy" (yes!) because its inner metal band was typically removed to permit earphones to be worn, all of which exuded glamour. It was my thought, however, that many wanted the air corps simply because they remembered movie pilots and their look of devil-may-care as they headed for the sky, silk scarves flowing. Whatever the motive, in the face of extended delays, Jack and others agreed to a one-page test, the results of which sent them off not to pilot training but to bombardier or navigator school, and in the end, Jack became a bombardier.

THE DEPRESSION IS OUT, WORLD WAR II IS IN

When war was declared, Americans hit the ground running. We had to. Our country was ill-prepared for a war, especially one as big as this one promised to be. As evidence, we had only to think of the outdated cavalry unit at the University of Florida, and the military posts whose main functions were to provide ceremonial settings, not to provide infantry and artillery training. Planes were not only inadequate in numbers but, more often than not, were of World War I vintage. The navy fleet, never considerable, was now almost skeletal: the Japanese had seen to that at Pearl Harbor. What all this meant was that we had to start from scratch—and right now—to build planes, naval vessels, tanks and guns, and the myriad other items required for a serious war. And no one doubted that this was a serious war.

And what did this mean to the Depression? It meant that the Depression had been suddenly thrown off the cliff. Factories began on the instant to turn out planes and ships and equipment, and training schools for technicians to service them sprang up. Jobs were advertised everywhere, in the papers, on the radio. And as if to affirm this, Will got a job at a Rhode Island plant producing some cog in the war machine, and yes, he had been hired as an engineer. It was wartime, customs and rules were upside down, and nobody was asking your religion. All at once the Depression and the thinking we expended on it were no more; the Depression was the past, the war was the present and the future.

President Roosevelt's fireside chats no longer concerned themselves with finding jobs for the unemployed. There *were* no unemployed. Things were boom, boom, booming all over the country. Jobs were opening up, adding to the jobs left vacant by those in service. And so the fireside chats of President Roosevelt now concerned themselves with how many planes were being turned out, how many ships were being built, how many war bonds were being sold. And they did something else that meant something to a lot of us: they told us of the women who had now entered the work-force, women who worked on the planes and on the ships. And if Betty Grable was the pinup girl for GIs, "Rosie the Riveter," the lady wearing the hair snood and holding the riveting gun as she worked in a war plant alongside men, was the pinup girl for American women.

TRAVELS WITH JACK

From the very beginning of Jack's service—except for his cadet training—I traveled around with him from air base to air base until he was "shipped out," an expression I purely despised, connoting to me as it did a box of life-less things being sent to a final destination. I was with him in Victorville, California; Salt Lake City, Utah; Tucson, Arizona; and four towns in Kansas of four different names but otherwise indistinguishable. It was in Tucson that Rick was born and where we decided that his name would be Rick, so taken were we with the noble and patriotic hero Rick Blaine, Humphrey Bogart's character in *Casablanca,* the movie nobody could get enough of. Well, it was wartime, and noble and patriotic heroes were just what we needed. And it was in Kansas, near Wichita, that Jack's plane was being readied at the Boeing plant for its date with the Japanese enemy.

While Jack and I were traveling around, what had happened to talk of money, cash, dollars? If during the Depression we had to parse our spend-ing, we didn't now. We didn't now make elaborate plans before we spent it, we didn't save it, we didn't even think about it. We spent even more lavishly than we had pre-Depression. Jack no longer talked about the "tyrant," and I tried not to think that it might someday again stalk us. There being so many things to think about, to worry about, money was now something to be spent without niggling it to death. Jack's seventy-five-dollars-per-month cadet stipend had always been adequate, but after he became an officer, money was in the category of confetti.

Indeed, after Jack became an officer, money was scarcely mentioned between us. We spent as we pleased, Jack gambled as *he* pleased (who could argue with a man slated for combat?) and though there was nothing much to buy in the way of apparel—all cottons and wools were now going toward the manufacture of army uniforms, and all silk toward the manufacture of parachutes—we found ways to spend. When going with Jack from post to post, I never argued when civilians overcharged us for housing. I just didn't care. My Depression lifestyle in which decisions were money-based had morphed into one of easy come, easy go.

MIAMI BEACH GOES TO WAR

When Jack left the country and flew to India to join his B-29 group, I returned to Miami Beach. Jack was going to India to take part in missions over Japan; I was going to Miami Beach to wait and to worry. And it was at that point that I discovered that frivolous, playful Miami Beach had gone to war.

It went to war because of the very thing that had made it an unserious town—because it had hotel rooms in spectacularly large numbers. And acting with (unusual) common sense and not with their "sit-downs," as my mother would have said, the army decided that the rooms would serve nicely as barracks for the Officers Candidate School they were planning. The hotels, to be sure, were paid a very respectable sum and were duly commandeered by the army for its plans for the OCS, as everybody called it.

With the coming of the OCS, Miami Beach—including all businesses—was transformed. OCS attendance came to almost thirty thousand, and what could be better for business than an infusion of thirty thousand men with money in their pockets and the belief that they deserved to spend it as they wished?

So if Miami Beach merchants had feared that when war was declared, a resort town like theirs would be brought to its knees, they had to think again. Never had business been so good; never had they made so much money. Indeed, businesses were flourishing as never before, even pre-Depression. All this owed, as everyone knew, to the presence of the men in khaki.

My father was one of the ones reaping the rewards of the new reality. It scarcely mattered that the army had taken over Hialeah and Tropical Parks and that racetrack habitués had stopped coming down. And if my father had been worried that the soldiers would not trade with him—the store being a few long blocks from their barracks—that worry too went nowhere. Business was booming off the charts.

Even his stores on Twenty-third Street were no longer begging for tenants; they now had waiting lists. Military clothiers had moved in as suppliers to the boys who wanted an extra uniform or another pair of shoes, and tailors rented spaces to serve fashion-conscious officers who wanted their uniforms to actually fit. Souvenir shops rented a store or two. The OCS boys would want to send mementoes, wouldn't they?

The souvenir shops in my father's stores on Twenty-third Street had a different clientele from the ones on Lincoln Road. The Lincoln Road customer shopped for Seminole Indian dresses to wear at parties up north, and the Twenty-third Street stores' soldier/customer wanted key rings adorned with bathing beauties and trinkets made of alligator skin. The target customer of these stores was the ordinary GI, the enlisted man—there were many of those at OCS, needed as they were for auxiliary services—who had in his pocket a monthly check of twenty-one dollars. Still, although GI enlisted men sang a wry little song called "Twenty-one Dollars a Day Once a Month," when you thought about it, it was twenty-one dollars more than they might have had before the war.

With all the OCS boys milling around, stock on our drugstore shelves that perhaps dated to the previous owner flew out the door. Hair gels, which through the years had sat forlorn and forsaken, were now snapped up by GIs looking to give their crew cuts a sheen; deodorants were sniffed and purchased in multiples to assure the right scent for every occasion. The main attraction, however, no surprise here, was the drawer in the back, the one that was available only to my father and clerks of the male persuasion. The store, in sum, was not only "doing a good business," it was doing it "in spades," as my father would say.

My mother, wanting to contribute to what everybody was calling "the war effort," did it in her own way—with mangoes. She brought most of her crop to the soda fountain and instructed the soda jerks to put them on the boys' ice cream and, "Don't charge them extra," she would say. Because mangoes were considered a south Florida specialty and thought to be unknown in other parts of the country, the soda jerks were skeptical, but my mother insisted that when the GIs got to know mangoes, they would go "plumb wild" about them. My mother was happy with having made a contribution, and she would say, "They sure don't get mangoes in their mess tents." Well, mess tents were actually unknown to OCS boys; they ate in gilt-emblazoned Miami Beach hotel ballrooms under crystal chandeliers.

Jack's father was not left out of the new wartime Miami Beach prosperity. In the year before the OCS takeover, he had been given a tip from one of the men at his bridge club that a well-known Miami Beach hotel, the Boulevard, was for sale cheap, and longing to be back in the give and take of business (though he would deny this), he had put up a little of his remaining capital. He hoped for the best, but of course he feared the worst: It was an old hotel, and tourists had started bypassing it, something Mr. Suberman attributed to the small closets characteristic of old hotels. "So small," he explained, "the women can't hang their fur coats." It was an irony, I thought, that fur coats, Mr. Suberman's undoing, had also been the hotel's. Still, in the end Mr. Suberman lucked out: OCS leased the hotel at a "very attractive price," as Mr. Suberman said, adding, "You think the boys are going to notice small closets?" Thus was Alex Suberman once again a player in the world of business.

When we came back to Miami Beach, Rick and I were to live with my parents, where my sister Ruth was also living. Ruth was now married, even though her husband was out of the country, so Ruth and I were both now in the "wife" category. We had also changed in another important way—in our racial views. Mine had undergone a radical shift because of Johnny Bulla; and Ruth's because when she had lived in New York, no one was impressed with her racial philosophy. "Nobody thought I was cute for saying the things I said," she told me. "They truly thought I was as stupid as a stick." So neither of us any longer spewed out racist mantras—like, "Don't be ugly to darkies but keep them in their place"—and we forgave each other for ever having done so.

PHIL HECKERLING

As had so many of our friends during this time, Ruth had had a quick courtship and marriage. When she finished school in New York, she had come home and was quickly pressed into service as a dancing partner down at the OCS ballroom on the pier, and there she had met Philip Heckerling, ex–New Yorker and now of the U.S. Army and an OCS candidate. And a few weeks after they met, they married.

I had been surprised to get Ruth's letter telling me that she was married, though if I was surprised, my mother wasn't. Phil had apparently been coming over for Friday night dinners, and my mother had seen enough of the two of them together to realize that Phil and her second daughter were in love. And when Phil asked Ruth to marry him, my mother, perhaps factoring in that Phil had been complimentary about her chopped liver and her fruit *tzimmes,* into which she had put not only the traditional dried fruits but also some mango that she had dried herself, she no doubt concluded that he was "a good Jewish boy" whose second lieutenant's salary could support a wife, and "So why not?" she said.

Even if very soon after they were married, Phil graduated from OCS and was sent to Hickam Field in Hawaii, my mother said, "At least they're all married." Yes, my mother's Tennessee imperatives had been answered: Minna, Ruth, and I had husbands. And all Jewish ones. Minna and I had already provided grandchildren—my Rick and Minna's Major. Major was so named, we all thought, because Minna and Mike were caught up in the military mindset sweeping the country, but Minna said no, she just liked the name. (Hm-m-m.) Ruth was now pregnant and on track to follow Minna and me. Will too was married and to a Jewish girl, had a child, and still had his job with the Rhode Island war plant.

When I told Doris about our marriages, I wrote, "Ruth is married to this Yankee soldier," which probably made him sound as if he was fighting the rebels in the Civil War. Did I forget that I too was married to a Yankee soldier?

Ruth didn't worry as much about Phil in Hawaii as I did about Jack in god-knows-where. I had always been anxious about Jack's involvement with dangerous airplanes, but because I was no longer in spitting distance of where he was stationed and where he was daily engaged in dangerous training exercises, I had to settle for being anxious long-distance. Still, I and the other wives, and the other families, were in constant contact with the war—in letters, in newspaper accounts, on radio newscasts, in newsreels. The war was ever-present. It was everybody's war, and we were working toward ending it as soon as possible. We wanted our boys home. We wanted to pamper them and love them. And after that? Well, we didn't talk about "after that." It seemed a totally inappropriate subject.

THE MIAMI BEACH HOME FRONT

Back again in Miami Beach, I soon saw how OCS had turned the town up-side down and backward. The streets of Miami Beach were now drill fields and its sands were rifle ranges. I no longer counted the number of Auburns and Cords rolling along; I now watched feisty jeeps bounding by. Most ob-vious of all, of course, were the thousands of men in khaki now around us, marching and singing as they went to class. How often did Rick and I wake to the sounds of "I've got sixpence/Jolly, jolly sixpence," and how often did I try to explain to Rick what the heck sixpences were, and how often did I fail? And how often did I look for that OCS candidate Clark Gable marching along with the others? Well, anytime I could. It was thrilling to me that the boys—Clark Gable included—were so upbeat and determined. It was also thrilling that the signs in front of the hotels had disappeared. It may have taken a war to do it, but they were gone.

If the physical city of Miami Beach had gone to war, so had its people, and they did it in their own way, one of which was trying to spot subma-rines. My father was a submarine spotter, and he stood for hours on the roof of some seaside hotel or another scanning the seas for the "weasels," the German submarines. When he was to report for duty, he took his Bausch & Lomb binoculars ("Bush & Lawn," as he pronounced them) from their tissue-lined drawer, and he would say that maybe today he would get his "big laugh" by spotting a German submarine with his German-made binoculars. Though he never had his laugh, he had the satisfaction of knowing that when a German submarine actually landed spies on Florida shores, the spies were caught immediately, all due, my father proclaimed, to his fellow spotters.

Ruth and I spent a lot of time working in the store because it needed us. As we said during those days, the joint was jumpin', and as the daughters of a retail merchant, we knew when we were needed and what we had to do. Furthermore, we wanted to be helpful and good company to the sol-diers who came in. We felt they were far away from home and no doubt homesick.

For some part of every day I plunked Rick in his playpen, left him to be amused by the soldiers—I knew from the GIs I had known when I traveled around with Jack that it was a duty they delighted in—and I stationed my-self at the cash register while Ruth went to work behind the fountain. When we were off-duty at the store, we went to the pier to be dance partners for the OCS boys—yes, plenty of married women were on the scene—and be-cause nurses were in fierce demand, we pitched in at Jackson Memorial

Hospital and wherever else war effort was called for. Wives, garment worker retirees, expatriate Cubans, maybe even the Capone contingent were part of the effort. It was a matter of pitching in to bring the boys home. No complaints. Lights were not allowed at night? Rations cut? So what?

WHERE HAVE YOU GONE, BOBBY RIGGS?

When Ruth started having labor pains, we knew where to go—to the Biltmore Hotel. Need I point out that the Biltmore was no longer a hotel but was now a military hospital? And need I point out that Bobby Riggs was now in service and nowhere to be seen? The tennis courts were still there, however, if unrecognizable. The once groomed and tailored courts were now chockablock with little shacks serving as military offices of one kind or another, and the clay was marked by the tracks of army boots going this way and that. As to Ruth and her imminent delivery, her son Dale soon came along, and it was now decided that because he and his mother would be staying with my parents, Rick and I would move in with Jack's.

And that's why I was living at the Suberman house as I waited and worried. And that's why it was the Suberman mailbox that I went to twice a day in the hope that I would find a letter from Jack telling me he was safe—well, that he had been safe when the letter had been written two weeks earlier. And that's why I was in the kitchen of the Subermans' house when I got the telephone call.

10

Reassignment

The call came on November 27, 1944, as I was padding around barefoot getting Rick's midmorning snack. After the phone call, after I had put the phone down, ten minutes later Rick was in his grandmother Frieda's arms, and I was driving the family Ford north out of Miami. I was in a tizzy—so tizzied that as I was driving and looked down, I saw two bare feet. It didn't matter. The phone call was the one I had been waiting for: the one from Jack telling me he was home. And waiting for me to come get him.

Where he was waiting was at Morrison Field in West Palm Beach. We had been apart for just about a year, and as with all of us on the home front who had loved ones overseas, that separation had controlled my life. I had found myself constantly veering between an ecstasy and a funk, an ecstasy because I had received a letter, a funk because of something I had read in the paper. In the months before that phone call, I had been in a funk a lot. Because the B-29s were the biggest bombers of them all, they were such media stars that newspapers had taken to reporting in full everything they did. Thus I was daily treated to a rundown of B-29 missions and, in a sidebar story just for me, of their casualties. But at this moment I was in nothing but a happy delirium as I raced up the road.

Perhaps "racing" is not quite what I was doing. U.S. 1 was crowded, not as crowded as it might have been if gasoline rationing had not still been with us, but U.S. 1 was the only north-south artery through southeast Florida, so it was pretty congested. So racing was out, and frustration was in. As I made my way up the road, I imagined that the crews in the planes flying over me and heading as I was for Morrison Field were laughing and pointing at this pathetic young lady in the Ford trying to put on some speed. I wanted to tell those mighty roaring things that my heart was going faster than their planes were flying, so fast in fact that I had some feeling it might leap out the window and beat me up there. At that moment in time, if there was a future to be thought of, it was the one that would happen in about an hour, the one when I would have Jack safely in my arms.

Then all at once I was there, past the MPs at the gate, and there Jack was, in my sights, looking at me with that Jack look that always made me go funny whenever we had been apart, if only for hours. There was my Jack with that familiar rangy frame, the crumpled shirt tucked and untucked by turns, the hat in the flying officer's signature "raunchiness."

Had he changed at all? When I had last seen him, his six foot two frame was equipped with two hundred pounds, and now he was thinner, though the lost weight made him look somehow fitter, as if he had gotten himself into fighting form for his job. Well, there was also a change in his officer status. He now wore a captain's "railroad tracks" instead of a lieutenant's single one, but who cared?

We got into the car and went to an orange juice stand because orange juice was what Jack wanted "ASAP," he said, which was another new expression for me to file away. And then we went to the hotel in West Palm Beach where we had spent our honeymoon—the one we were reduced to after we had lost most of our money at the dog track, the hotel that overlooked not a lake lapping at the mansions of Palm Beach but a parking lot. Actually it didn't matter which hotel we chose. What mattered was that Jack was in the room with me and there was a bathroom where I could wash my feet and a bed that we could throw ourselves into.

The next morning we went back down U.S. 1, Jack driving, me sitting as close as I could without actually being in his lap. We needed gas, and I had enough coupons to fill the tank, but Jack had his own ideas. "What do you say we fill it only half-way?" he asked me. "How would you like to run out of gas?" *What?* Well, I wouldn't like it. But I soon understood that running out of gas would, to Jack, be a great joke. Having recently been inhabiting planes in which running out of gas would mean disaster, he thought that running out of gas on U.S. 1 would be a lot of fun. He could just casually step out the car and hitch a ride to the nearest gas station, laughing all the way.

Jack had been sent home on reassignment, which meant that he would be posted to wherever in the States he was needed. When he told me this, did I believe it? Well, I believed that he was being reassigned but did I believe it was to stateside duty? Not when I knew by now that to depend on army plans showed a weakness of mind. I knew very well that if an urgency arose in any of the theaters of war, original army air corps plans could slide right off the desk and into the black hole that was the wastebasket. So, I wondered, couldn't "reassignment" mean he might get sent back into the maelstrom from which he had just escaped? Could his being home be just a respite? The war was still on, our boys were still fighting, so why not?

But of course when I said, "Don't tell me there's a chance you'll be going overseas again," Jack joked it away and said something like, "All right, I won't tell you." As usual Jack wanted no part of the wringing of hands. He tried to soothe me with a happy story of our life in the foreseeable future, which included being posted to an agreeable place and having the fun we had not had for long months.

We didn't run out of gas, and Jack said it was okay, that anyway he was in a hurry to get home to Rick. Rick was now two years old, and though I knew that his memory of his father was dim, I hoped that some semblance remained. I wanted Rick to have a memory of lying on Jack's chest while the two of them slept on the sofa, and though I couldn't promise that, I could promise Jack a conversation with the smartest, most charming child this side of Hollywood.

I should have had no fears that there would be any moment of awkwardness, for it seemed that Rick knew Jack at once. When Jack came into the house, Rick was instantly in motion, rushing at Jack, the blue eyes very like his dad's fixed on his target, and hair, curly and blond (further evidence of Cossack infusion into the gene pool?) a-bounce. And then in no time at all they were wrestling around—tussling around—the two turning and twisting, laughing and shouting as if they could do what they were doing forever.

Jack had a week's leave before his reassignment notice was to arrive, and we stayed at his family's house in Miami. His younger brother Irwin was in service, stationed somewhere, and his young sister Sheila at home. Jack's mother Frieda went into an ecstasy over having her "soldier boy" back, and went instantly to forage for steaks. Steaks not being available at her local Piggly Wiggly—the Piggly Wiggly not having had much in the way of beef except soup bones for a couple of years—she knew to get them from a black marketeer butcher and without having to fork over ration stamps, something she knew to be a criminal act but that in no way deterred her. "Pooh," she said to us, "They're going to arrest a mother for getting a steak for her soldier boy? Don't talk foolish."

Awaiting reassignment, in the mornings when Rick was napping, we sat on the porch, and Alex and Frieda sat with us. We sat in a routine formation—Alex in his rattan chaise longue; Jack, Frieda, and me at the card table—and we listened while Jack told us things: why he had been sent home for reassignment, how it was to be a bombardier on a B-29 stationed in India, how it was to sit for eighteen hours at a stretch in the nose of a B-29, and how it was to bomb targets in Japan. And why it was not all guts and glory.

* * *

It started out with glory, in the successful bombings of railroad yards in Bangkok and Japanese-held Mukden, which were raids that seriously interrupted Japanese supply lines. But in the missions over Japan, glory was apparently hard to come by.

The source of the problems, Jack told us, was that the B-29s were stationed in India, near Calcutta, and far away from their targets in Japan, indeed too far away for direct strikes. The solution was an advance base in western China—Chengdu—where fuel and bombs could be stored. The fuel and bombs had to be ferried to Chengdu by the planes and the crews themselves, which meant flights from India over the Himalayas, over the three mountain ranges called the Hump. The trouble here was that these ferrying trips to the advance base consumed about as much fuel as they delivered. "When we added and subtracted," Jack said, "in the end we were barely in the black."

The missions over Japan itself were seldom in the glory category. The planes were to rendezvous near the target, and on the way from Chengdu, planes got lost, were shot down, had malfunctions, ran out of gas. In the end the rendezvous was comprised of a fraction of the original groups— "We looked like poor little lambs who had lost our way," Jack said—and without the support of a surround of planes, over the target they were at the mercy of enemy fighter attacks and the always present antiaircraft fire—the *ack-ack,* as Jack called it.

Another misfire: because B-29s flew at extremely high altitudes, hitting the target squarely was a rare occurrence. And when Jack asked us, "How do you hit the oven of a steel mill in Yawata or Omura from twenty thousand feet?" we could only exchange looks. Place your always fluctuating bomb into an oven when you're twenty thousand feet above it? How was this possible? Sometimes, Jack said, with winds buffeting and the hitherto unknown jet stream adding a hundred or more miles to the air speed, the bombsight couldn't compute, and the men often found themselves dropping their bombs into the sea, sometimes a few hundred yards from the steel mills. Telling these stories out there on the porch, at this point Jack's sense of the ridiculous would kick in, and he would say, cheerfully, "Sometimes we not only missed the oven, we missed Japan."

It was apparently obvious to all at the base in India—it was constant bull-session talk among the crews—that the B-29s could be more effective if they were closer to Japan. The whole installation was thus finally moved from India to the newly secured Mariana Islands, and Jack, having served his tour of duty, was sent home, and fresh crews took over in the Marianas. "We did the experiments," Jack said. "Now let's see what the new boys can do."

So it was not all windswept banners and triumphal huzzahs, though there was some of that as well. There was a banner and a huzzah from the country in the huge psychological lift that had come from the B-29s. We civilians looked on our B-29 crews as knights in shining armor, though it was true that the planes shone only because their aluminum skins had been denied the camouflage paint that would have added unwanted extra weight. Like the Doolittle raid in 1942, the B-29 raids over Japan were morale builders.

Jack took a lot of pride in what he and his B-29 buddies had done. They had been asked to do a job and they had done it. If some wanted to call them heroes, he would not argue with them.

* * *

Waiting for reassignment, Jack mostly took it easy. He taught Rick a few things—how to sit in a barber's chair to get his curls cut; how to comfort Mommy afterward; how to say "Joe DiMaggio," whose hitting streak in 1941, as I had been informed only too often, lasted for fifty-six games, and if it weren't for two "supernatural" backhand stops by the Cleveland Indians' third baseman Ken Keltner, the streak apparently would have continued into infinity. Add to this that Joe DiMaggio's team was the New York Yankees, and for Jack—bred in the place that Yankee Stadium sat in the middle of—the New York Yankees were right up there with books and liberty and justice for all.

Because no major-league baseball teams existed in Tennessee, we took a proprietary interest in the St. Louis Cardinals, and when Sportsman Park, the Cardinals' new field, rose up in 1920, a special train was arranged for Union City fans who wanted to view it. The trip was set for a Saturday, so my father couldn't go, not only because it was a Saturday—when the store typically stayed open until two or three in the morning—but because the store was also having a first-anniversary sale. My father made up for it on buying trips to St. Louis, when he saw many a game and came home with many a tale, all of which pretty much focused on the star of the team, the Rajah, as Rogers Hornsby was known. Sadly, the Rajah was traded in 1927 to the New York Giants, and everybody said, *New York Giants?* Lord, they sent our boy to *New York?*

* * *

On his second day home, so keen was Jack to have the feel of books in his hands that he was out of the house and off to the library, where the librarian allowed him to take home as many books as he could carry. "We've all missed you," she was reported by Jack to have said to him. "Even the books missed you." And so, between telling war tales and teaching two-year-old Rick to throw a baseball without falling over, Jack spent long moments on the porch with good books and bad ones.

To use my mother's expression, I *qvelled* seeing Jack like this; I trembled with pride to see him reading again, to giving himself over once more to his favorite hobby, which, to say the least, he had had little time for recently. And I couldn't stop myself from replaying that fantasy of mine where Jack was on a college campus, talking to students, pearls of wisdom dropping one after the other from his lips.

When we went out, I always held tightly to Jack's hand as if he might disappear back into the nose of that B-29. At the movies I gripped even more tightly, if for a different reason. The newsreels had begun to show General Eisenhower at the concentration camp ovens, and as Jack and I sat watching, we realized that pain and misgivings had diluted the old movie-going pleasures. Later, at home, the bad feelings would overcome us as we talked about the pictures we had just seen, and we would rail about those who should have known and didn't speak out. But the hardest part was that we knew that we were to blame as well.

Finally the reassignment came: Jack was being sent to Maxwell Field in Montgomery, Alabama, and Jack said, "Didn't I say we'd have a choice posting?" Well, I did know that Maxwell Field was a storied air corps installation, and Jack kept assuring me that we could take advantage of its many splendors. More seriously, we hoped we'd find in Montgomery a decent place to live and see some old friends. Even I admitted that it might be fun, this reassignment of Jack's. Now that he was home, I had to say the future was looking good. But hold on. We were talking about the *immediate* future, weren't we? Wasn't there another future to contemplate? Wasn't there a future having to do with the rest of our lives?

Indeed there was. And it was a big subject—so big that it demanded a big question. Actually, it demanded two big ones, and Jack's father asked them. The first big one: If Jack had been sent home, was the war winding down? And the second: If it was, what did the two of us plan to do next? From his place in his rattan chaise longue, Jack's father asked, "You got some plans?"

Plans? What plans? Had we ever considered what we would do after the war? Had we ever had a *plan?* Had anybody we knew thought of one? The answer to all these questions was definitely in the negative. All we had ever talked about were current war matters. So when Mr. Suberman asked the question, we could only look at him in bewilderment.

But still. If the war was or wasn't winding down—and the case was being made either way—it was going to be over soon, and what *were* we going to do then?

MONTGOMERY, ALABAMA

But why worry about all that now? Jack's reassignment suited us. Maxwell Field in Montgomery was a perfect place for getting the kinks out, Jack said, and he set himself to weaving me a happy tale of our life in the days ahead. "High living all the way," Jack said, referring to the amenities at Maxwell. Rick and I, following our custom, were going with Jack to Montgomery. Because we had gone with him from posting to posting before he had been shipped out, I saw no reason to abandon the practice now. I told Rick, who seemed pleased to hear it, that it was our job, that we were just plain old tacky camp followers. "Just two disreputable so-and-so's," I told him, "making a soldier happy."

We departed for Montgomery not only in high spirits but in our newly purchased 1941 Lincoln Zephyr. We had bought the Lincoln Zephyr because of the falling apart of our first car, a 1939 Pontiac Silver Streak, which we had bought the instant Jack had put on his officer's bars and been handed the relatively bountiful officer's check that allowed us without further ado to go into debt. Because no new cars or parts were being

manufactured—all automobile plants were now set up for military needs—
we hadn't been able to cure the Silver Streak, and so we settled for the
Zephyr, which though two years younger, was even so not a spring chicken.

If the Pontiac Silver Streak had been conspicuously black and big, the
Lincoln Zephyr, if not blacker, was bigger, and its twelve cylinders knocked
back a lot of gasoline. With these drawbacks in mind, we could only afford
to buy the car if we got a bargain, and a bargain we got because there were
few bidders for a car that got seven miles to the gallon in a rationed four-
gallon-a-week world.

Maxwell was a relatively harmless posting compared with the earlier
ones that inexorably brought Jack one step closer to being shipped out. At
Maxwell, he had no flying assignments, in fact didn't even venture onto
the tarmac. He filled his time with "scut" work, which meant he tossed
papers from this bin to that one.

For military men awaiting reassignment, Maxwell offered many a recreation, and the men indulged themselves without making excuses. After
"work," they gathered with other officers in the officers' club, and for an
hour or so they played a couple of hands of gin rummy. At lunch they indulged at the bar in a little liar's poker. They played golf every Sunday.
"It's R and R for us heroes," Jack would joke. I was having a bit of R and R
myself. Considering that Jack was doing no flying, my anxiety mechanism
was as always primed, but it was not on a hair trigger.

Nonetheless, I was able to find a few things to unsettle me. Where we
were living, for example, was a great unsettler, because where we were living was bad even by my standards, and my wartime housing standards
were about as low as you could get. When I had been traveling around with
Jack, I learned early on not to expect too much from wartime housing, and
had often been grateful for rooms in auto camps so bleak and seedy that
John Steinbeck in his best days could not have done justice to them. But
those "cesspools," as Jack called them, were not the worst. There was that
basement in Salina, Kansas, which was a space so dank that nothing made
of cloth ever dried, the blackness so deep that a miner's headlight would
have been helpful, the configuration so strange that you could sit on the
toilet and take a shower at the same time. And there was more.

The "more" came when our good friends Peg and Bill O'Connor (whom
we had known at Davis-Monthan base in Tucson) couldn't find housing
and had to stay with us. When the landlady agreed and said it was her "patriotic duty" to cooperate, Peg and I rolled our eyes at each other, for we

knew from experience that when "patriotic duty" was so ceremoniously invoked, you were in for a very bad resolution.

The resolution involved a flurry of activity. Announcing that she was providing privacy, the landlady divided the space by dangling a dividing curtain, reminiscent of the one in the movie *It Happened One Night* but without the aura of romance between Clark Gable and Claudette Colbert. "No such thing as too much privacy," the landlady said, winking at us, apparently not bothered by the fact that you could not only hear through the curtain but *see* through it. When satisfied that she had done the job, she decreed that the space was now two apartments and—"You girls understand, what's fair is fair"—she doubled the rent.

And now here we were in Montgomery, set up in a southern mansion in the posh Cloverdale suburb. If the Depression had touched the lady who owned it, there was no evidence of it, for the place was in all respects an homage to plantation living, including the obligatory white columns. Ornamental bushes of great size covered the front yard, and an ancient black gardener came every day to tend them. On the porch, wrought iron furniture of such weight as to be unmovable by anything short of a crane was positioned apparently for the ages, and over them hung an intricately ornamented iron chandelier of terrifying mass. If this description of a typical southern manse makes it sound as if we had landed in hog heaven, we definitely had not. What we had landed in was the servants' quarters, which meant a room and a bath.

We didn't even get a welcome, perfunctory or otherwise, at our Montgomery housing. In other places we got welcomes, even from the Kansas lady, though it came rather curiously in the form of an invitation, one which Peg and I declined with some horror, for Peg and me to join her and her women friends in a game of strip poker. After we had fled the scene, after we had laughed fit to die, after we had collapsed in a spluttering pile, Peg said to me, "Sit around with hags having to look at their bags and sags? No thanks."

But there was no welcome from the owner of this southern mansion. We didn't expect strip poker, but perhaps a traditional southern welcome of a pie, and since we were in Alabama, a pecan one?

No, it was clear from the beginning that this Montgomery lady was barely suffering our presence. Living now in her other house in a mountain resort near Birmingham, she left us a note that gave little doubt of her feelings: We were to give our rental checks (weekly, exorbitant) to her longtime maid, Maudie Lee, who would come by every Friday. Further instructions followed: "Please do not bring any appliances into your room other than those supplied you. Please do not try to get into the kitchen. Please do not venture into any of the other rooms. If you have any colored acquaintances, please do not invite them into the house."

A lot of polite southern "pleases," but what it amounted to was that a returning soldier and his wife and child were consigned to holing up in a room with one bed, one window, and a bathroom with a single-stream shower. Plus a note about "coloreds" that, with me now an active, outspoken RSB, just about set my hair on fire. What did it tell us that the "colored" maid might read the note? Like as not she had been born and raised in Alabama, a part and parcel of the deepest South, and so it's true that she was probably illiterate. But if she was not, did it mean that she was inured to this kind of talk?

At any rate, keeping "coloreds" out of our room didn't pose much of a problem considering that the Maxwell military, despite our landlady's suspicions, was strictly segregated. The result was that "coloreds" were not seen except as air base workers, and Jack really didn't know any well enough to do any inviting. In the end, as I considered our comfortless accommodations and a southern landlady with surprisingly few southern gifts for graciousness, I concluded that none of the places we had stayed in during the war had promised so much—the innards of an imposing southern mansion—and had delivered so little.

CHECKING OUT MONTGOMERY

So Jack's reassignment found me in the Deep South making noises to him about the shame of separation of the races and the practice of second-class citizenship. For an issue that had not been a concern of mine since . . . well, since I was born—it was suddenly front and center. And I decided to make it my business to find out how these things stood in Montgomery.

When Jack took the Zephyr to Maxwell every morning, Rick and I were left to walk or to take buses. Because we saw the town in this manner, and because Montgomery took no pains to hide its attitudes and customs, I saw Montgomery as the kind of place I formerly wouldn't have seen anything wrong with but now deplored. Nothing surprised me. Not the "White" and "Colored" signs, not when I asked directions of people on the street and got answers like, "You turn left where you see that bunch of niggers over there." On buses, I was aware that the custom of blacks to the rear was strictly adhered to—and enforced. Civility to blacks was so rare that on the one occasion that I had heard a bus driver addressing a black passenger in ordinary tones, I thought it worth mentioning to Jack.

On some days I would walk Rick uptown, sometimes just for the exercise, but always to notice things. On occasion I would tour around the Alabama state government complex up on Goat Hill to try to divine what was going on inside. It gave me a pang that here I was in a southern state, walking around its capital grounds, and I had never once done this in Nashville, my own state's capital. But I had seen many a picture of its buildings, and darned if they didn't look just like these in Montgomery, except that the Nashville capitol was domeless. I had also been well taught at Westover Elementary in Union City that on the Nashville grounds was the tomb of James Polk, one of the three Tennesseans to serve as president, the others being the two Andrews—Jackson and Johnson. Still, for me and my friends, the all-time Tennessee hero was Sergeant Alvin York, the soldier who had received the Congressional Medal of Honor after World War I for having led an attack on a German machine gun nest during the Meuse-Argonne offensive, and in the process had killed twenty-five German soldiers and captured 132 others. It was no surprise to any of us kids. After all, Alvin York was a good old Tennessee country boy, and we knew that all Tennessee country boys could shoot a rifle with deadly accuracy from the time they first drew breath.

Goat Hill was dominated by the capitol building, a Greek Revival edifice of the mid-nineteenth century appropriately columned, and the state legislative building was right behind it. I tried to intuit what was going on in the state of Alabama from the buildings I visited and from the state workers I encountered, and in the end I took the capitol's color—very, very white—to be one of the messages.

CYRUS

Despite orders from the owner of our "mansion," we managed to have an unauthorized interaction with a "colored" person when Maudie Lee brought her son Cyrus around. Cyrus was in service, stationed in New Jersey, and he was home on leave. Fearing being reported by the neighbors to Miz Arundell as harboring "coloreds," we did not invite Cyrus into the house or sit with him in the wrought iron furniture on the front porch. We hosted him in our Lincoln Zephyr parked in the backyard.

It took only a few minutes to understand why we were meeting Cyrus: Maudie Lee had determined that Jack and I were "commonsensical," and she wanted us to talk to Cyrus about his wish to go to college. My father always believed that blacks had an intuitive sense about which whites were approachable and which were not, and Maudie Lee had obviously concluded that Jack and I were.

Cyrus was aware of things. He knew that the southern doctrine of "separate but equal" schools was a sham, and he had stories about his own school that proved it. One of his stories was about the most basic school need—desks and chairs. "They finally got us some desks," he told Jack and me, "but they never got us any chairs." So students and teachers had apparently brought in some chairs from their churches, wood-slatted things offering nothing but sore "sit-downs," Cyrus said, using that expression I knew so well.

Cyrus also knew that the state-supported school, Alabama State College for Negroes, in Montgomery across town, was vastly inferior to the white students' University of Alabama in Tuscaloosa. Yes, Alabama State got some appropriations, Cyrus said, but when you got right down to it, he told us, "the money always goes to band uniforms," and about lab equipment, he said, "It just sits there all busted up and rusty."

Memories of the Depression still clung to Cyrus. If those times were to return—and no one, black or white, was speaking with any confidence that they would not—Cyrus did not want to be living in Montgomery when it did. If the Depression had been bad for southern whites, even I, with my early tendency not to notice racial injustices, could not deny that it had been horrific for southern blacks. Discrimination and exploitation, somewhat tempered in good times, in the Depression were rampant.

Cyrus, having had his fill of it, thought that going to college in the North might be the answer. "Is it true what I heard?" Cyrus asked. "Colored boys sittin' next to white boys up there?" Jack didn't say, "Well, in the North, colored boys have their problems too." He just said, "Yes, it's true."

Pursuing the thought, Cyrus wanted to know about scholarships for black students, for impoverished students, for students who were grandsons of slaves. "Anything like that?" he asked. We couldn't answer; all we could offer was the hope that after the war, perhaps black military service would be acknowledged and that southern universities would open their doors to all. Did we believe this? I have to say that behind my rosy glasses, I did; but Jack, behind his clear ones, did not.

I learned other things from Cyrus. I learned that there was a Montgomery Women's Political Council, and that it met in the basement of a black church and that many white women met with them. Cyrus gave me a long look and told me he thought I should go. "They'd sure make a place for you," he said.

And I did go. With the women gathering in the evenings, Jack babysat Rick, and I went to the meetings. Cyrus had said that white women attended the meetings, but I did not anticipate so many. And black or white, the women spoke out for the same thing—opportunity for blacks commensurate with their numbers.

The black members of the council had stories and anecdotes: of insult, of discrimination, of frustration. "It's like bumpin' up against a brick wall," they would say. And others would agree and say, "Well, that's so, but we got to keep tryin'." And then would come cautions against wasting time with too many anecdotes. "We all know how it is," they would say. "We've all had that happen to us a million times."

If one of the black women offered, "We got to get us some important somebody to talk about how it's jus' race plain and simple," it would be answered with a laugh and the remark, "You got as much chance of gettin' somebody to do that as gettin' a white lady to do your laundry." What the women knew was that despite their population majority, they had no political leverage, and so most ideas were discarded as impossible dreams. Even so, dreams were allowed. "Sweet Jesus," they would say, "help us get where we want to go and make it soon."

I felt inadequate in the face of such need. It was not my town, and even if in some sense it was, it was only a temporary one, and I soon stopped attending the meetings. But the other white women—some of whose husbands were pillars of the community—stayed on, and they were important to the plan the women were beginning to hatch. It was a plan that would shake not only the town but the entire country. And when it came to pass, I remembered with admiration the women in the basement of that black church.

We saw Cyrus a couple of times before his leave was up, but we didn't talk much more about things that might happen after the war. We told him to write to us, and he did, and his letters would always refer to "our visits in the Lincoln Zephyr."

FT. MYERS BEACH

One of the reasons Jack was spending so much time at the officers' club was that when he came "home" for dinner, he came home to a cell-like room and to dinner at a drugstore down the street. The store had no pharmacy for dispensing prescriptions—it carried patent medicines—and it had a fountain and kitchen that offered meals, which were called "blue plate specials." So it was a misnomered "drug store" like my father's in Miami Beach, and like that one, tables were scattered around for sitting, drinking "dopes," eating meat loaf with mashed potatoes and snap beans, and talking.

Sometimes others from the base—many who had just come back from combat and, like Jack, were awaiting further reassignment—joined us. The Battle of the Bulge, the battle that had come at us just as we had thought the war was on the verge of ending, had finally been won, and the prevailing opinion among those sitting around the drugstore tables was that the war in Europe was winding down. Still, there was another prevailing opinion, and it was that the war with Japan was not. The consensus was that the Japanese were fighters so dedicated to their cause they would fight on until the last man.

The boys were optimistic, however, that the last man would go toes up in a reasonable time, and there was a little, mostly jokey, discussion of what everybody was going to do afterward. Jack would say, "Tell them to call me if they need somebody to put figures into a bombsight." And somebody like Arnie Lorgan might laugh and say, "If they want somebody who knows how to bail out at six thousand feet, I'm their guy." And someone else, maybe Marty Rutner, said he could offer his services spotting Japanese fighter planes. "I got the know-how," whoever it was said. "If they're out there, they're mine."

Listening to the boys, I felt I was back in the fraternity house. They seemed a bunch of kids having fun with each other, and I laughed with them. But once more, that subliminal nudge was making its presence known. I sensed that somewhere deep in the subconscious of these boys was the thought that the realities of the future were waiting. But was there a feeling of urgency? I'd have to say there wasn't, and after a while, drugstore conversations about the future—facetious or otherwise—just died. Of malnutrition, I suppose.

There was no urgency for Jack and me, for now was now, and we were about to leave Montgomery. When we left, we left with no real regrets. From my point of view there was nothing much to feel regretful about. The rigid racial code? The thought that Cyrus was trapped by an unjust system? No, leaving Montgomery set off no sentimental throbbing in me, and as we rode off in our Lincoln Zephyr, I waved goodbye out the window and cheerfully called out, "Goodbye Montgomery. Goodbye forever. Hope never to see you again." And, I probably said in my head, "Hope never to think about you again."

Still, I have to say that Montgomery fooled us. In later years, we not only thought about Montgomery again, we thought about it in as different a context as could be imagined. How could we know that Montgomery, Alabama, that bastion of tradition, would down the road become a leader in a movement that would shake the country?

* * *

And so, equipped with a ration book that allowed extra gasoline for getting to a new posting, we headed out in our Lincoln Zephyr to Buckingham Field in Fort Myers Beach, Florida, where Jack would become chief of a gunnery training program for bombing crews.

Ft. Myers was a Florida beach town, but accustomed as I was to the east side of the state, this west side beach town was decidedly different. The surf did not roll out of the mighty Atlantic Ocean but out of the unassuming Gulf of Mexico, and its sands were not coarse and yellow—what the Miami Beach public relations people called "golden"—but soft and white. Walking on them was like walking on Willie Arnold's angel food cake.

In Ft. Myers we took up residence in an army wife's dream—a shingled beachfront cottage on stilts, with a wraparound porch and a full view of the gulf. The upstairs bedrooms looked out at the water, and as we slept, the gulf murmured to us and plied us with soft breezes. We spent our Sundays in hammocks on the wraparound porches and watched as Rick and a next-door friend played on the shore. Well, it's true that we had to share the house with the "no-see-ums," those little flying—and biting—things that flew with impunity through the screens and made themselves at home; but pesky little flying things aside, the house just plumb beat all, as I might have said in Union City.

Ft. Myers turned out to be another of Jack's postings that qualified, according to my way of looking at things, as a very good one, meaning no danger. Indeed Buckingham Field rivaled Maxwell in offering pleasant distractions. At the field, Jack could schmooze away his lunch hours at the officers' club, and in the evenings play softball on the base team. Or he and two-year-old Rick could spend time in the water, Rick floating and Jack swimming. Jack didn't float. He couldn't. When he tried, he may have trimmed and toned himself to 180 pounds, but he sank like a stone, and when he struggled up, there would be Rick doing his baby dolphin float, smiling his baby dolphin smile.

It was in Ft. Myers, it has to be told, that our big bargain of an automobile turned into a big misery, for soon after we arrived, we had to sell the Zephyr and doom ourselves to wheel-lessness. The Zephyr wasn't exactly falling apart like the Silver Streak; it was falling to a gambling debt Jack had incurred while he was overseas, the result of one of those poker games where a guy lost one night, won the next, and everything sort of evened up in the end, except for those who knew to quit when they had won enough to buy that yacht or Lamborghini or whatever else they had been dreaming of.

And so, as the story went, on one particular money-gone-wild night, Jack lost to a guy who didn't come back, but then he did, and while we were in Ft. Myers, he called Jack from his stateside hospital to say he was okay, even if the doctors had said that he had "gone bonkers." Well, he apparently hadn't gone so bonkers that he didn't remember the debt, so it was the end of the Lincoln Zephyr and the end of my being amused at Jack's family's gambling gene.

The loss of the Zephyr was not as devastating as it might seem. With our meager gasoline ration, the Zephyr had stayed motionless quite a bit, and surrounded as we were by men who had served overseas tours of duty and whose women had "done their part" on the home front, wartime gambling debts and wartime behavior were familiar to all. The result was that judgments were withheld and somebody's car was always at our disposal.

We liked our Ft. Myers neighbors, and we came to know each other's parents, siblings, education, political party affiliation. There was even a little talk of race and religion. Only one subject was scrupulously avoided, and that was the future, the "after the war" thing. It was terra incognita, perhaps a forbidding terra. It seemed a topic that demanded too much of the men. They had answered enough demands to last them a while.

A LOSS UNLIKE ANY OTHER

It was in April of that year, 1945, while we were in Ft. Myers, that something happened that was never going to happen. But it was true—the radio said so—that President Roosevelt had died. When my father called from Miami Beach and said, in a sad, sad voice, "We've lost our best friend," I could only agree with him. And that night, in our Ft. Myers enclave, Republican or Democrat, Jew or gentile, Catholic or Protestant, we mourned together.

It was only later that I thought "best friend" for what? For the war? Definitely. For the economy? Of course. But best friend for the Jews? The answer, long a subject for debate, was still not clear. Whether Roosevelt was personally anti-Semitic—and his Jewish brain truster, Felix Frankfurter, had written in no uncertain terms that Roosevelt was not—did not enter into it. What did enter into it was that he had dragged his feet on easing the immigration quotas on Jews desperately trying to escape Nazi-held Europe. Was it political expediency or personal resistance? Whatever, it was a puzzlement.

The majority of us Roosevelt-lovers tried to put the best light on it—our hero must have something clever in mind, we told each other, and some said, "Stupid he's not. He doesn't want to win a battle and lose the war." And when Roosevelt finally, in 1944, acted on the pressure from his treasury secretary, Henry Morgenthau Jr., and issued an executive order establishing the War Refugee Board to oversee and liberalize admission of Jewish refugees "and other persecuted minorities in Europe," some said "too little, too late," but some of us—my father, me, maybe Mr. Zimmerman—said better late than never. Although the board was subsequently credited with rescuing as many as 200,000 Jews, in the scheme of things the board had limited success, for the reason that its hands were shackled by political realities. It seemed that to get what it wanted, the United States, despite being engaged in do-or-die war, still must not offend nations that didn't want to offend Germany.

It was an intriguing subject for discussion, but at this moment we couldn't spend too much time on it. Roosevelt was gone and Vice-President Harry Truman (Harry who?) was suddenly the man in the White House. This new state of affairs brought no change to the progress of the war, only in personalities. We found ourselves having to adjust to a mild-mannered leader of conventional origins instead of a confidently assertive one of origins most aristocratic.

World War II was on a steady course toward its end. The war in Europe was in fact over on May 8 of that year—1945—and to celebrate what was called V-E Day, we gathered around while our neighbor Captain Marvel fired a rifle into the air. Captain Marvel no doubt had a first name, but "Marvel" was his last, he was a captain, and Captain Marvel was a celebrated comic strip hero, so "Captain Marvel" was—naturally—what we called him. And because Jack Suberman was often jokingly called "Superman," it created a nice coincidence. "Two super-heroes in the neighborhood," Captain Marvel said to the neighbors. "You guys never had it so good."

After V-E Day, after Captain Marvel had fired his rifle, we had only to wait for Japan to call it quits. And in May of that year President Truman, in a surprising action for the tepid temperament we had assigned to him, made a decision to drop the big bombs, the atomic ones, on Hiroshima and Nagasaki—one each—and the war was over.

CHAPTER

11

After the War

NOW WHAT?

So now what? Good question. To avoid answering it, we in the Ft. Myers contingent settled on talking about "de-mobbing," as the discharge from service was generally called, though for officers it was service "separation," not "discharge." Jack and I talked about this insistence on different terms for officers and men, and we agreed that death on the battlefield was very democratic, and it didn't care if you went down with a corporal's stripes on your sleeve or a general's star on your hat. The big question thereby successfully put off once again, we spoke instead about who would be "de-mobbed" and who would be asked to stay on while the military figured out how to handle the minutiae of ending a war.

Jack and most of the boys were not among those asked to stay on, and we said goodbye to each other and went our ways, which meant we were going to wherever we called "home" to await word that the separation papers were ready to be picked up at whatever separation center was nearby. Nobody was talking seriously about plans. If the boys were asked what they were going to do, some would say, "Just see the folks," and some, "Guess I'll look for a job." But what job? And where? The boys weren't talking. They were just happy to be going home.

Jack and I lucked out with a neighbor family who lived in Homestead just south of Miami, and we rode down with them. It had been decided that we would stay with the Subermans, and we were dropped off at their house in Miami. It was the logical place: My sister Ruth's husband Phil was en route from Hawaii, and Ruth and Dale were living with my parents in

Miami Beach. So the Suberman house it was, and Jack and I said to each other, "Until things are settled and we know what we're going to do."

LIVING THE DREAM

Jack was happy. He joked that having three months' leave on full pay was not bad, not bad at all. Mostly, he was happy that he was free, as he had not been for a long time—free of having to wake up knowing that a combat mission awaited and, not to be underestimated, free of duties and free of orders. He was relaxed and funny and playful and occasionally serious, although never serious about personal matters, only about books or politics or "When the hell are they going to desegregate the armed forces?"

Jack felt good about the war and about himself. He was coming off a once-in-a-lifetime experience, and he had come out a winner. Indeed, he felt super-lucky to be home at all and not, as he said, "crashing into some pagoda and being carted off in a wheelbarrow." He thought that what he and the rest of the boys had done was a marvelous achievement, and wanting to put a bit of drama into it, he would say, "We were the good triumphing over the evil."

He was impatient for the announcement that his separation papers were ready, and he would also say that the only thing standing between him and happiness forever was those papers, and he would say that his life was "sitting there in some moldy desk drawer at an old army base in Waldo, Florida," Waldo, Florida, being the location of Camp Blanding, our nearest separation center. No doubt the separation was awaiting him up there at Camp Blanding, but ultimate freedom and happiness forever?

As Jack and the boys waited, they got out and about. Jack kept to his uniform—like most of the other boys, his prewar clothes no longer fit—and when they went about the town, they drew a lot of attention. When they walked along the downtown Miami streets, they were often stopped and greeted and asked for handshakes, or at the very least were smiled at, and little boys dashed up to touch them. Shouts of congratulations and thanks came from those in cars and buses. If we were in a restaurant, diners stopped at our table to slap Jack on the shoulder or, sometimes, to tell their own tales. Everybody loved Rick and me as well, and they asked us questions, and when they asked Rick if he knew his father was a hero, Rick replied with a no-nonsense, "Sure." Without embarrassment, the townspeople called the boys heroes, and without embarrassment the boys accepted the accolade.

Officially, the town responded to the veterans' return with great fanfare. The Miami/Miami Beach city fathers hosted ceremonies at city parks and presented the boys with an assortment of certificates, documents, and plaques. They asked for wives and children to be on hand, and Rick and I obliged and were introduced and applauded. Not to be outclassed by his uniformed father, Rick wore an overseas cap, and I must say he wore it with distinction, but if it was one Jack had given him or one from my stash of World War I souvenirs is a memory lost in the mists of time.

Jack picked up on familiar things. He went around the neighborhood to renew acquaintances and to be introduced to any baby born in his absence. Unlike other Miami boys, he had no high school teachers to check in with, so he made do by going over to Miami Beach to try to find his old construction buddies. Though he knew that they too had served, he figured that once home they would make a beeline for one of the beer joints they had frequented after work, one, Jack hoped, that was not *our* drugstore. Where he found them was at a beer joint on Third and Washington, and after a long, beery afternoon, the men said, "You notice Jack's not so jumpy anymore? Wonder why that is." All followed, of course, by those well-remembered guffaws.

We went with other Jewish boys to restaurants whose food had been eaten only in their dreams, and they ordered anything that was corned, pickled, or shot through with chicken fat. I for one was amazed that the menu was offering such a formidable array of meats. While the war was on, while Jack had been overseas and I had been home, meat or fish offerings were rarely seen on menus, only little notes that read "Sorry. Our corned beef has gone to war," or "Close your eyes and our canned salmon will taste to you like Nova." Well, it didn't, but rationing was the order of the day, and meats and fish were the number one scarcity. Still, with the war's ending, a big release from the local government warehouse had put a lot of the foodstuffs you had thought were gone forever into the public domain. And here they were, on the Wolfie's menu—the brisket, the chopped liver, the Hungarian steak, the smoked salmon.

Parties, planned or spontaneous, popped up everywhere. Parents gave parties for their sons, clubs gave parties for returning members. Jack was gung ho for most of them. Like the other boys, he could not pass up a chance to see old friends and tell war stories, to hoist one or two, and, it must be said, to grieve with others for those who didn't come back. And so we went to the party given by his softball league, to the one thrown by his fraternity, to the one at the library. If any of the boys had worked before the war, they went to a party given by their ex-bosses. The ex-boss didn't offer you your old job, but he gave you a party.

The Harvey Seeds Post 29 of the American Legion was always open to the boys, and if the boys were looking for a place where libations were a little harder, its restaurant-bar was at their disposal. The boys went there often, and sometimes I went with them. We were all familiar with the story of the Harvey Seeds Post having been named for the first Miami doughboy casualty, and how the post kept in mind veterans of that war. I had often seen the men of the post come into the store and point to my father's little collection boxes with the sign that said, "Give to our boys," and I would listen when they said, "Thanks for your long memory, Mr. Kaufman."

Our visit to the Harvey Seeds Post brought all this to mind, and as usual I thought about how those earlier veterans upon their return had no doubt been surrounded by the same hoopla and hullabaloo now surrounding the current returning veterans. But I was remembering as well the hard times that followed and the Bonus March and the struggles. No slack had been cut then for veterans, no special allowances given. In time, it seemed, the custom of showing gratitude and respect to veterans was no longer an imperative, and their deeds were all but forgotten. Indeed, weren't they called "forgotten men"? I did not begrudge the attention being enjoyed by the boys now around me at the Harvey Seeds Post—the ones taking a beer or two or three—but if hard times came again, did I hope that they would not have to depend on somebody's "long memory"? Most definitely I did.

WHAT JUST HAPPENED?

To get to my parents' house on Miami Beach, Jack and Rick and I had to weave our way through a lot of commotion. Miami Beach was now dismantling its once-elaborate military facility and in so doing had become a study in movement and sound. MPs were on every corner, blowing their whistles at careening trucks and skittering jeeps and anything else that moved. I have to say, however, that I missed the uniformed boys marching down Collins Avenue singing, "I've got sixpence/jolly, jolly sixpence."

Jack thought the commotion was great, that it was a sign that the war was indeed over. And it was true that the rifle ranges were being packed up, and all the beaches were once again public property. "How do you know the war's over?" Jack would joke. "Because the kids are necking again on the Fourteenth Street beach." Fourteenth Street beach, prewar the venue of choice for lovers, was once again the setting for necking, smooching, petting, call it what you will.

When I first walked into the drugstore after the war had ended, however, I was aware that it too was reflecting the war's end, and not in a good way. The store was empty. The race tracks still being closed, there was no calling out of "Didja have him?" and "Didja get the double?" And no GIs either. No boys shouting, "Hi there, Buster" to Rick, no asking for extra mango slices on their ice cream, no ordering of hamburgers "rare enough to talk back." No boys milling around the drawer in the back as they anticipated a rewarding night under the moon over Miami.

The drugstore was not alone in its decline: most Miami Beach commercial enterprises had taken a hit, and the owners commiserated with one another. "Look, we agree it's good that the war's over," they might say. "But good for business? Not so much." It had to be faced: when the military pulled out, the commercial life of Miami Beach sank back to the prewar state of "just getting along."

And the Twenty-third Street stores? Bad news there as well. Renters were reneging on their leases—"sneaking out in the dead of night, and taking their *tchochkes* with them," my father said. And no one was begging to get in. I knew that my father was worried, and whenever my ebullient father worried, I worried as well, for I knew there was something to worry about.

POSTWAR JITTERS ON THE SUBERMAN PORCH

The boys, however—we still called them "boys" although they were now mature men, some even fathers—were home and they were content. The welcome they had received on their reentry into the world had made them feel honored and, above all, valued. What could be more satisfying, they asked themselves and each other, than to know you did a good job and to have that good job acknowledged? They laughed and they joked. "Look at us," they might say. "Nothing to do but cash monthly checks." They were enjoying, enjoying it all.

Well, they enjoyed it all for a while. They enjoyed it until one day the "Is that all there is?" moment arrived—the moment when all the buddies had been schmoozed with, the pickles at Miami Beach delicatessens tasted like pickles and not gifts of the gods, the freedom to do as one wished—to fish, to read, to go to the movies—was all at once curiously confining. At this point the sense of needing a "next" became acute.

I had been doing some wondering about a "next" as well, and it had set me to thinking about the separation and how the boys were talking about it as a goal. How often had I heard in some words or another, "My goal is having the separation papers in my hands"? What kind of "goal" was that? It occurred to me that separation was not an end in itself; it was a rite of passage. All of which led me to say to Jack, "If the separation is a rite of passage, what's it a rite of passage *to?*"

There was no answer, of course. Jack's answer should have been "to a secure future," but at this point in time, there was no future, secure or not. Few of the returning soldiers had a firm grasp of what the future—when their check would not be waiting for them at the finance office—would look like.

The future, then, was a riddle, and not just for Jack but for other Miami boys who were now gathering routinely on the Suberman porch to talk things over. According to the papers, it was a riddle for vast numbers of others—those who had served and who, like Jack and his buddies, were beginning to understand that serving their country was all well and good, but had it equipped them for a postwar life? Well, no. Those who had no prewar careers—and that would be the majority of them—could not resume their old jobs because they *had* no old jobs. Or their old jobs were now filled by others. And money? Ha. In service the boys had spent their money like, um, drunken sailors, and most came out of the war with debts.

Jack fit only too well into the category of skill-less, moneyless returning veterans. Like the majority of others, we had zilch in the bank. I didn't blame this entirely on Jack's penchant for gambling because I knew that much of the fault lay with me. With the war raging and Jack's captain's check at my disposal, I had persistently ignored my mother's lessons in thrift and spent as I wished.

The boys on the porch could no longer kid around, not as the boys around the drugstore table in Montgomery had kidded around. They could no longer tell jokes about a possible postwar need for men experienced in bailing out of planes or putting figures into bombsights. Suddenly joking was out, and earnestness was in. Out there on the Suberman porch, the boys had real questions, and the one that they asked over and over was, "Can any of you guys tell me of what use is battlefield know-how in the real world?"

It became a daily routine: Jack and the boys gathering on the porch of Jack's family house in Miami, Jack's father in his rattan lounge chair, and a goodly number of returning veterans filling the remaining chairs or sitting on the tile floor. Jack's brother Irwin, married and newly the father of a daughter, Lee, was among them. Ruth's husband Phil, having apparently fallen in love not only with my sister but with all that Miami had to offer, was planning to make Miami home and came every day.

Some of the boys we knew well, some scarcely at all. A number were Jack's fraternity brothers, and some I knew from high school or wherever. All were Jewish, and most were sons of previously well-to-do business-men who had fallen hard in the Depression and had fallen again when the military installations left town. And now, things being what they were, the sons could expect little from their fathers.

My schoolmate Jack Rubin, who had been a prisoner of war during the Battle of the Bulge, was a regular porch-sitter. Jack Rubin had a lot of sto-ries to tell—he was, after all, a Jew who had been captured at the Battle of the Bulge and held in a Nazi prison—but Jack Rubin was not in the mood to tell his war stories. Like all the others, he was worried about his future. If Jack Rubin had left tensions behind him when he was freed from the prison camp, he would say that the present ones would serve.

When Rick was napping, I sat on the porch as well, though I was usu-ally the only wife out there. Some of the wives were at home child-caring, and if they had held jobs during the war, they were still at work, for when the war came to a close, the women—primed by the Depression and sens-ing an uncertainty—had held on fast. Jack's mother came out occasionally to offer soft drinks and cake, but she didn't enter into the conversation, no doubt feeling that any decisions about jobs and futures were to be made by the men, as my own mother would have felt. I didn't quite feel that way. I understood that Rick and I had a big stake in this and that I had every right—maybe even a duty—to participate. From the moment Jack and I had come out of the movie, to that newspaper boy shouting the news about Pearl Harbor, I had been part of the team.

As I listened to the boys, I needed no super-sensitive antenna to recog-nize how moods had changed, how anxieties had overtaken euphoria. And the irony was great: the boys had only months earlier, maybe days earlier, been living with their adrenaline always stuck on high, and they had come back to a plodding discussion of "Where do we go from here?"

There was some talk about help from the government, but Jack's father for one was not impressed with the rumor of government help. "What kind of help are you expecting?" he asked the boys. "A job with the WPA? With the post office maybe? Are these the kind of jobs you want?"

The boys didn't know. They didn't know what kind of jobs they wanted; they only knew they needed jobs, and if they had families, they were get-ting perilously close to panic.

* * *

When I saw my father pull up in his 1941 emerald green Buick, I felt a glow of optimism. My view of my father as a begetter of good ideas and as a fountain of good cheer had not diminished, and as if to affirm this, before he had even jumped out of the car, he was in full cry. "Why is everybody just sitting?" he shouted toward the porch. "You don't sit. You talk." It was Jack's father who answered, and he said, "Listen, Morris, these boys have talked so much they don't have to talk again until next year." On the porch, as I waited for a solution or two from my father, I realized that he was not at his best. "I'll think of something," he kept saying, and though he was indeed "thinking," he was not coming up with much. And Mr. Suberman, thinking as well, wasn't coming up with much either.

My father fell into telling tales of what he knew about the problems of World War I veterans. His stories were, of course, about their struggles, and he would say to the boys on the porch, "So bad it was, it was like America wasn't who it was anymore." These words would bring me back to those days in Union City when we sat at the breakfast table and my father passed around pictures of the doomed Bonus Marchers, and I had to wonder about the stories my father was now telling: They might have been relevant, but were they helping? Not so you could tell.

I had taken one thing for granted and that was that those boys who had gone into service before they got their degrees would go back to college, and I was surprised to discover there was little support for this. When they had been in college, most of them had never chomped at the bit, had never said, "Can't wait to finish and dive into my job." Classes had been tedious, mainly, they would say, because they were so useless. Now they were saying something different, and it was, "What's a man with a war under his belt doing in college?" Going to college now, even if they had a way to do it, made no practical sense to them, especially if they had become family men with wives and children.

Never mind about those boys. I had every confidence that my Jack would go back. He would finish that last semester and get that degree in English. As it turned out, however, if I had every confidence, Jack had none, even when his father offered to pay for the missing semester. "Why should I go back?" Jack said to his father, his point being, as always, that a bachelor of arts degree with a major in English meant nothing on the job market. "I could say I have a college degree," he said to his father, as his father *utched*—fidgeted—around in his rattan chair, "but will it get me a de-

cent job? No, it won't. An undergraduate degree would be just a starter."
Did his father take the hint? I'd have to say he didn't. There was more from
Jack of a discouraging nature. "And who will be paying the bills while I'm
taking this useless degree?" he asked. "I've got a wife and a kid, and they
need me to have a job."

It was becoming clear that the very idea of going back to college was,
for Jack, less than appealing. "Go into a situation meant for students still
wet behind the ears?" he said to his father, and maybe to me. "Stand in
line and deal with admissions people who've heard it all and don't want to
hear it again? Answer to requirements and deadlines, and try to decipher
what the hell the professor really wants? Sit in the library for hours?" Jack
was full of objections, and with each one, he seemed to convince himself
further. "Are you asking me to do all this scut stuff?" he said finally. "After
what I've just come through?"

Afterward, at night in bed, there would be more of the same, and Jack
would say to me, "Going back to college—it's for kids. I can't see myself
doing it." He would not say that he *would* go back if the kind of job he
wanted was in the cards, *would* go back for the kind of job I had been fan-
tasizing. In other words, would he go back if there was a way for him to get
those higher degrees and become a college professor?

ONE FLICK AFTER THE OTHER

Jack and the boys (and I) sat on. Ideas were thrown about, chewed over,
spit out. And then came a letter from Bill O'Connor, our behind-the-
curtain basement-mate in Great Bend, Kansas, to give the boys yet another
painful flick.

Bill had been with Jack in India as a B-29 bombardier, had been shot
down over the Yellow Sea, and had finally been sneaked to safety by
Chinese guerrillas in a long, dangerous journey through Japanese lines.
When we had last seen Bill, he had come to Miami after being liberated
and had sat with us on the porch where we now sat. All he wanted to do
at that moment, he had said, was to get back to Boston and Peg.

Now he wanted something else. He wanted a job. Any job. In his letter, he said that he and Peg were on their way to a third child ("still good
Catholics doing what good Catholics do," he wrote), but his main message
was about finding a paying job. "I really need a job bad," he wrote. "I can't
take sitting around much longer, what with Peg expecting and all. . . .
When you got nothing to offer, nobody wants you so fast."

Bill was one of those who had never been to college, and he wasn't thinking of going now, even though it was no longer as sacrosanct, as unthinkable as it had once been. For boys like Bill, their time in service had taught them that you didn't have to be super-smart to own a college degree, and they had seen the proof of this in their college-educated buddies and superiors. Still, Bill was not thinking of college; he was thinking of a job.

It was in Bill's last paragraph that the flick was delivered. "Jobs are scarce up here," he wrote. "The plants making war stuff are closed or closing, so no jobs there. And if they had been making other stuff before the war, they don't seem to be going back to it. . . . There's an Irish guy owns a bar down the street and I'm going to ask him—one mick to another—if he needs somebody to help out."

We all understood that the "bugouts" of the country's military installations had forced some local businesses to the brink of collapse, as it had with my father's. But a nationwide slowdown? On the porch we were suddenly jolted: More hard times? Was the tyrant pulling himself up from the abyss and climbing up the cliff? Could we be in for another—I could hardly allow myself to think the word—*Depression?*

"No jobs" Bill had written. Not even jobs with an hourly wage. It seemed unthinkable. During the war, the boys had gotten used to hearing that the economy was "flourishing," "going gangbusters." Factories had been turning out war equipment as fast as humanly possible, and what followed was a phenomenally prosperous economy, so prosperous that the Great Depression had abruptly turned tail and run. And here was a returning veteran writing about factories closing, and saying "no jobs." That factories making war matériel had closed down didn't surprise us, but we had confidently believed that they would automatically go back to turning out beds and cooking stoves. As this seemed not to be the case, however, we had to consider that the prosperous wartime economy just been a placeholder for a Depression on furlough.

Unlike the rest of us, Mr. Suberman was not surprised by this turn of events. "When a war ends, you think everything just automatically goes back to normal?" he asked us. "You think somebody's waiting for you with a job?" And after some *utching,* he would say, "What makes you think the bosses have to wait? Boys like you looking for jobs are lined up around the block."

Newspapers picked up the job story: "Jobs Hard to Come By," the *Herald* headlines might read. "Veterans Looking, Not Finding," they might say, and they pointed out that for every available job, four or five returning veterans wanted it. In sidebar stories, reporters interviewed bosses who said they couldn't make room for veterans. Sorry about that, they all said, but "I've got a business to run, and the men I've got [usually men who had been classified as 4F—a classification for those ineligible for the draft because they were too old, too sick, or too conscientious an objector] know their jobs. I can't afford to let seasoned workers go." And sometimes, usually unmentioned, those seasoned workers were women.

And then, as if to give evidence, here came my brother Will at the wheel of my father's Buick to join us on the porch. Will had lost his job when his war equipment plant had closed, and he had come down to see what he could find. "Nothing doing up North," Will said to us assembled ones. "So I thought I'd test the Miami waters."

Well, the Miami waters, the boys told him, weren't quite navigable either, and Will took his place among all the others looking for answers. With both Will and Jack's brother Irwin having careers in engineering in mind, they had that special worry—whether after the war the field would revert to its Jew-aversion policies.

The boys often used Yiddish locutions, perhaps feeling that they were particularly appropriate for expressing hopelessness, and somebody like Jerry Snyder, who spoke, as my mother would say, "a very good Yiddish," might say, "What are we jerks doing? We're just *schlepping* around, turning into *schlubs,* and *spieling* about how it was in the Depression. What's with us?" It was what they all felt: that they were dragging themselves around, turning into losers dwelling on the bad times of the past.

Soon the boys would say they were on *shpilkes,* on pins and needles, and they would leave, apparently deciding to *schlep* their *shpilkes* elsewhere. It was as if wherever they were, somewhere else was calling them. They spent their days like this, visiting with us and then milling about town, seeking a place where a special sunbeam might suddenly shine down and show them the way.

After the boys had left, after Will and my father had departed in the Buick, after Phil had gone as well, the talk on the porch would narrow to Jack and Irwin. I knew what to expect: ideas would come and go like so many wind gusts, and we would flail about in them.

Still, on one of these days, Irwin's problem was more or less worked out. Mr. Suberman said he would support Irwin in finishing off his degree in engineering, with the hope that maybe—maybe—Irwin would afterward find a job. This was all right with Irwin. He could see a path. He would have a degree that promised a set of skills useful in the marketplace. It was a plausible way to go. "Okay with me," Irwin said to us. "Maybe by the time I graduate Jewish engineers can get a job without a war." One Suberman boy down and one to go.

Push now having come to shove, Mr. Suberman began to warm to the idea of a job in business for Jack, although he knew Jack's limitations in that world. Jack had often told me that he was not what his father would call "a crackerjack businessman," and, more important, he remembered when his father, in a moment of gloom at Jack's lack of competence, plus his lack of enthusiasm, had turned to him and said, "In my opinion you're too light for heavy work and too heavy for light work." They were words, Jack said, that he didn't forget.

Now, however, Mr. Suberman was going to approach a New York business acquaintance, Leonard Berkman by name, who was, as he himself had been, in the fur import business and was still importing from a place in Manchuria called Mukden. "Maybe he needs somebody over there," Mr. Suberman said to Jack. "It might be something for you. It's got some adventure. You'll see."

It was, however, not the kind of adventure Jack would be drawn to. In a strange coincidence, Jack had had experience with Mukden: During the war Mukden had been in Japanese hands, and Jack had in fact bombed it. In a letter to his father, he had said, "I can't imagine that you ever visited in this place. If Mukden is what it looks like from the air, it's as cold and dreary as a tomb." So now, to the adventure that Mr. Suberman thought might intrigue Jack, his son said, "I didn't spend eighteen hours fighting off Zeros to haggle over animal skins in an igloo called Mukden." And so Mukden became another idea that went by without leaving a trace.

Then there was that one return trip of my father's when he thought he had a viable scheme. Was it a prospect I could fall in love with? No, it was not. The scheme involved Will, Jack, and Phil and grew out of the particular needs of south Florida. My brother Will had apparently been taken with the amount of rusting he had seen in Florida's salt air, and he remembered a certain product that claimed to prevent metal from rusting. When he wondered if the New York company that made it might be interested in a south Florida franchise, my father jumped on it, sent Will to New York to check on the product, and told him to report back. I listened to all this with my heart in my mouth. Would Jack find charm in selling anti-rust stuff?

To my surprise, Jack did. He thought that selling anti-rust stuff might not be such a bad idea. After all, if he could make a living for his family and be his own boss, what was wrong with *that?* And he liked the product. "How can you not like something that's going to make lives better?"

he asked us. "It's a thing of value." In the end, it didn't matter if Jack was charmed or not. Will's report from New York did in the project: the product was only for new construction, and considering that there was at this point no new construction, rust-proofing went the way of all the other ideas.

So we sat, and we thought. Ideas got wilder. Jack mentioned that he had taken some agriculture courses at the University of Florida, one of which dealt with growing hydroponic tomatoes. He had read that hydroponics were a coming industry, and would his father subsidize a small hydroponics plant?

The idea of being a farmer seemed to Jack both romantic and useful, and it seemed that way to me as well. I saw Rick running between corn stalks, planting his own garden, petting the livestock. I was remembering my visits to farms around Union City, all of which had offered splendid entertainments. One of them was picking strawberries, which paid a penny for two boxes. I was not very good at it, having "neatened" the strawberries by pulling out the stems, and when I presented my boxes to the farmer for my pennies, he just smiled and said to take them home and enjoy them. Moreover, I had never actually performed any of the onerous tasks required on a farm, but I was, like Jack, romantically taken with the word "farm."

Jack's father was not romantically taken with either the word or what it connoted, and he declined to stake Jack to a small hydroponics plant. "I don't think of you as a farmer," he said to him. And Jack said, "Okay, so what do you think of me as?" To which Jack's father said once more, "All I know is that you're too light for heavy work and too heavy for light work." And out there on the porch, that's when Jack said, "All I want is to make a living for my family." To which his father answered with a dry, very dry, "I think that's the idea."

FACING FACTS

I kept asking myself things like, "In the event that jobs are available, what aptitudes, what qualifications does Jack have that could help?" Well, he had been a lead bombardier. Um. What else had he been? President of a fraternity? Sports cup winner? Varsity basketball player? Um, um, and um. Book lover?

Book-lover? "Book-lover" was, of course, the operative word for that wartime fantasy of mine, and even if Jack had laughed at me and said that my head was just "a jumble of movie plots," I knew he shared it. I was not deterred, and I determined to talk again of the logic of Jack's getting an undergraduate degree. Still, when I did, I made a mistake. What I said was,

"Let's get the degree, and then we'll hope for something to come along to get you higher ones."

Whoops. I had said the word "hope," and Jack had immediately said, "Hope? Where's this hope you keep talking about?" He had more: "Do you expect me to subject you and Rick to one room in Gainesville?" And when I suggested that Rick and I could stay in Miami while he was up there, Jack was definitely outdone. "Haven't we been apart enough?" he asked me. "And what about Rick? I guarantee he will forget all about me if I'm in Gainesville and he's down here."

It was hard to let go of my fantasy. I knew the odds: we were in a real world, and in a real world such a goal would need hard support. I could only rev up my courage and ask Jack's father if he could stake Jack to those succeeding years. The answer was, quickly, "No." Maybe Mr. Suberman was thinking of Jack's lackluster prewar college years, or maybe he was thinking of his own bank balance, but whatever the reason, he said, "A semester, yes. More than that, I can't do."

My father? I knew he couldn't help. When the anti-rust project fell through, his means were going toward something for Will. What Will would be doing was redesigning one of the Twenty-third Street stores for a restaurant that had shown a bit of interest in locating there. It was make-work, but it was work.

Finally, Jack had had enough. He was mad at me and he was mad at his father. Surprisingly, he was also mad at the military. "How could they turn us loose like this?" he would ask of anybody who might be around. "How could they not offer some sort of easing out? Some promise of something?" When somebody might remind him that he had three-months' leave and the pay that went with it, he said, "In three months I'm supposed to forget I was an officer with an officer's pay, a husband and a father, and just make believe the past years never happened?"

It was obvious he was mainly mad at himself: he was asking himself why he had been so smart-alecky in college, why he had "larked around," why he had joked about "indulging a hobby." And was he also asking why he had taken so many courses in English literature, knowing they held such little promise? And, ultimately, he had to be wondering why he had been so *enamored* of English literature.

Jack may not have shared his insights with others—not even with me—but I was on to him. I knew why he loved literature: I knew he felt it was the basic, the essential, the indispensable tool for informing one's life. I also knew that Jack wanted what I wanted for him—to communicate his love of literature, and to do it by teaching. When he talked about being a teacher, he would say, trying to keep me from going giddy with hope, "Yeah, teaching is great, but you got to have the right students." And when I would ask who those right students might be, he would say, "Mature ones. Students open to new ideas and not closed up in what they were learning in their schools." These were the students he had in mind—young people fresh to college that he could open to the enlightening ways of literature and the humanities. And this meant. . . . Well, this meant something seemingly beyond reach.

And then came the day when Jack decided he had had enough. "Enough talking, enough everything," he said to us. "See you later." And that's when he got up, got into his father's Ford, and went out and got a job.

The job Jack got was absolutely the worst, so bad that I wondered if he had taken it to teach his father a lesson, to show him that he was not too heavy for light work or too light for heavy work, the meaning of which I had never quite worked out. The job was in a storage warehouse hauling rugs out and returning them to the hotels that had stored them there during the military takeover. Now the hotels were hoping for a business revival and wanted the rugs back. It seemed that the warehouse people didn't fall in love with Jack's brains as I had; they fell in love with his brawn.

Jack didn't care that it was a terrible job. Well, he *did* care, but he was in no mood to explain why he had taken such a job. Mainly, I suppose, like myriad other returning veterans, he didn't know what else to do. He might also have felt that one terrible job was as good—or as bad—as another. But it broke my heart. My wonderful, handsome, accomplished Jack fooling around with rugs destined for cushioning tourists' feet in some Miami Beach hotel room.

MY FATHER PUTS IN HIS TWO CENTS

Despite that Jack was now a jobholder, the porch gatherings did not come to an end. Mr. Suberman and I—and the occasional veteran—sat together as often as we could, sat and stared at each other, as if willing the other to produce a bit of inspired thinking. It would be a few weeks before inspired thinking would show up, and when it did, it was courtesy of my father. This time, he didn't disappoint.

Going up the walk to the porch, my father was already firing questions: "Are y'all still sittin'?" and "You think roast chickens gonna fly in your mouth?" We in the Kaufman family, accustomed as we were to my father's adages and sayings, knew this one very well. And no, we didn't expect roast chickens to fly into our mouths; we didn't even know there were roast chickens out there.

My father was still yelling as he came through the screen door. Hadn't we *dumkopfs*, we dumbbells, heard on the radio, as he had, that there was some kind of something in Washington meant to help GIs? A bill for veterans? And being pushed by the American Legion? My father had heard something from his favorite radio commentator, Gabriel Heatter, whose sign-on phrase—"Ah, there's good news tonight"—had made him a loyal listener, so it was not so much what he had heard but whom it had come from that had made him, as my mother would say, so *meshugeh*. In fact, so *meshugeh* was he, so overexcited at this moment, his Savannah-learned grammar as usual went to pieces. "Don't nobody here know nothin' about it?" he asked us. "I was the only one heard Gabriel Heatter?"

Well, we *dumkopfs* didn't much listen to Gabriel Heatter, but we had a dim recollection of what he might have been talking about. President Roosevelt had said in one of his early wartime chats that he did not "intend" to let current veterans go the sad way of the veterans of World War I, and he had signed a bill that was supposed to have veterans in mind. But with other things pressing, we had no time for it, and we concluded that it was just another bit of the scuttlebutt that continuously made the rounds.

Still, in a letter, I had offhandedly mentioned to Jack both President Roosevelt's remarks and the passage of the bill, and Jack had written back, "It's probably nothing to think about. Just somebody's idea of rallying the troops." It was a typical response. In the letters between Jack and me, little was written of plans for the future. My letters were chiefly of Rick and of longing and hoping. Help from the government at that point was the answer to a question that had yet to be asked. Our focus was elsewhere, and that one exchange of letters seemed to be the end of it. Out there on that Miami porch, however, amid the welter of propositions, courtesy of my father, it had a revival. And we began to wonder if the rumor had turned into something viable, or had my father, in his trust in Gabriel Heatter, gotten it wrong?

When Jack came home from his skirmishes with rugs, he wasn't terribly interested in what my father had told us. "Why take off one uniform just to put on another?" he asked. To Jack, government-sponsored help meant more rules, more orders to be followed.

SEPARATION AT CAMP BLANDING

When Jack was notified that his separation papers were ready, he went up to Camp Blanding with no discernible enthusiasm. Camp Blanding, in north Florida, had served in many capacities during the war. It had been an induction center, then an infantry replacement training center—with a mission to train filler personnel for overseas forces—and it was now a separation center where Florida boys got "separated" or "discharged," as the case might be.

We all knew things about Camp Blanding. When I had been at FSCW, I knew that many of the girls' boyfriends had been stationed there, and we knew about it from the Florida newspapers, all of whom had followed closely its development as a full-service facility. It was full-service in every way, from a post exchange to juke joints to a vast choice of bordellos.

In the later war years, Camp Blanding held German and Italian prisoners of war, and a small POW cemetery had been established there. Well, Camp Blanding had nothing on Miami Beach. We had German POWs in Miami Beach as well, and don't think it wasn't "aggravatin'," as we would have said in Union City, that German soldiers were so openly in the midst of a rather substantial Jewish community. Had some military someone thought it a truly clever idea to have German POWs paying for their transgressions by repairing the streets of Miami Beach? If this was the idea, it didn't work out too well. When they leaned on their shovels and flirted with Miami Beach girls in heavily accented "hubba hubbas," those wolf whistles in words, Miami Beach was mightily offended. The POWs may have been called heroes in their own country, but in Miami Beach, they were called—loudly and to their faces—*schwein*. Pigs.

* * *

When Jack left for Blanding, he had little thought of anything beyond his separation papers. Well, he had promised me that he would look into the thing my father was on about, but he thought he would just get his papers, come home, and resume his . . . um . . . job. Still, at Blanding, after he had signed his papers, he was surprised to get an offer that he spent more than a little time thinking over.

Tucked among his papers was an invitation from the active reserves to join up and a promise of a promotion if he did. It was hard for Jack to dismiss the offer. Being an officer again—if only on the weekends—had its appeal, especially after a week of hauling rugs around. And that sizable major's stipend! Still, if he said yes, he would be agreeing to weekend duty at various bases and to temporary assignments that could send him anywhere in the world.

It was tempting, but it was a no-go. Any affection Jack had felt for the military was fast declining. The original job that he had been called upon to do—and which he and the other boys had accepted with enthusiasm—was no longer a part of the military mission. He believed, as we civilians did, that the military had performed brilliantly when it counted, and it had counted when a madman and his people had gone amok and had to be stopped, but that particular circumstance no longer pertained.

There were the other reasons. Jack, like most of the boys, knew from experience that military orders sometimes seemed to come from an unhinged brain, and it had led them to believe that the military and the government that oversaw it were not among the most trustworthy or efficient of institutions. Otherwise, why was the acronym SNAFU—Situation Normal, All F——ed Up—so often invoked? Why trust your future to such an uncertain hand?

In the end, with some reluctance, Jack left the form unsigned and turned his attention to that other thing he had to do at Camp Blanding. What was that again? Oh, yes, he was supposed to find out about government help for returning veterans.

Jack walked over to the bulletin board to take a look, and he saw notices and notices, all thumbtacked helter-skelter, as if they were saying "Here's something you won't be interested in but we were told to put it up." He searched among them, at first finding nothing to pause over. And then, as he was about to turn away, a thick stack of notices on a hook caught his eye. The lettering across the top read SERVICEMEN'S READJUSTMENT ACT, and Jack ripped one off and put it in the inside pocket of his jacket. Then he got back into his father's 1940 Ford and headed back toward U.S. 1.

At home, Jack threw his discharge papers into a drawer and hung his jacket in the closet. He was distinctly out of sorts. He was tired, and he was cranky. It had been a long trip through the long stretch of the Florida peninsula, and he was still uncertain of his decision to decline the reserves. In short, he felt he had nothing of interest, certainly not of importance, to impart. He didn't want to ask or to answer questions. He wanted to nurse his wounds.

I let him alone. For a while. And then, not able to resist, I asked him, "What did you find out about that thing my father was talking about?" Jack gave me a look that said, Oh, yeah, that thing, went to the closet, got the paper out of his jacket, and tossed it to me. I tried to find something in it to read, some figures maybe, but there was almost nothing. Well, it said that more information could be found at the post office.

When I asked at the post office for information, I was handed a brochure whose cover read, "Servicemen's Readjustment Act," and I began to read. What I seemed to be reading was of an act whose purpose was to assist returning war veterans. Was this the bill my father had been talking about? I decided to read on and find out.

12

The GI Bill

As I read on, if the paper in my hands had said, "Jack Suberman, this is for you and all those other guys who have been sitting on your porch," I would not have been surprised. What it was telling Jack, what it was shouting to Jack and to those other returning veterans and to whoever else had worn a military uniform, was that because of their military service, they had rights. And what they had rights to was a fruitful life. When Jack had been at Camp Blanding, when he had scrounged around among the scraps of paper on the bulletin board, he had found the GI Bill.

As I continued to read, I thought of what this bill would mean to Jack and me, and to all those boys waiting and wondering on the porch, and, for that matter, to all those waiting and wondering veterans in the whole country. Did the other boys already know about it? If they didn't, they would know soon, and when they did, they would know that what they were going to do with their lives had been decided.

As I stood in the post office, I read and reread, and though there were items to be considered carefully, this was not the moment for that. It was a moment for me to take that precious brochure home to Jack.

Jack, however, was still not ready to discuss a government-sponsored anything. And when calls started coming in from the boys to say that they were getting on board, the other Jack showed up, the one who wouldn't learn to march, and this Jack said to me, "Just because everybody else is doing it doesn't mean it's a good thing for me." It sounded to me, as always, like the thing my mother used to say—"Just because the other kids are swimming in their underwear doesn't mean you have to do it too," which I had heard more times than I could count.

It was the appearance of this Jack that had me pitching a fit—though not the fit with the tail on it that I would produce in the future. I just thought to remind Jack that we were still living with his folks and that Rick was being raised by two sets of advisors, and how long could we live like this? And when I had stomped around, threatened, and drawn what lines I could, Jack finally gave in. "I guess I could take a look," he said.

* * *

After a hurricane, the air becomes very still and crisp and when the storm has finally whirled itself out of town, the moon glides out and bathes the land in a brightness so luminous that Mother Nature seems to be saying, "I can get tough, but I can be tender as well." And what Jack learned in the brochure produced in him the same effect: the storm was gone, the moon was aglow, the light was the brightest ever. Somebody—some thing—had brought to our lives a new radiance.

We never once overestimated what was in the brochure; it was impossible to overestimate it. It told us, first of all, that we were not alone, that our government was with us, that we had its guidance and support. Was this the bill that President Roosevelt had signed in 1944—when most of us had been too otherwise engaged to take notice? The one where he gave "emphatic notice" that America did not intend to let its veterans down? Yes, it apparently was. This Servicemen's Readjustment Act, or the GI Bill, as it was already being called, had put bones and meat on President Roosevelt's emphatic notice.

The post office finally had the full text of the bill, the boys got a copy, and now when we gathered on the porch and talked, spirits were once more a-zoom. We read and reread the bill aloud and to ourselves. Jack and I took pages of it to bed and read it to each other. When we woke up, we grabbed for the copy on the nightstand. We told Rick about it as he ate his breakfast, and he seemed delighted. We summarized it to Jack's father as he lounged in his rattan chair, and for the first time I saw the pre-Depression grin that I had only heard about. We lectured on it to Jack's mother as she fixed *matzo-brei,* the matzos and egg mixture that Jack's sister Sheila daily breakfasted on. All the while we tried to zero in on how we could best take advantage of what we had in our hands.

THE CLAUSES

The bill was in fact full of clauses that told us how it could be of help. The clauses were famous, and if in Union City, my friends could quote Bible passages chapter and verse, I could quote chapter and verse GI Bill clauses, as could most of the boys and their wives. We discarded some clauses as not pertinent, but some were very pertinent indeed.

The bill's guidelines were artfully simple and written in all positives. We read not a torrent of bureau-speak but the straightforward words of what seemed a benevolent older family member speaking to praiseworthy younger ones. Furthermore, we saw the bill as all democratic all the time, and it went to great pains to make that clear. What was impressive from the first reading was just how democratic the bill was: all enrollees got the same benefits, no matter their rank (though those above the rank of, say, lieutenant colonel, were likely to be regular army and would have no need for the bill). So no matter how you exited the service—wearing an officer's insignia or an enlisted man's stripes—you got the same deal. Furthermore, the bill did not state who were not eligible but who were. And it seemed that everybody was, anyone who had served ninety days or more, and who hadn't done that?

For Jack and me, and without doubt for all who were Jewish, when we looked reflexively to see if there were any coy quotas, we did not find any. Aware that discrimination was still showing up—in Miami Beach, hotels were again sporting signs proclaiming themselves to be Jew-free—for us to find no hint of it was, well, refreshing. And when I looked for black quotas, I didn't find those either.

The GI Bill benefits, contrary to what had been feared, did not come in the form of advice; they came in the form of money: Each of the clauses promised financial support in one way or another. For us, one stood out. In fact, it not only stood out, it stomped around and shouted. It was of course the clause that offered the way to an education. When Jack and the thousands of others who took advantage of the education clause read carefully, what they found was a munificent program offering funding for tuition, fees, books, and seemingly whatever else was needed to get yourself educated. And—were they reading right?—a stipend of sixty dollars a month for living expenses, plus a little more for dependents.

Still, Jack and I had to wonder if colleges were on board with all of this. The GI Bill may have been staunchly nonrestrictive, but it did not lay down rules that said colleges were obliged to admit any qualified veteran who applied. And so, the Jewish boys had reason to believe that the colleges that had quota systems would still have them; and I had every feeling as well that Cyrus, our black friend in Montgomery, would find white colleges in the South still barred to him. I couldn't imagine that such schools had undergone a change of heart. Jack would say to me, "Can you find anything in the bill that tells colleges to take their quotas and shove 'em?" But though I looked with hope in my heart, I couldn't find anything that said that.

We decided to concentrate on all the bright things in the bill. With a year on the GI Bill available for every year served, Jack would be provided with four years of college, and wouldn't that cover a Ph.D.? It would. It would also cover four years—enough to get an undergraduate diploma—for those entering college for the first time. It seemed to cover everything necessary to get you and all your first cousins, and first cousins once removed, educated. And get this! It covers on-the-job training! My gosh, the boys said to one another, what didn't it cover? All in all, it was a deal to take your breath away. It was even family-friendly. Perhaps the bill preparers understood that families had endured a gracious plenty of being apart, and the family provision was enough to enable families to come along. Jack and I figured we would have enough for Rick and me to be in on Jack's GI Bill adventure.

Veterans who used the education clause did not all want to be teachers. The goals of those who opted for the education clause were as diverse as they were, and, as we learned, many veterans—the majority of the boys on the porch, in fact—intended to pursue professional degrees. "What are we going to do with all those lawyers and doctors?" Mr. Suberman would ask. Was he perhaps rueful that his sons would not be among them?

Of course, Jack and Irwin both were planning on professional degrees, but they were not going to be among the lawyers and doctors. And Ruth's husband, Phil Heckerling, knew he wanted to have a profession, and though he didn't know which one, having the education clause at his disposal, he would have the luxury of choice. Something was becoming obvious: a whole new class was being created—a class of boys who would become first-generation professionals.

For the boys who wanted to try their luck at operating their own businesses, the business clause popped out at them. It was the clause that offered low-interest loans and the promise of experienced advisors, and our former prisoner of war Jack Rubin, not being under the direct influence of that anti-business crusader, Jack's father, took the business clause to his heart. He wanted a printing press, some advice, and some start-up money. "When you guys get rich and need some advertising," he announced to the other boys, "look for me in my office." My father, who took proprietary interest in the bill, claiming to have "discovered" it, was especially taken with the business clause, and he would say, "Believe me, the government is some banker. If I had that kind of banker, I could be Neiman and Marcus by now."

If a veteran entertained nothing more lofty than finding a job, a GI Bill clause protected him or her as well. Everybody called it the "52-20 Club" because of its guarantee of twenty dollars a week for fifty-two weeks to any-body out looking for work. It was a clause that was talked about more than it was used, and in fact it barely got off the ground. As we learned, only about 20 percent of veterans actually asked to be in the "club." Still, it was good to have it as a fallback position.

And then there was the housing clause. Ah, the housing clause. Even though Jack and I had no intention of buying a house, we of course read the clause, and when we did, our minds went a-boggling. "Look here, you guys," I can hear myself saying to any of the boys who might be around, "this is really some kind of something." And it *was* some kind of something. How could it not be when it offered a guaranteed home loan with zero down payment and an interest rate so low that my father maintained that even with his "Bush & Lawn" glasses, he couldn't find it?

Sociologists, economists, and all the other professionals whose job it was to research such things fell all over themselves in describing the hous-ing clause. The *New York Times* quoted them as saying it would "spark an ex-plosion," that it would "break the grip of paternalism," but what was said about the middle class seemed most important—that the housing clause would allow the expansion—actually the creation—of the middle class.

Jack's father didn't need scholars to tell him the benefits of the housing clause. The minute he read about it, he began *utching* around in his porch chair. "You'll see," he said to us as he *utched*. "When people buy houses, they need things to put in them. Mark my words, we're going to have smokestacks again. Lots of them."

Even as we were trying to fully understand the housing clause, a Long Island development called Levittown was under construction and being called "the beginning of a new trend." Although we were aware of what critics were saying about Levittown and other such developments—that the houses were "ticky-tacky" in style, small and uniform, and lacked aesthetic appeal—would veterans and their families care? Unless they were holding onto their movie standards, they wouldn't. It was enough for them that the houses were affordable and offered privacy and a backyard.

Jack was not surprised, therefore, when an old Bronx friend, a former B-17 pilot, who in his previous life had shared with his brother a convertible sofa in the living room, wrote to tell him that he had already made the dash to Levittown. "Come on up and visit," he had written. "We've got a guest room, and we've got a backyard and grass. Did you ever play badminton?" No, as Jack's friend knew very well, he and Jack had not played badminton in the Bronx; they had played stickball on asphalt streets with sewer covers as bases.

So, as we were learning, houses were being built and veterans were buying them. Sometimes, according to the papers, if they were veterans, construction workers bought the very houses they had worked on. Mr. Suberman crowed about having figured it all out. "Didn't I tell you?" he said to us. "Now you'll see factories, real factories making real things that people need."

What Mr. Suberman was predicting began almost at once to happen, and factory and service jobs were once again being advertised in the *Herald*. "WORKERS WANTED," the want ads called out, "LOOKING FOR WORKERS." It was a stunning turn of events, and when it happened, workers became once again the hot topic for the retired garment workers, so hot a topic that when they came into the store now, they talked of their hopes that unions would finally find a degree of welcome in the South. "Let's see a little southern hospitality," they said to whoever might be in the store. "Looks like bosses are making money. So maybe they should give their workers a voice, no?"

Yes, the economy was on the rebound, and our fear of a return of the Great Depression had subsided. Not that we forgot, not that we ever forgot, but it was not on our minds in the same dark and relentless way of the past. Now if I sang "We're in the Money" to Rick—as I often did—I sang it not with a misplaced confidence but with conviction.

It was not until much later that we thought about those predictions, about the GI Bill making possible, among other things, a "dramatically changed society." We of the multitudes of returning veterans and their wives who intended to use the GI Bill were not particularly interested in the bill's role in bringing about a changed society. We were interested in what it meant to us and to our well-being and, perhaps most of all, what it would mean to our children.

IT'S 1946, AND THE GI BILL LIFE BEGINS

Even though the GI Bill had opened the doors to other universities, to nobody's surprise Jack decided to return to the University of Florida. When its students left for service, the university had promised that when they came back, their credits would be waiting, and Jack didn't want to waste a single one. Moreover, Jack felt at home on the Florida campus, even as he recognized that he would no longer be in the familiar role of frat boy and athlete but in the unfamiliar one of husband and father. And so we—Jack, Jack's father, and Rick and I—set out for Gainesville, and as we went, we were fully armed with goals. My fantasy, I thought, was becoming real life.

As it was to turn out, however, what I was picturing as real life was itself a fantasy, one that went like this: Jack would snap his fingers and get his undergraduate degree, glide into his master's, and because the University of Florida did not offer a Ph.D., would then slip seamlessly into another university for the ultimate degree. And after that? Why, after that he would begin to teach. As I saw it, Jack just had to put in a lot of studying and good things would happen. Nothing to it.

Of course, there was a lot to it. If I had substituted reality for fantasy, if I had substituted maturity for naiveté, I would have known that we were not going to be waved through any toll gates. For Jack, and for all those GI Bill boys who had chosen to go to college, the coming years would present many a struggle. They would have to acquaint themselves with their strengths and their limitations and learn to factor them in; they would have to learn that their lives would revolve around study hours, and library carrels, and 3 x 5 file cards, and if they, like Jack, were hoping for advanced degrees, they would have to deal with the pressure of examinations—the "prelims," the "writtens," and the "orals," and if the Ph.D. was the ultimate goal, the dissertation would be ever on the mind. There was also the factor not to be underestimated: the question of whether the goal was worth the investment of many years.

And the wives? We wives would be doing what we had done on the home front, which was, as we all described it, "helping to get the boys home." But if, during the war, this meant pitching in to shorten the boys' exposure to danger, it now meant doing our best to keep the boat from rocking.

THE UNIVERSITY OF FLORIDA, IN GAINESVILLE

Jack and I were still car-less, so we were going up to Gainesville in Jack's father's 1940 Ford, and going slowly in deference to the tires. The ban on buying a spare tire was still in effect, and all the tires Mr. Suberman had in the world were on the four wheels of this vehicle. It had always surprised me that Mr. Suberman owned a Ford. Henry Ford was well known among Jews as the world's biggest anti-Semite (until Hitler came along), and most Jews boycotted Ford cars. I had not known in any detail how Henry Ford got his reputation as the "biggest," and Jack, once again not letting a teaching opportunity go to waste, had once explained it to me. And that's how I had found out about the *Protocols of the Elders of Zion,* that it was a treatise purported by anti-Semites to reveal how the Jews were planning to take over the world, and how despite its being proven a hoax, Henry Ford had published it in 1920 in his own newspaper, the *Dearborn Independent,* and how the hoax thereby went on to gain widespread acceptance. So I guessed that Henry Ford was the "biggest" because he had the money to buy him the biggest mouth. But when I had learned it all and had asked Mr. Suberman why he was putting money into the pockets of the world's biggest Jew-hater, he said they were all the biggest, and that was that.

Traveling at forty-five miles per hour had its pluses: it allowed us to check out who and what were on the roads with us. It was January, registration for the spring semester was upon us, and Florida roads were filled with men and conveyances—beat-up cars, motorcycles, pickup trucks, even horses—and the dress of the day appeared to be bits and pieces of World War II uniforms. What was abundantly clear was that registration was going to be a mob scene of returning veterans.

We spent the night at the Thomas Hotel. The next morning Jack was up early and off to register at the campus admissions office, where he would also rescue his old credits and sign up for new ones. But what he had to do first was to attend to that little life-altering item that had actually put him in the admissions office in the first place—the presentation of his separation papers and, in turn, to receive the official recognition that he was being admitted to school under the GI Bill.

True to our predictions, Jack was one of a multitude of veterans in the admissions office qualifying under the GI Bill, and they were all, Jack explained, very happy to see each other if they had known each other prewar or not. And they all wanted to talk. Not about the expected—war deeds and exploits—but about schedules and degrees. And GI Bill benefits. "Believe it or not, I haven't been asked for a dime," they all said. And then they would laugh and say, "Uncle Sam, I love ya."

RICK AND I SEEK SHELTER

As soon as Jack's father went back to Miami, Rick and I began our job, which was to find us a place to live. Acting on a rumor of special housing for GI families, we went around to the so-called campus housing office, where we learned that the print on the GI Bill was still drying and government-subsidized housing units had only just broken ground. We put our names on a list.

In Gainesville proper we found nothing, and we went further afield. As we walked and we walked, Rick, three years old, was up for it. We didn't walk alone. Dozens of wives, some with children, were also walking, and we would call out "Finding anything?" to one another, to which the answer was invariably a "Not yet." As in most college towns, Gainesville housing had always been tight, but no vacancies at all?

Paradoxically, "For Rent" signs were everywhere, which suggested that the town was well aware of the massive infusion of shelter-seeking veterans. The signs, however, which at first glimpse gave such hope, turned out to be nothing more than a snare and a delusion: when inquiries were made, the place was already taken—"You're the tenth [twentieth, thirtieth] I've turned away," the owner would say—and I'd mutter to Rick, "So why don't you take the golderned sign down?" Rick and I were not deterred—at least not terminally—but as we moved to outlying Gainesville and the pebbly clay roads, the feeling grew in me that finding housing in Gainesville was going to be a matter of doggedness and/or luck.

If doggedness was the trick, Rick and I could have won the doggedness cup. I dragged him along to garage apartments, trailers parked in yards, any house, shack, or cabin that looked habitable; and Rick, no doubt feeling that desperate times called for desperate measures, dragged me along to his find—a tireless and rusting car sitting among Gainesville's spindly slash pines. Well, why not? Hadn't I dragged him to a wood cabin with no screens and an icebox in the yard?

A sign nailed to a tree, on it an arrow and the words SEEK HERE, sent me dashing forward. Seek a job? Seek salvation? I didn't know, but I had hopes. If it was to be shelter, even if was another basement room like the one in Kansas, I'd jump at it. Well, it turned out to be two rooms and a hot plate in a structure no doubt once the family garage.

Even if the former garage was not exactly the Roney Plaza, Miami Beach's most sumptuous hotel, I would have happily signed up for it if an Ocala wife and her infant son hadn't gotten there first. Awash in empathy, the young woman offered to share it—"We could have a schedule and take turns at things," she said—and although I said no thanks, I appreciated her kindred spirit-ness. I somehow knew that she and I were kindred spirits twice over: her offer suggested that she, like me, had once been a traveling-around military wife, and now she, like me, was a GI Bill one.

IN THE PI LAMBDA PHI FRATERNITY HOUSE

The day ground on. We had found nothing, and Rick was no longer the cheerful companion he had been when we had set out on our quest, and it seemed to me a good time for our rendezvous with Jack at the Pi Lambda Phi house.

As was the norm at this time of day, the fraternity house living room was empty, and as ever dark and dank, as if under no circumstances was sunshine to be allowed in. It didn't matter. I was grateful to be limping into it and plopping down into the cushions of one of the numerous sofas, and I was grateful when Rick put his head in my lap and went instantly, magically, to sleep.

I had no doubt that in the way of most fraternity houses, the sofa upon which we sat had not undergone a cleaning since I had last sat upon it, and I suspected that it was now so dirty "you could plant petunias in them," as my mother would have said. And there was also that familiar smell in the air, that combination of stale beer and overused sports socks. None of these things offended me. Indeed they were in some ways welcome, for they spiked memories of the boys I knew in that house and the good times I had there.

I had not been in the fraternity house since the month after Pearl Harbor. Jack had been fraternity president that last year, and I had gotten to know the boys. They came from all over the state, chiefly from Dade County (Miami/Miami Beach) and Duval County (Jacksonville), but from little towns as well. Many of the small-town boys, like Irv Rubin of Cocoa, were from "Jew store" families like my own. And many of those, again like us, were among the rare Jews in town. The Jew store boys and I called each other "Jew babies," as we had in Tennessee, and we told each other stories of our lives as we had lived them as our hometowns' most exotic residents.

There was another Jewish fraternity at the university—Tau Epsilon Phi—and you were always aware of the competition between the two. At a Fall Frolics before I met Jack, I had gone as the date of a member of Tau Epsilon Phi—the TEPs—and I had learned there had been a rivalry between the two in about every direction possible. When it came to grades, however, there was no contest: Pi Lambda Phi's not only made better grades than the TEPs, they invariably won the university academic achievement cup, a feat of some campus interest. The faculty was particularly interested, and one of the professors was so interested that when he noted in his class a Pi Lam of indifferent intellectual ability, he called Jack in for a conference and advised him to drum the boy out. "Not up to your standards," he told Jack. "You Pi Lams have to guard any distinction you might have, you know." Whether this meant that the Pi Lams, being Jewish, had no other positive distinctions, Jack didn't care to pursue at that moment. He just took it on board.

Even if scholastic achievements could not be argued with, the TEPs could deride them. The next year, when I went to Fall Frolics as Jack's date, my TEP friends told me how to have a good time with Pi Lams. "Bring a book," they said.

As I sat in the Pi Lam living room, I wondered about those rivalries. Postwar, would they still exist? Would the camps still be arguing over which one could boast the most scintillating wits, dated the best-looking girls, possessed the most in-depth knowledge of the big bands? I guessed they would not. Certainly not the fraternity boys I knew, the ones back in school under the GI Bill. Those war veterans had made it plain that they were back in school for one reason and one reason alone—to prepare themselves for a future.

As I sat in the fraternity house living room, with Rick's head on my lap, I glanced around at the things I was deeply familiar with: the magazine pictures of pinup girls tacked on the walls, the plants underwatered and overwatered by turns, the cigarette burns on the tables. It was when I looked out at the ping-pong table on the side porch that I took my deepest plunge into nostalgia. That table loomed large in the life of the fraternity. It had been in constant use, the paddles so fiercely fought over that occasionally only a wrestling match would settle it. For the boys who lived far from Gainesville, too far to go home on the weekend, ping-pong play was continuous from Friday afternoon until Sunday night.

I began to consider the boys who had played at that table. Some had gone to war, some had not. And which of the boys among those who had gone would be back to play at that table once again? I already knew with a terrible certainty those who wouldn't.

Miami and Miami Beach had their share of those who wouldn't. Alfred Kohn, the diminutive guy whose nickname, "Alfy," fit him so perfectly, wouldn't be back. He had been the editor of the Italian edition of the military newspaper *Yank*, had volunteered to join the fight in the south of France, and had been killed there. Bob Richter, whom every Fall Frolics date wanted to dance with, wouldn't be back. I wanted to dance with him too, not because he was movie star handsome—which he was—but because he would dance a dynamic Lindy Hop, which Jack couldn't or, more like it, wouldn't. But Bob had been killed in the retaking of the Philippines toward the end of the war. Lee Silver, a classmate of mine from Miami Beach Senior who had volunteered for parachute duty, had died in a jump over France. Nathan Aronovitz, who was from Miami but, having lived his early years in the more exotic Key West, always liked to say he was from that city, was one of those who wouldn't be back.

Jacksonville also had its share. Simon Rothstein wouldn't be back. He had been killed in a flight training accident in Savannah, in much the same way that my friend Johnny Bulla had died in Victorville, California. Louis Dwoskin wouldn't be back, and neither would Billy Mayer. Billy had been killed on the very last day of the war. There were others that I knew about from other Florida towns, and others that I didn't.

What was I doing with all these memories? Didn't I have plans to think about, like where we were going to live? I pulled myself out of my nostalgia and straight into one of my funks.

I knew what my father would do. He would do what he always did when things weren't going his way: he would call on his special helpers, one of which was his *zutz*, his hustle, a word he always insisted he had himself made up, as I always insisted I had made up *utch*. The other was his *mazel*, and who knows who made that one up; it was just in common use as an all-purpose Yiddish word meaning "luck." He knew these two well when he was trying to establish his little Jew store in Union City, and "Such good workers they are," he would say. "I should only have a dozen like them."

All right, I was thinking, I had given ample opportunity to my *zutz*—what my father might call "hustle" but what I would call "doggedness"—and it was a no-show. And my *mazel*? Well, my *mazel* was this moment sitting down on the sofa across from mine.

Who was sitting down was the university's engineering dean, Dean Weil, the fraternity's faculty sponsor. I had never met the dean, but I had heard a lot about him, including that during the war, he had left the university to work for the War Department. As my brother Will had found out, during wartime, if you had skills the military was looking for, you got hired. Even Jewish engineers got hired.

Dean Weil and I greeted each other, and he said, Yes, he was happy indeed that Jack had come home safe and sound. Yes, he had thought constantly of the boys all during the war. Yes, it was great that Jack and many of the old fraternity boys were back in Gainesville. And yes, he had a house to rent. And yes, I took it.

Full of my news and wanting to hear Jack's, I waited for him to come in. The living room was filling up, and though it might have seemed a typical fall reunion, it was more than that. It was also a reunion of boys coming back not from a summer vacation but from a war. I knew some of the boys, for sure those who had sat with us on the Suberman porch in Miami, and we greeted each other in the way of people who had gone through tough times together and come out on the upside—with an "okay, we did it" kind of smile. You couldn't miss any of the boys who were back in school under the GI Bill. Their ways were self-assured, confident. You could almost see the GI Bill's pages sticking out of their pockets.

Jack's brother Irwin was not there, nor was my brother-in-law Phil. For various reasons, they had decided to wait out this semester and come up for the next one. But Jerry Snyder, the good Yiddish talker, was there and still studding his conversation with Yiddish. "What a *machiah*," he said to me. "Who'd have thought we'd finally get our *tuchesses* off that porch?" Who indeed? As we sat on that porch, who would have thought that in a short while the boys would be off their sit-downs and enrolled in college?

But they had done just that. One of the boys might say to me, "Never thought I'd be studying architecture, but here I am," and somebody else who knew Jack's father's hostility to business and its natural companion, the stock market, might joke, "Tell Jack's old man I'm taking business administration. That ought to get him going." How many times had the boys heard Mr. Suberman say, "Business is like the racetrack without the fresh air"?

And here came Jack. Here he came with a big smile that stayed put, and here he came ready to clap shoulders and feint jabs like everybody else. He looked, I thought, GI–Billish, a locution I had that minute coined. Finally,

finally, I was seeing Jack the way I had longed for so long to see him—cheerful and at ease, as if that postwar dejection had never happened.

When we finally had a chance to talk, I waited with my news until he had told his, and what I learned was that he had totaled his old credits, and although he discovered that a single English literature class would get him his B.A., he said he intended this semester to take all–English literature courses all the time. "If you're shooting for higher degrees," he said to me, "you want all the ammunition you can get." Higher degrees! Yes! And though he had no regrets about those agriculture courses he had taken prewar, his schedule now contained no courses in castrating pigs or rotating crops, and I gathered that there would be no more "larking around" or "indulging a hobby." Listening to Jack, I couldn't keep an Ira Gershwin lyric out of my head—the one that went, "I got rhythm and who could ask for anything more?" I mean, like the song said, Jack and I definitely had "rhythm," and could we ask for anything more? So far, I didn't think we could.

Jack reported running into a lot of guys at admissions that he had known before the war—not fraternity brothers, just boys he had been with in this class and that, and who were now going back to school under the bill. I wouldn't have bothered to ask Jack if he had seen any blacks at admissions because I felt sure that the educational facilities of the state of Florida (lower, higher, whatever) had not changed their whites-only admissions policy. And I hadn't heard that it was any different in any of the other southern white universities. So the two million or so African Americans who had been in service in the all-black platoons provided for them were still locked out of white colleges. Though the black GIs might have lost a limb or two or escaped with their lives in ambushes that had killed their buddies, southern custom was not to be deterred. These were all thoughts to consider more fully at a later date. For the present, we were content with our exchange of news—Jack's that he was on his way to a career; mine that I was on my way to a house.

As we all talked, a couple of boys walked out to the porch to the ping-pong table, and someone else went into an adjoining room to the piano, a never-tuned thing that the boys liked to bang on, though a few could actually play. Good, I thought, as tunes drifted out, somebody is pretty good, and when Jack got up to schmooze with the boys, I sat back and listened. Whoever was playing was sticking with the songs that had seen us through the war—songs we had danced to, made love by, dreamed with. They were songs of longing and loss, and they were songs of country. Here came "I'll be seeing you / in all the old familiar places," and here came "I'll never smile again / until I smile at you," and here came "It's a grand old flag / It's a high-flyin' flag." And here came the tears. Like my mother, I cried easily, and Jack would laugh at me just as father laughed at my mother. If my father said that my mother cried when somebody missed the bus, Jack said I cried listening to the alma mater of some school I never heard of.

But what was wrong with a show of tears at this moment? I was grateful, wasn't I? I was proud, wasn't I? I was proud of myself for finding us a place to live—for opening up to my *mazel*, my luck—proud of Jack for deciding he could learn to march after all, proud of those special boys in the room who knew what they wanted and who knew that what they wanted was a good thing. And I was proud of my country.

Why such pride and, especially, why such patriotism? It was easy to explain in this room filled with boys who had fought a just war and had defeated a cruel enemy. And, more to the present point, hadn't our country stepped up to the plate? Had it not seen the boys' needs and had it not found a way to fill them? And so as I sat on a sofa in that fraternity house living room, as I sat with my son asleep in my lap, loving my country had never seemed so right.

OUR HOUSE ON HERNANDO STREET

The dean's rental house was a small, wood-sided one, and it sat on a small plot of dirt studded with scrub. The rent was twenty dollars a month. The house was on Hernando Street, a few blocks from the campus, a block from University Avenue, and almost immediately behind the Pi Lam fraternity house. It was mostly furnished, and with very dark things that I supposed "Miz Dean," as I called the dean's wife—if only to Jack—had cast away. As I was currently a member of the Miami Beach diaspora accustomed to wicker and fabrics a-splash with lighthearted palm fronds and hibiscus blossoms, very dark things were not what I had in mind. The only suggestion of plants, real or fake, in or out of the house, was a rose of Sharon bush in the front yard.

Miz Dean gave me forty dollars to "fill in," as she said, and she directed me to a couple of used furniture places. I searched in them for something in the Miami Beach mode, but Gainesville's used furniture stores seemed only to carry things of a brooding nature, and I finally bought two mahogany chairs and tried to buy into the idea that the little pinched roses of the fabric suggested hibiscus blossoms. The chairs were also so severely upright that I concluded—too late!—that they were designed to give the sitter a serious pain in the back.

With the twenty dollars that remained from the chair purchase, I bought a cot for Rick and a mirrored dresser. The trouble here was that the mirror's taut paper backing managed to echo with a thump-thump-thump whenever Gainesville's signature palmetto bugs (read: great big roaches) had a mind to go marching across it.

Settling in required little more on my part than trying to work out how to live on the GI Bill's seventy-five dollars a month, instead of a captain's pay of four hundred. We would either live on that amount—augmented by an occasional bill slipped into a letter from our families—or I would go to work.

I didn't know if there were jobs available in Gainesville—after all, it had been Depression-hit like any other town, and as a college town had suffered when the student population went to war—but I might ask at one of the stores downtown, maybe at Silverman's Men's Store or Rudderman's Department Store. Though both of them, as I learned, were run by Jews, they were not, strictly speaking, Jew stores, because Jews stores, at least by my definition, were not specialty or department stores but modest dry goods stores. I was qualified, however, to work in either store because I had been familiar with the workings of a retail store from birth. I could even pass the ultimate test of the retail clerk: I could re-pin an opened-up shirt so adroitly that I could say without fear of confrontation, "Yes, Miz Ponder, it's fresh from the box."

Or I might try for a job at the CI, the College Inn, the college hamburger joint of choice just down from us on University Avenue. Maybe part-time? But wait. Didn't I have a child at home? Wasn't I needed there full-time? If somewhere a system of mutual assistance mother-pools had been worked out, it had not yet put in an appearance in Gainesville, and more to the point, I concluded that I didn't really need a job. I could put to work the gene that I had inherited from my mother and find a way to live on our stipend.

Our house was in the middle of a GI Bill enclave. Houses all around us—or at least rooms in them—were occupied by veterans and their families, all of them taking advantage of the GI Bill's education clause. Well, all of our neighbors except our next-door ones, Ralph and Helen Bradbeer from Jacksonville. The Bradbeers were not actually in Gainesville because of the education clause; they were in Gainesville because of Sears and

Roebuck. Still, the GI Bill was in their lives, and it was because the housing clause had bought them a house.

Ralph was following generations of family tradition by working for Sears and Roebuck. The Bradbeer men and their families were firm believers in the beneficence of Sears and Roebuck, and Ralph had come back from the war eager to rejoin the company. Still, Sears and Roebuck might have been a great company, but it could not have bought—at such rock-bottom interest rates—the house that the Bradbeers were living in. For a lot of things that counted in life, Sears and Roebuck was second best to the GI Bill.

When the Bradbeers bought their house, it confirmed what Mr. Suberman had said about how when you buy a house, you have to buy things to put in it, and that would lead to a revival of "smokestack America." And here was the example: the Bradbeers bought a house, and they then bought a refrigerator and a stove and other things to put in it. The Bradbeers had done their part. Wanting to get my little light to shine, I thought, well, Jack and I hadn't bought a house, but we had bought those chairs and that cot and that dresser. And without further deliberation, I gave us all a star.

JACK GOES (BACK) TO SCHOOL

The focus of the families in the GI Bill enclave was on the head of the household and his schooling. This was certainly true in our particular household, and when Jack set off for class in the early morning of the first day, it was a moment full of drama. Pulling on an old air corps shirt, snatching up his beat-up flight jacket, Jack was off to the campus, and as he made his dash across the backyard, it seemed to me that a new air of purpose was dashing with him. As I stood at the door watching, I thought of the wife in *How Green Was My Valley* seeing her husband off to the mines. Well, my husband wasn't going down a mine shaft; he was going to a class in Old English literature with an emphasis on *Beowulf.*

Jack's classes might have seemed at first glance to be much the same as before the war in that they were held in the same classrooms and were taught by the same professors. Despite the current massive demand for graduate classes, the university had little time to devise separate ones, so as before the war, graduate and undergraduate students sat together. Still, there were many differences between prewar and postwar classes, and I understood that they were different because the students were different.

In the days before Jack was consumed by the studying, he had a bit of time to tell me about his classes—what the professors were like, including their mannerisms and their tics, and what his fellow GI students were like. According to Jack, the latter were so different from prewar students they might have been a different breed. They engaged the professors, and not reverentially. Jack didn't have to remind me that in the prewar days, open disagreement with a professor instantly tagged you as an eccentric with suspect views. But now, he said, the practice of "brown-nosing," so routinely engaged in by prewar students, was no longer the classroom custom. Humoring professors was out, and stating your own view was in. The boys apparently understood that they were now free not only to ask questions but to challenge.

What it amounted to was that the GI Bill boys were having a very good time. As I explained to myself, they no doubt felt that having at last thrown off the burden of authority, they declined to let another impose itself. What or who could do them harm? The GI Bill was there to defend and protect them. It was a security they may have never known before.

The GIs were eager to talk, and they talked walking to class, in the halls before class, and in class. "You can't shut 'em up," Jack told me. "It's like they spent their lives bottled up, and they're pouring it all out now." They wanted to talk about why they wanted an education, and they decided there was nothing "corny," a word that had just come into usage, about discussing "truths" and "ideals." They discovered that the principles and attitudes they had held as unchallengeable could—and would—be challenged. From their enthusiasm, from their lively participation in class discussion, when I thought back on it in later years, I had to believe that many of these GI Bill boys were having a first experience in critical thinking.

PROFESSOR LYONS

English Literature 401 (Shakespeare's tragedies) was taught by Professor Clifford Lyons, coincidentally the professor who had urged Jack to infuse his big-city education with something rural. He too was back from the war, having served in the navy as a commander, and he was surprised to see Jack. He was not surprised that Jack was back as a student; he was surprised that Jack was back studying English literature. He had known Jack as an athlete and a nonstudent, and that Jack would be serious about a degree in English literature struck him as somewhat odd. "Did they mix you up at admissions?" Jack remembered him asking. "Maybe," Jack answered him. "I guess you'll have to tell me."

Almost at once Jack established something of a relationship with Professor Lyons. Professor Lyons had been a college football lineman turned serious scholar, so it may have been sports that initially bonded them, but for whatever reason, talk between them flowed. Sometimes they talked about what they had done in the war, at other times books, occasionally the Depression, and often the quality of the GI Bill students.

It was a sign of the times that in-house, man-to-man discussions between a professor and a student could take place, and it seemed to me yet another change brought about by the transformation of the student body. Dr. Lyons often talked with Jack about what the GI Bill boys had brought to the classroom. "They test our mettle," he would say cheerfully, the "our" meaning the faculty. The faculty, having in the past known only uninterested students bogged down by the weight of the Depression, were apparently now, like the GI Bill boys, having the time of their lives. "These students are curious and eager," Dr. Lyons said, "and I might never have known them without the GI Bill."

Jack always enjoyed his chats with Dr. Lyons, but as a veteran of the New York Jewish wars and equipped with an abiding awareness of anti-Semitism, he never left home, as they say, without it. He was compelled to look for it in just about every non-Jew he met, and Professor Lyons was no exception. Deplore the Holocaust though everyone might, Jack was still not persuaded that anti-Semitism was a thing of the past.

It was true that anti-Semitism was alive and well in many places, as in those Miami Beach hotels that were once again proclaiming their Jewlessness, and it was also in good health in Gainesville. This was confirmed in a chance meeting Jack had with an old New York friend, a member of Jack's *mischpoucha*, his extended family, whom Jack had known in the Bronx as Herschel Walcoffsky but who was now Harvey Walcott and, according to Herschel, Jewish no longer. "From now on," Herschel had said to Jack when they crossed paths on the campus, "you don't know me. From now on, don't nod, don't wink, don't wave; just walk on." As "Harvey" himself walked on, he turned back to Jack and said, "And don't hold it against me."

Jack was not surprised, and he didn't hold it against him. He understood Herschel's plight. And Herschel's plight might explain why Jack took a lot of measurements before issuing a pass to a WASP.

Jack thought that I and my fantasy would be interested in Professor Lyons's teaching style, and I was. Everything about it was movie-like. Dr. Lyons's office apparently adjoined the room in which he taught, and with a table in the center and the students sitting around it, the classroom channeled Oxford University more than it did the University of Florida. At the appointed hour, Professor Lyons strolled in from his office and, first things first, knocked his pipe against an ashtray, noisily expelling the ashes, then sat down and, before proceeding, offered a witticism or two. It was Jack's first intimation that if you were going to have a career in English literature, the English way of doing things was the one true way.

GEORGE AND BOBBY HARPER

Jack's fellow students were mostly from Florida, among them one or two fraternity brothers, but many were from out-of-state, though even so from the Deep South. One out-of-stater, however, was a graduate student from Missouri, and he was George Harper, home from his stint in the navy and looking forward to a Ph.D. and a job of distinction.

Jack and George had shared those mixed classes before the war and had had a nodding acquaintance. But now they were becoming close friends. This despite their having had altogether different backstories: Jack had grown up in the big-city ambiance of New York, which was evident in the New York flavor to his speech; George had been born on a Missouri farm and spoke with a Midwest twang.

Was Jack's antenna catching any sounds of anti-Semitism emanating from George? George knew Jack was Jewish, not from his own deductions, but because Jack had told him. George having had little or no experience with Jews—there had been no Jews in George's hometown, and he had met few in the navy—Jack gave him the benefit of the doubt. "Could be that George doesn't know that anti-Semitism is part of the Zeitgeist," Jack would say to me. Still, Jack sensed that even if George knew, it would mean little to him.

George had reported something else to consider: he apparently had had a close friend who was the son of a Lebanese storekeeper, and Jack wondered if maybe being friends with an Arab had prepared George for being friends with a Jew. "After all, we're kin with the Lebanese, aren't we?" Jack would say. "Aren't we Semites one and all?"

I heard a lot about George Harper. George was a serious scholar, I was told, and when he caught Jack sneaking in a page or two of what George thought profligate reading—reading that was not required—he was quick to chide him. George was concerned that when the time came, Jack might choose to write his master's thesis on some contemporary writer, which George thought a distinct waste of time. "Shoot," he would say to Jack, in as scoffing a tone as George could muster, which wasn't very scoffing, "you want to be a scholar, you stick with the masters." George, the son of a cattleman, knew the value of good stock.

It was a different experience for Jack—this being close friends with a non-Jew, especially a non-Jew from the Midwest. In the air corps Jack had been close to some who were not Jewish, but they were not friends, they were "army buddies," and that was not the same. Before the war, the majority of Jack's natural companions were fraternity brothers or hometown pals. Establishing a close relationship with a non-Jewish fellow student was a first for Jack, and it seemed to mark his new direction. For all the veterans who came to college under the GI Bill, new directions were there for the taking, and the boys were beginning to pull away from their previous lifestyles and to get on with their new ones. It was another sign of the times.

I liked hearing stories about George, and I was especially interested in that Lebanese friend of his, the son of the storekeeper. I knew something about Arab merchants. When Jew store owners in Tennessee got together, they liked to talk about anything related to their little piece of the mercantile business, and of course they delighted in stories of "the big guys"—Neiman-Marcus in Dallas and Rich's in Atlanta—both of which had started as Jew stores; but they also told stories about Arabs—which they pronounced "Ay-rabs"—who came as peddlers from New York selling their wares from wagons, eventually settling down and opening their own modest stores, much like Jews had. And one of the Jew store owners would always say, "Derned if you can tell an Ay-rab from a Jew."

I met George's wife Bobby one afternoon when they came to call on somebody across the street. We went out to greet them, and I immediately learned a couple of things: I learned that Bobby was from Jacksonville and that the Harpers owned the car we were standing next to. It was a brand-new Chevrolet—a "Chivy," George pronounced it—obtained in Jacksonville through the pull of Bobby's father. As we stood beside this gleaming symbol of good connections, we could only think of our departed Lincoln Zephyr and of the used bicycle that had replaced it.

Through the months, Bobby and I became very close, although we were as different in our own ways as Jack and George were in theirs. On the face of it, we did not fit at all. Bobby had "come out" as a debutante; my goals vis-à-vis "society" were somewhere between zero and zilch. Her father was a well-fixed community leader in staid, respectable Jacksonville; my father was a drugstore owner and sometime–real estate player in glitzy Miami Beach.

As for religion, need I tell of the many ways we were different? When I first "interviewed" her, I learned that Bobby, if not strongly religious, was not irreligious. She went without fail to her Presbyterian church every Sunday, where, she told me, she prayed "just enough" to keep her in good standing. All in all, she seemed serene about her beliefs.

I was not at all serene about my beliefs. I had heard my father preaching the gospel of "God is just a rumor agreed on by everybody" since I could remember, and it rang in my ears. And my mother? Well, though my mother liked Jewish rites and observances, she herself would say that truly knowing her religion was beyond her grasp. I was confused and torn, and Jack was no help.

Jack and I both held to our *yiddishekeit*—our Jewishness—though deistic belief remained outside our lives. Jack never bothered, never worried, never doubted, but I had to wait for Albert Einstein to come along and save me. When I read that he had said that being Jewish meant you belonged to a worthy and valued *tradition,* I felt I was home free. And when I described for Bobby the long route I had taken, she said, "Jews are so interesting. They just take things so to heart."

Bobby and George had had a typical wartime romance. They had met when George was stationed at Mayport, the Jacksonville naval base, and Bobby said she was "simply overcome" by George in his navy whites. "Those whites just dazzled me," Bobby joked, "and George thought I was the sophisticated girl of his dreams." And she would laugh and say, "After all, he was from a rural someplace in Missouri, and I was from Jacksonville, the glamour capital of the world." George and Bobby were yet another example of "mixed" marriages—in this case, country boy/city girl—which the woods, postwar, were full of.

Bobby and I got along very well. Even though she came from a well-to-do family, she was a Democrat, and I was not surprised at this. All southerners I knew—Tennesseans or Floridians—were Democrats even if they were Republicans in Democratic clothing. But they called themselves Democrats and voted that way, with the exception of the 1928 election when, as I knew only too well, anti-Catholic voters thought Al Smith and his open phone line to the Pope were too much to sit still for. I of course knew

Republicans in Miami Beach, but they were snowbirds who didn't vote in Florida, so they didn't much count.

THE GI BILL BOYS KNUCKLE DOWN, AND SO DO THE GI BILL WIVES

After the boys had put in a day in class, they went to the library for a couple of hours, and then came home to dinner. After dinner they studied at their makeshift desks, and they studied alone and long and hard. It was the routine. No going to the movies, no card playing, no listening to the radio. A telephone call, even one about a school matter, would be cut short with "We'll talk about it in class."

Jack's desk was in the bedroom. It was one he had "built" himself of concrete blocks topped by two planks placed side by side, and he was proud of it even as he knew that it would have provided a good laugh for his buddies at the Miami Beach construction sites. He went to his desk right after dinner and stayed there with his books and his 3 x 5 file cards until one or two in the morning. Sometimes he would jump up and dash off to the library, and though he would say, "Be back in a minute," he often didn't come home until the library—now open late to keep pace with the growth of the student population—had closed. Sometimes when Jack came home, he would go right back to his desk. It was something we wives talked about—how we had become accustomed to sleeping with the light on while our husbands bent their heads over their books.

If in earlier days we couples had a nightly bedtime routine that involved the basic delights of a husband and wife, we didn't have it now. These delights now took place whenever the boys could steal a moment or two away from the campus, or on Friday nights. Definitely on Friday nights. Because Friday night was the eve of blissfully unstructured Saturdays.

* * *

We wives were not idle while our husbands went about doing what they had to do. Wives who typed did their husbands' typing. Bobby Harper typed for George, and I typed for Jack. And thanks to my experience in the office of the NYA, I typed fast and made not too many typos even when I was engrossed in what I was typing, as I often was when I typed Jack's stuff. I typed on a used L.C. Smith typewriter bought at the local office supply store for five dollars, and of course we called it "Elsie."

Jack's classes, being almost all English ones, required a lot of paper writing, so I kept telling him how lucky he was to have a wife who could type. Very few veterans could type, and some who couldn't hired typists, though this was a service not covered by the GI Bill. We all said that overlooking a small thing like typing services was to be expected amid all the other services the bill provided, and we forgave it, but it meant that some veterans were turning in term papers written in longhand.

The wives who typed, even if thrilled by the goals of their typing, were not thrilled by the onerousness of it. An original and a copy! Or—groan—two copies. Carbon paper! Corrections, corrections! I consulted Bobby on the last, and she told me of her trick. To make corrections, she said, "without wishing you were dead," you rub a piece of chalk over the offending typo and type over the chalk. From that moment on, I was never without a stick of chalk at my elbow, even if the faculty wondered why white dust kept flying off Jack's papers. "Where have you been keeping this?" one professor asked Jack. "In an Egyptian tomb?"

However papers were written, it caused no problems with the faculty. According to Dr. Lyons, veterans' papers were so superior to those of the past, he said he would have read them if they had been inscribed on rocks.

THE NEW YORK TIMES

At night after I had finished my typing, I indulged in my one extravagance—*The New York Times*. The reading of it was not the extravagance; the extravagance was that it cost at least twice as much as the *Gainesville Sun*. Extravagant or not, I had to have it. If I did not read a paper to keep up with national and world news, my father would have, to use an old southern expression, "plumb wore me out," or to use another old southern expression (which means the same thing), "give me a good whuppin'." More likely, however, he would have gotten to me with something even less welcome than a good whuppin'—filling the mail trains with hectoring letters.

I had developed a relationship with the *Times* when Jack was overseas and I was living with the Subermans. They had stayed with it despite the Jewish rage against it for its disinclination to carry full stories of the Nazi atrocities, and I understood the rage. Still, the *Times* seemed to me so plainly superior to all other papers that even if I did not forgive the paper's bosses—who were themselves Jews—then (or later) for their sorry role in the Holocaust story, I had to have it. I was as interested in politics and world doings as ever, and if I was to keep up, the *Times* was indispensable. For me, not knowing what was going on in the political life of the United States, not to say the planet, was to let go of what was a very dear and meaningful Kaufman tradition.

And so it was that every Tuesday morning, Rick and I walked down to the College Inn and picked up the Sunday edition of the *New York Times*, and in the rare moment that I felt flush, I would splurge on a weekday one. I spent a full week finishing the Sunday edition, and even then I wouldn't have finished it. But throw it out? Never. I simply kept a stash of them, carefully organized by dates, and made a promise to myself to read them thoroughly later.

It was the *Times* that confirmed that our Gainesville lifestyle (though wives were not mentioned) was echoed by GI Bill boys throughout the country. One item quoted an educator as saying, "Lights stay on late at night in many rooms. The quietness of the dormitories is enough to sober the most chronic of noisemakers. The library is filled with diligent seekers of knowledge. Little interest in anything but studies has been exhibited. The veteran realizes he has a golden opportunity and a well-earned one and he is out to make the most of it."

And then there was this from the *Times* education editor: "The GIs are hogging the honor rolls and the Dean's lists," he wrote, and went on to say that of the nearly eight thousand veterans studying at New York's Columbia University "none is in serious academic difficulty." He then quoted the president of Harvard as saying that "for seriousness, perceptiveness, steadiness, and all other [academic] virtues," the veterans were "the best in Harvard's history."

So hello to you, Harvard President James B. Conant. Looks like you changed your tune. Do you think we don't remember that you and University of Chicago President Robert Hutchins were among the many notable academic and political leaders who vehemently opposed the bill? We remember that the last time you were heard from, President Conant, you were speaking against the educational provisions of the GI bill and were quoted as saying that veterans would be unable to meet academic standards. And now we say, See? See? How wrong you were!

Nothing I read told me anything I didn't know, but I read the pieces over and over until at some point I would feel tears running. I supposed I was beginning to understand something very true and very poignant—that America had put its faith in its veterans and its veterans did not intend to let America down.

THE WEEKENDS

The boys took Saturday as a holiday and did not bury themselves in studies. At our house, Saturday mornings meant Jack did something with Rick, usually plopping him into the basket of the bicycle and the two of them tooling around the neighborhood before heading to the CI for hamburgers.

On Saturday afternoons, if there was a football game, we all—*all*—went to the Swamp, officially named Florida Field. Going to the games was a longtime Gainesville tradition: students, townspeople, and out-of-town alumni went to each and every game despite that the University of Florida invariably had a breathtakingly dismal football record. Some years, even if picked by every sportswriter in the country to win its conference—the Southeastern—in the end the championship was carried off by most any SEC team except Florida. In 1946 I had hopes, but it was not for the University of Florida. I liked the University of Florida, but I *loved* the University of Tennessee, which was also a member of the Southeastern Conference, and in 1946 my favorite team stood a very good chance. And wouldn't you know? The University of Tennessee won the 1946 Southeastern Conference trophy! Yes! With nobody to crow to, I sent a fallback letter to Doris, and I wrote, with what was no doubt deep emotion, "Those UT boys just did me proud. I reckon they showed what Tennesseans can do when they put their mind to it."

Even before the war, when the University of Florida student body was comprised of a mere 2,800, Florida Field stands had always been full. Now, with what was called "the GI Bulge," students numbered more than 9,000, and the stands were fuller, much fuller, hanging-from-the-press-boxes fuller. It was a development that no doubt held for all stadiums where football was played. Universities, with the backing of GI Bill–provided tuition, were now full fit to bust.

Because tickets were free to all students, GI Bill boys turned out to the Swamp en masse and became instant and rabid fans. Those who had not been to college thrilled to the idea of rooting for their very own college team, especially a team belonging to a prestigious conference, and they stomped and they yelled, and they followed cheerleading instructions, and they sang the alma mater. They also happily sang "We are the boys from old Florida, F-L-0-R-I-D-A / Where the girls are the fairest / The boys are the squarest / Of any old state down our way . . . ," and happily joined in on the traditional swaying that accompanied the singing.

Of course when they sang of "the girls," they were not singing of coeds because precious few coeds were enrolled at the University of Florida, the university still being wedded to all-male schooling. The few coeds were in the pharmacy school, there being no pharmacy school at FSCW, though it was a mystery as to why they were not admitted to other schools not at FSCW, like law and agriculture. To follow this wobbly thing to the end, where did black students go when there was no state-supported school for some career they wanted to follow? Good question.

Still, all-male exclusivity came back to bite schools adhering to the practice when GI Bill boys started clamoring to get in and schools began to run out of room. The Florida solution was simple: press FSCW into service. Whoops. Florida State College for *Women?* Well, just change the name. In 1947, the state legislature changed Florida State College for Women to Florida State University, and a female bastion was no more. It was another sign of the times.

If the University of Florida had been and still was a school for boys, it also had been and still was a school for white boys. When the fans in the stands in Florida Field sang of "the boys from old Florida," black boys were not what they had in mind. Even with the GI Bill at their disposal, black boys were not the boys of old Florida—not in story or in song.

Nor had the race policy changed at the newly named Florida State University. GI Bill boys or not, black students who wanted to go to a state school did not go to the University of Florida or to Florida State University; they went to Florida Agricultural and Mechanical University in Tallahassee, the historically black school where they had always gone.

THE SATURDAY NIGHT PARTIES

The first of our Gainesville Saturday night parties came when one of the GI Bill boys said, "Why don't we go get us a bottle and get drunk in a pile?" and the other boys answered, "Count me in." Though they might have been studying in various disciplines, from economics to animal husbandry, the boys were ever united in being ready for a party, and a party meant a drinking party. Among most GI Bill boys, "party" was synonymous with drinking, and preparation for the party meant you chipped in for the requirements.

GI Bill boys had been ready for parties from the moment the war was over, though there had been that pause between the end of the war and before the GI Bill had come into their lives, that unsettling time when parties were the last things on their minds. But that was long ago and far away, and they were now ready to let go, to joke, to celebrate.

The boys would have agreed that they were celebrating several things. The big one, of course, was that they had made it. They had been in a situation where they had bet their lives and they had won. The smaller reason was that they were celebrating the simple fact of being out of military service. They were at last free of commands, of being at the mercy of decisions made by others. These veterans were calling their own shots, and it seemed to them that so far, their aim was true.

Rick looked forward to the parties. He looked forward to seeing all the other what we called "war babies" and to be allowed a party presence for an hour or so before being sent off to play somewhere else. The war babies played far into the night, and when they at last couldn't stand another minute of fun, they dropped off to sleep in the bedroom of whatever domicile they found themselves in, usually on the floor on pallets built up of army blankets. Everybody who had an army blanket—and most everyone did—brought it, and by the time the kids went to sleep, the pallet was layered in six or seven of those ugly olive drab scratchy things. It didn't matter. The kids fell asleep on whatever was there and stayed that way until they were carried home.

During the war, I had gone with Jack to many parties, but those had been very different from these Gainesville ones. In the army there was little liquor—except in Tucson when Bill O'Connor brought out his much-loved cocktail shaker and dispensed a concoction of tequila and pink grapefruit juice and christened it "the Arizona Sunset"—just beer, beer, beer. Some beer appeared at our Gainesville parties as well, and when it did, I was always reminded of my second landlady, Midge Folsom in Victorville, California, where Jack had trained as a cadet. She was the first one to tell me what I was to hear a million times—that you don't buy beer, you just rent it. I remembered Midge Folsom for other things as well. She was the landlady who had rescued me from my first landlady, the one who, when she found out I was Jewish, had said, "Well, I'll just have to make the best of it."

Unlike these Gainesville parties, those during the war, though intense, were not very joyful. Granted that arguments did sometimes erupt at these Gainesville parties, but they were good-natured, and no hard feelings were carried over. On the other hand, hovering over the wartime ones was the knowledge that it was only a matter of time before you or somebody you loved would be shipped out, and the result was that more people got drunk in less time, and arguments were angry and personal.

My own drinking habits derived from my being a businessman's daughter who had learned never to overpay; at one point, I pretty much stopped overpartying when I realized I was not willing to overpay on Sunday morning for my good time on Saturday night. I also monitored myself pretty closely during and after pregnancy. My tolerance for messing with my stomach was apparently on the level of my mother's, who was family-famous for becoming instantly nauseous if she rode in the backseat of the car, if she didn't have her morning coffee at exactly seven o'clock, and when she fasted on Yom Kippur, the Day of Atonement. She finally gave up on the last when my father asked her what she was atoning for and she couldn't think of anything.

Gainesville was in Alachua County, and county laws kept it dry, so to get a bottle for those Gainesville parties, a strategy had to be devised. In Union City, among my sister Minna's crowd, the strategy involved a moonshiner—each boy had his favorite among the many moonshiners in the county—and "white lightnin' " was bought to "spike" the grape juice punch, which then turned into a drink called Purple Jesus. The GI Bill boys, however, were in too much of a hurry to waste time hunting for the local moonshiner, and so everybody contributed to the bottle pool and to the cost of gas, and somebody (usually the Harpers in their "Chivy") drove over to the next wet county, specifically to a liquor store named Ruby's on the county line cheek by jowl with Alachua. There they would pick up as many bottles of bourbon and Southern Comfort as the pool permitted.

The custom of the South prevailed at these parties, which meant that the boys stood around the kitchen sink and drank bourbon and water ("bourbon and branch," the boys called it) and the wives in the living room drank Southern Comfort made even less palatable with Coca-Cola, pronounced as it was in Tennessee as "co-cola." The scheme of boys in the kitchen, girls in the parlor made for conversational as well as physical apartheid. It didn't matter. We knew that the boys would be talking a lot about their war experiences—what they called "shop talk"—and there would be stories of triumph and defeat, of comical happenings and desperate ones, and I felt sure that Jack would be telling his story of that bombing mission, when, because of the hitherto unknown jet stream that played havoc with their calculations, they missed not only the steel mill oven, they missed Japan.

THE WIVES HAVE A LOT TO SAY

In the living room, what did we wives talk about? And in what accents? We all spoke "southern," but Florida accents differed from Tennessee ones, and my own accent had not yet been overwhelmed by Jack's and was still pretty much Tennessee. Our conversations usually began with making a jokey thing of how we couldn't count on our husbands during the week, and we put on a show of being "totally outdone" by their being so preoccupied. We pretended to envy the lifestyles of couples who lived in the outside world, and we said, "Can you imagine having a husband who takes you to the movies?" And someone would close her eyes as if dreaming, and say, "Or takes you *dancing?*"

When we talked, we told stories about what we had done during the war, and we found out that some of us had worked at jobs previously held by men—like delivering the mail, or in driving a fire truck. (Yes!) I got in my bit about having been a nurse's aide in a Miami hospital, but I wasn't even in the running: I was certainly outclassed by the woman who had gone out daily in her little Boston Whaler to spot German submarines—"Lord, what a day when I spied one," she told us. "I jes shook sumpin' awful afore I could tell on it." Another was a civilian pilot who had flown cargo planes not only stateside but to theaters of war. I had to admit that taking temperatures and counting out pulse beats, even on behalf of servicemen, didn't really cut it.

We would occasionally talk of things of national importance—about Winston Churchill's "iron curtain" speech, for example, which we understood as a warning against what was being called "the Communist peril," and we gave a lot of attention to the Nuremberg trials, in which Nazi leaders were being tried for "crimes against humanity." When we described how we personally felt about it, one of the women might say, "It serves them right, them lowdown, shifty old men. They otta be hung up by their thumbs."

As we sat and sipped on these Saturday nights, we didn't restrict ourselves to serious matters. We went into, yes, a swoon, at the mention of Frank Sinatra singing "Day by Day," and we might have stumbled about together in a chorus of Johnny Mercer's "Personality." I know for sure we would have discussed the Spock book of baby and child care that had just been published, and some of us would have said that we wished it had come out sooner, but some of us would have sniffed, "I'm fixin' to rear my kids just like my momma reared me. Cain't see nothin' wrong with that."

We for sure would have had a good time discussing the bikini bathing suit, which had just appeared on the scene, the one named after the atom bomb test on Bikini Atoll because its designer had said he wanted his creation to have a "similar explosive effect." Although we were intensely interested in this development, we all said we'd never wear such a thing—maybe because we were shy or prudish, or maybe it was fear of the "hubba hubba" test. As one woman put it, "Could y'all pass the 'hubba hubba' test? Lord, I know I couldn't by a mile."

When we read something in the paper about the "new look," it was soon a hot topic. It came from the French! It was by Christian Dior! We showed pictures to each other of full skirts and mid-calf hemlines, and we read out loud what the paper said—that the "new look" and its "wild extravagance of fabric" was a reaction to bare-bones wartime styles. We were certainly addicted to reading about it, but did the "new look" mean anything to our lives? Not really. Not when we were making do with seventy-five dollars a month (plus a bit for dependents).

We laughed about the things we got used to during the war—the penciled-in stocking seams and evaporated milk in everything. "Lord," one woman said, "we thought Spam with pineapple slices on top was real fancy eatin'." We joked about the toilet paper that felt like the morning newspaper and the oleo butter substitute that looked like a hunk of lard *before* we colored it with the yellow packet and looked like a hunk of lard with yellow stripes *after* we colored it. Somebody said that she had first learned to cook when she became a military wife, and she told the story of how she had saved up all her red stamps to buy a rib roast and then had set it on the stove, covered it with water, and left it to boil. Oh, wait, that was me.

We talked about who could serve the best for the least, though when somebody said she did a lot of spaghetti, we drew the line at her recipe. "Shucks," she said, "it's as easy as pie." And how easy was it? "All you do is boil your spaghetti," she said, "and pour your can of Campbell's tomato soup over it." We bought stringy, sinewy Florida beef, not because we were loyal to Florida but because it was cheaper, and never mind that you had to cut it on a power saw.

Talk of laundry was big. We washed anything washable, certainly our husbands' shirts, and on a metal washboard in a metal tub, and Lanie Bell, who lived behind me, said that she had "chloroxed the fool" out of Frank's shirts, only to find that the clay of Gainesville stayed put. We hung out our wash on the backyard clothesline, and when the Florida rains came, we rushed out and grabbed them, though usually not before they had been soaked through, and then we strew them on the beds and hoped they would dry before the bed was needed. The ironing board was always up, and when your child was napping, you ironed (yes, even your husband's starched, long-sleeved shirts), and you listened to *Stella Dallas* and *The Guiding Light* on the radio at your elbow.

Lest it seem that we were echoing the days of the Depression, we never thought of it that way. We did not consider ourselves victims of a catastrophe with no end in sight. No, when we saw the end, it was a bright one, and we wives thought of ourselves as part of what would get us there. We were living our lives under the GI Bill, and that made all the difference. If we had a new "home front," it was right here in Gainesville. The feeling was that if we had lived with anxieties when our husbands were in service, we now lived in a cheerful anticipation.

We dwelled only a bit on the time when the war had just ended and the boys had nothing to do and no place to turn. And when we told about it, we told it funny. "I reckoned if Avery hadn't found him somethin' soon," somebody said, "I'd have to hose him down and hang him out to dry. Sweet Jesus, thank you for the GI Bill." I don't think I thanked Jesus for the GI Bill; more likely I thanked Franklin D. Roosevelt and the American Legion, but I definitely thanked somebody.

We stayed away from the subject of race. Even I, the rabid RSB, did not bring it up. I told myself that I so liked being among these sisters that I did not want to put a wedge between us. And could I have changed minds? Probably not. My views were already a bit suspect: my being Jewish and having lived in Miami Beach pretty much saw to that.

On one occasion, however, I tempted fate. I had run across a race story in the *New York Times* about two black veterans and their wives who had been taken from their car by a white mob near Monroe, Georgia, and had been shot to death by the sixty bullets found in their bodies. The *Times* was calling it the "Moore's Ford Bridge Incident," and it seemed to me a story so outrageous as to defy keeping to myself. Still, nobody said, "How awful," and one woman said, "Mercy, sixty bullets! Those white boys were havin' themselves a damn good time." And one woman responded by picking up on the Georgia/Florida rivalry and said, "How could you 'spect anythin' better from those Georgy rednecks?"

In the South the expression "bless her heart" is often used in sincerity but often as a strategy—"Wilma, bless her heart, she's just plain ornery." But when Bobby Harper remembered the 1920s Florida atrocities in the hamlet of Rosewood, when blacks were beaten and their houses set to burning, and she said, "Not a scrap of difference between those folks in

Georgia and the ones in Florida. They're all white trash," I thought to my-self, "Bless her heart," with all the sincerity I could muster.

Some of the things the women talked about, however, were personal, and they were bothersome. I was definitely bothered when, in time, one or two said their husbands were having doubts. It hadn't occurred to me that anyone who had embarked on this scintillating voyage could be having sec-ond thoughts. Still, some apparently were, most notably the boys who had enrolled at relatively older ages—those in their late twenties and thirties, or even in their forties—and were in college as freshmen. These men had apparently been complaining to their wives that they were men with kids and in college as rank beginners, and it didn't feel good. And it was true that until they had made an awful fuss, they had been instructed to wear fresh-man "beanies," and they would say to their wives, "Here I am, a grown man with a damn good war record, and look at me—I'm fighting some damn fool eighteen-year-old who's trying to put some damn fool thing on my head."

Had these men realized what they had bought into? Had they fully understood the tyranny of the books and the studying? They had been in pressure situations for a long time, and they were now operating under a system almost as strict as the one they had known in service. Did they re-sent this new kind of stress? And there was yet another factor to be reck-oned with: jobs were opening up and beckoning them.

And Jack? Need I wonder about him? I remembered the blithe spirit of his undergraduate years, and I wondered if he was still vexed by the things he had stomped around about—those things he called "childish" before the GI Bill came along. Jack still seemed gung-ho, however, and I thought the better part of discretion was to forgo bringing up the subject.

At one o'clock or so, the Saturday night parties would wind down, and the boys would come in to join us, and we'd have a little male-female in-teraction. There was some flirting, but not much. There was the occasional exchange of a long look or a clutch in the backyard, but if a married man went home with a woman, it was his wife, or if he was unmarried, he went home with a woman who had no husband, perhaps someone on the uni-versity staff. It seemed a practical if unspoken rule that these Gainesville GI Bill boys were in college to get a degree and not to venture into complicated relationships.

Before the party was over, somebody would slur out a toast to the GI Bill. It usually came from Rusty Walker, a GI who before the war had been a gofer in his father's small drugstore in the middle of the state. We had known Rusty in Victorville, California, when he and Jack had been together in bombardier training, and we had known of his hopes to become what he had thought of as the most glamorous job in the world—that of pharmacist. And now with the GI Bill, he could live his dream. He didn't want to leave his hometown folks; he just wanted to fill their prescriptions.

Rusty's toast was, invariably, "To the GI Bill, which has given us a way to work our butts off," and we'd manage a version of a cheer; and then the party was over. And then, a little worse for the wear and tear of bourbon and branch and Southern Comfort, and toting our sleeping children, we'd all leave. Some of the women got up for church on Sunday, but most of the men just slept in.

SUNDAY AFTERNOONS

Most of the boys began their week of studying on Sunday and didn't venture out, but Sunday afternoon neighborly drop-bys were an option for others. Drop-bys often took place at our little gray house in the west (um, west Gainesville), and for a couple of reasons: for one, we had not just a room but a whole house; and for another, loud controversy was not only permitted but encouraged. The result was that the boys came in the door talking, didn't stop until they left, and everybody talked at once. The boys might have felt that they had whetted their appetites during the week and were ready for an all-you-can-eat feast.

War tales were last night's thing; pontification was today's. If in the kitchen around the sink on Saturday nights the boys had steered clear of topical events, topical events were front and center on Sunday afternoons. It seemed that the GI Bill boys were managing to keep an eye on what was happening on the world stage by some manner or another—by a quick look at the morning newspaper, by a more careful perusal of the Sunday one, or by a snatch heard on the radio. I assumed that they felt it was their duty to keep up, that they had made promises to the GI Bill, and one of the promises was to stay in touch with the world.

Bobby and George Harper always came, after Bobby had been to church in the morning. Like me, Bobby liked a good give-and-take, and on Sunday afternoons, unlike Saturday nights, we had good ones. Furthermore, we *always* got around to race, and Bobby and I were up to the task. We felt that this was our subject, one that we knew inside and out. Hadn't we—Bobby from Jacksonville, and I from Union City, Tennessee—been through it all, and at one time, as Bobby and I had talked about often, hadn't we once shared the views of certain people in the room? So didn't we have the right to challenge them? We felt we did, and we felt furthermore that we had the right to call those people "unenlightened." Smug we were.

The unenlightened ones, however, did not go quietly. They objected to the "unenlightened" tag and did not want to be told they were, variously, bigoted, fossilized, or uncaring. They said they were arguing from "the facts," and the facts were that "colored folks" were genetically disadvantaged, and they told such anecdotes as, "Our handyman Odas would do anything for us, but could he make a decision without asking my daddy? No indeed. He just doesn't have that capacity." At this, Bobby and I would say as one that this was nothing but "plantation twaddle."

But there was that one occasion when a G.I we might previously have identified as "unenlightened," one named Enos Thompson, remembered something from his combat days, and it was a recollection that had something to teach all, except perhaps those who had their brains under lock and key. Enos had been a B-24 pilot in Italy flying bombing missions over the Ploesti oil fields, and his story was of the fighter planes that had flown alongside him. When Enos asked us, "Who do you think the pilots of those planes were?" none of us had a clue, and Enos said, "I'll tell you who they were. They were black men, black as coal tar. And what were they doing?" Enos took a moment. "What they were doing," he said, "was covering the ass of every last one of us, that's what they were doing."

Enos need say no more, certainly not to Bobby and me. And it seemed to me that Enos's message had been received to some degree or another by others in the room. Maybe a little progress had been made, but when Bobby and I exchanged looks, the looks said, "One down and umpteen to go." Did we, however, treasure the "one down"? You bet we did.

I brought some other things to the Sunday afternoon drop-bys, usually courtesy of my father, who was still providing me with a steady stream of news, advice, and admonitions related to what was going on in our nation's capital or what he thought was going on. He wrote once a week without fail, in that self-taught looping handwriting of his, with asterisks looking like starfish splayed around the page. It took something for him to do this. He didn't like writing letters, but he had set out to write me regularly and had carved out an hour every Sunday morning for doing it. I saw him sitting down at the dining room table, moving everything around until he had enough room for his elbows to swing freely.

In one letter, he asked me if I had read where Wisconsin Senator Robert La Follette Jr. had been defeated for reelection by somebody named Joseph McCarthy. La Follette was not a Democrat but he had supported Roosevelt faithfully and had thereby endeared himself to my father and in turn to me.

212 The GI Bill

"He's a Republican but he's not a damned fool about it," my father said in his letter. "Too bad this McCarthy got the best of him. Better keep an eye on that guy."

Lots of people and topics found their way into our discussions. One was Truman's demand for a loyalty oath to be signed by all federal employees and thought by many to be in answer to the House Un-American Activities Committee (called HUAC in the papers), which had been ranting about the "untold and unknown numbers" of Communists in our midst and the dangers they presented.

As with many issues, there was a difference of opinion on HUAC. Jack, of course, and some of the other boys were outraged and declared that the Un-American Activities Committee was itself un-American; others said it was a prudent move that would ensure our "American way." I later personally experienced some fallout from the HUAC goings-on. That summer when we went to Miami for a visit, my Communist friends, who in the past had been the soul of (uninterruptible) loquaciousness, were not eager to talk to me. "If you want to talk," they said to me in an attempt at a joke, "better meet us in the alley next to the garbage dump."

* * *

One of the boys who came regularly to the Sunday afternoons was Ben Levin, who was in college as a freshman. He was from Miami Beach, where his grandparents were living in that South Beach enclave of retired New York garment workers, and I wasn't surprised that his main topic of conversation was unions. He was presently fired up because Congress had just passed what he considered an anti-union bill—the Taft-Hartley Act—and he wanted Truman to veto it. In the act was a provision called the Right-to-Work Act, and Ben said, "Right to work, my eye. It's the right to keep unions out, that's all it is."

Ben would have come by this position naturally because his grandfather was passionate about unions, and like most good Jewish boys, Ben was passionate about his grandfather. The grandfather was also passionate about the GI Bill. "The only thing my grandfather thinks is as good as a union pension is the GI Bill," Ben said. "And can I argue?"

On some Sunday afternoons, I slipped out of the drop-bys at our house and went to the one at the Tauntons' across the street. Jessie had been Jessie Bigelow, and she had met Peter Dexter Taunton of Boston when she worked at Camp Blanding. Jessie served nothing stronger than iced tea, which led Jack to call her afternoons "cold water sit-arounds," and which therefore led him to opt out.

Jessie was from Florida, and on Sundays her kin from all over the state regularly came to call. Many of them were doing something or other under the GI Bill, and they had stories to tell. Her cousin Dewey was from (I think) Tavares, and he was supported by the bill as he trained among the ovens of one of the town's bakeries, and he was proud of what he had learned. "I'll be blessed," he said, "if my angel food cakes don't float right up thar to heaven." I told him of my friends in Miami Beach who owned that town's bakery, though I didn't mention their Communist persuasion, and I asked him if he knew how to make *challahs* or *rugelachs*. He didn't, but he was interested, and I promised to get him some recipes from my friends. "You be sure to do that," he said. "Sure would like to do some Jew baking," and I understood that he wasn't trying to offend; he just didn't know better. At any rate, I went back to thinking what the GI Bill had done here: it had brought together a country boy from Tavares, Florida, and a Jewish girl from Union City, Tennessee, to share a few pleasant thoughts.

ENTERTAINING OURSELVES

With the coming of Monday, the husbands were off again to class, and we wives were left with ourselves and our children. After a little housekeeping—"rearranging the clay dust," we called it—we found company in each other. We sometimes sought each other out at night, and Bobby and I and a few others joined the campus Democratic Club. At this point in time the governor was no longer Dave Scholtz (whom my father had so approved of even when it turned out that he wasn't Jewish) but was now the unambiguously named Spessard Holland. Still, in between the two there had been Fred Cone, whose name also confused my father. No doubt having in his head that the name "Cohen" was and is the most recognizable of all Jewish names, my father would push it hard and say, "'Cone,' 'Cohen,' what's the difference? He's Jewish, no?" Well, my always hopeful father, the answer was "No."

Florida was Democrat-dominated from the Panhandle to the Keys—congressional delegation, state legislature, and governor—even though in my opinion, and in the opinions of many, Florida's elected ones held views more Republican than Democrat. Still, they were officially Democrats and they made up majorities, and many agreed that it was better to have a doubtful Democrat than a "high and mighty" Republican, "high and mighty" being among Democrats the default adjectives for Republicans. As to the Democratic Club, it had few goals to work toward, and we simply congratulated each other over and over for being on the winning ticket.

On some nights, when the need to see a movie was overpowering, we wives went with each other. Movies were no longer showing extravagantly staged escapist fare, and Busby Berkeley movies were a thing of the past. Musicals were still popular, however, though they were now more intimate, and the twosome of Fred Astaire and Ginger Rogers had taken the place of the hundreds of Busby Berkeley boys and girls fanning across giant piano keyboards or climbing stairs to some kind of heaven. And we never again experienced pig latin as practiced by Ginger Rogers. We all saw *It's a Wonderful Life,* and we might have seen it a couple of times because our husbands were home safe and sound and in good spirits, and we were in the mood for sentiment.

I visited almost every weekday morning with Lanie Bell, the one who said she had "chloroxed the fool" out of her husband's shirts, and Rick visited with her son Travis, with whom he had frequently shared those scratchy olive drab army blankets. I tried to get to Lanie's before Frank had left for class because I wanted to see the Travis show, which took place as soon as his father started off for class. Travis, having apparently kept an eye out for Frank's appearance, took it as his cue to run into the house, bring out the big textbook that always accompanied his father, and tuck it under his father's arm. "Lord have mercy," Lanie said to me, "if Travis don't think that book is one of Frank's body parts."

I had known Lanie at the University of Miami, and I knew that she was from Alabama, or 'Bama, as she called it. She had been Lanie Travis, and considering her son was "Travis," I guessed that she had followed the southern custom of giving your firstborn your maiden name. In her case it was "Travis," but in the South it could have been "Hunter," or "Winborne," or "Darden," or some such, and sometimes it didn't matter if the firstborn was male or female, that's the name it got. A girl would often be given a double-barreled first name like one of my best friends from the past, Mary Reeves Groome, and we all knew that little-jack-little the "Mary" would be dropped and she'd be known the rest of her life as "Reeves." And sure enough, when I saw her in later years, she was Reeves Something-or-Other.

Lanie would often turn nostalgic, for 'Bama, for the University of Miami, for how things had been before the war; and she would stare out at the cars passing on University Avenue and say, "Gainesville sure is different, don't you think?" I took "different" to mean from how it had been when you were single. Lanie would follow up with memories of previous Gainesville days when she had been the date of an SAE or an ATO, those fraternities of glittery social standing, and when she had been one of the "cute" girls dancing at Fall Frolics parties and being cut in on before she could take two steps.

It's true that life in Gainesville was very different for all of us girls who had known Gainesville before the war. Still, I thought we took it in stride nicely. Lanie was not complaining; she was commenting. Lanie Bell, in a previous life the exemplar of the captivating "young thing," was now a typical GI Bill wife.

Lanie's ideas for recreation, however, were hers and hers alone. Often when the kids were napping, she would telephone me to come over. She wanted to dance. "Get your little self over here," she would say, "there's gonna be a whole lot of jitterbuggin' today." And I'd dash over there and she'd bring out the radio, run its wire from a wall outlet through a window, and we'd dance up a storm to the big bands like Harry James and Benny Goodman. Occasionally other girls would join us and we'd be in one of the FSCW rec rooms again, girls dancing with girls, doing the Lindy Hop and jitterbugging. And then we'd rush back home to be there when the kids woke up.

Lanie was the one who clued me in on our rose of Sharon bush. I had been in despair over its habit of shedding its blossoms every night, and when I wondered to Lanie if on my hand my mother's green thumb had turned black, she reassured me. "Not at all, you silly thing," she said to me. "Haven't you noticed the blossoms come back every single morning?" Well, I had, sort of. Lanie said her mother called the rose of Sharon the Easter bush. "It's the story of Jesus, don't you see?" she explained to me. And why? The answer shouldn't have surprised me. "Shoot," Lanie said, "don't you know a rose of Sharon dies one day and resurrects itself on the next?"

If I didn't quite enter into the spirit of Lanie's mother's metaphor, down the road I devised one of my own. In my metaphor, the shedding of the blossoms was the catastrophes we had just experienced—the Depression, the war, the terrible postwar period—and the return of the blossoms was the righting of things. I felt the metaphor was apt and also backed by evidence. Weren't things righting? Shoot, didn't we have the GI Bill?

GAINESVILLE'S SOCIAL SCENE

Visiting with Lanie also meant a visit with Stuart Weinstein. Stuart, previously a lieutenant in the infantry, now lived in the apartment next to the Bells. When Stuart came back from class, there Lanie and I would be, on the steps, fired up for conversation with him. Stuart was also in school on the GI Bill, and like Frank Bell, he came from a family whose patriarch was a lawyer. But unlike Frank Bell, as I found out when I "interviewed" him, Stuart had no interest in the law. He didn't want to be a lawyer; he wanted to grow orange trees. Stuart, though not a Pi Lam, was Jewish and from New York, and—mercy!—he wanted to grow orange trees.

A bit of fine dining, Gainesville style, came our way from knowing Stuart Weinstein. Stuart's parents came often from New York to visit him, and they always invited Jack and me to dinner at the Thomas Hotel. I think Mrs. Weinstein thought that Jack, as a fellow New Yorker, would support her view of Gainesville as a town visited by plagues. "Why would my son pick such a place," she would ask Jack in a mournful tone, "so far from everything, so far from New York and us?" Why indeed?

Most glaring among Gainesville's flaws as perceived by Mrs. Weinstein was that, during the winter, Gainesville was neither hot nor cold. "At least you could have gone to the University of Miami," Mrs. Weinstein complained to Stuart. "In Miami we could have had some good weather and some good food."

It was true that in Gainesville the weather was foul, and a fine restaurant was a contradiction in terms. The Weinsteins had all their meals at the Thomas Hotel, though it in no way pleased them. No doubt accustomed to the generosity of New York delicatessens, where sandwiches and pies sat on the plate like skyscrapers, Mrs. Weinstein would look at Mr. Weinstein's plate, on which a slice of Thomas Hotel cherry pie rested, and say severely to her son, "Just look at that piece of pie, Stuart. It's so thin your father could read his *Times* through it."

When they had left, Stuart would explain to us why he was on the GI Bill and not on his "father's dime," as he would say. He maintained that if his education was paid for by his father, his mother would be in control of it. "Can you see my mother letting me go my own way?" Stuart asked us. Stuart's own way, as it turned out, had put him at the University of Florida to study citrus culture. And Jack remembered the advice he had been given when he had been hitching rides, and he joked to Stuart, "Look into orange juice concentrate."

* * *

Other than the occasional dinner with the Weinsteins, none of us ever ate out, except at the CI once in a while. Dinners out were exchanges with other GI Bill people, and we exchanged often with Harold and Margie Retman, in whose apartment the Harpers had a room. Harold was a returning infantryman going to college under the GI Bill, and to afford the apartment, he had only to rent out a room, which required all the effort of hanging out a sign.

Harold was Jewish, Margie was not. Theirs was another of those wartime "mixed marriages"—Jewish/non-Jewish—that would have brought a lot of attention prewar and no longer did—well, not as much. Harold was one of those Jewish boys who had been stationed in lonely outposts where the Jewish population was slim to none, and he had discovered that the non-Jewish town girls were not only friendly but downright cordial. The girls invited the boys into their homes and made a fuss over them and called them "heroes," and pretty soon Harold had written home that he had "met a girl." Many a family, like Harold's, was in for a surprise. Most, but not all, got over it.

We often had dinner at the Retmans,' and when we dined with them, we dined, invariably, on Margie's much applauded tuna casserole. We knew that Harold was a collector of war mementos, so we were not surprised to be at a table fitted out with candleholders fashioned from artillery shells and, after dinner, to put our cigarettes out in a German soldier's shoe. We were surrounded by mementos: plants growing in German helmets, and what had been wartime parachutes now at the windows as draperies. Need I say that it was not only interesting but unnerving to be so close to stuff that had actually been on the battlefield, perhaps on some combatant's body? And so I tried not to think of that poor soldier—German enemy though he might have been—and the manner in which he had lost his shoe.

13

Drinks at the Professor's

When we got the invitation for "pre-dinner" drinks at the home of one of Jack's professors (English 412, Nineteenth-Century English Poetry), we knew it was not going to be a "Let's get a bottle and get drunk in a pile" party, nor its variation, the BYOB, which meant, depending on where in the state you called home, "Bring Your Own Bottle" or "Bring Your Own Booze." Nor would it be a tuna casserole dinner among the artillery shells at the Retmans'. Because the invitation made a point of saying "pre-dinner" drinks, we were clearly not going to get dinner at all. Furthermore, unlike typical Saturday night parties, where all attendees were GI Bill boys and their wives, this event was limited to undergraduate and graduate students in English literature.

It was the kind of party that was brand new to me, and I was in a state. It was at a professor's house! Lord, what would I wear? I finally accepted that we couldn't not go: if Jack was going to be a professor of English, he—and I—were going to have to learn how that life was lived.

Just going up to the house in the Harper's "Chivy" was unnerving. If I had been panicked about what to wear, going out there I was panicked by what I had chosen. I did not have anything that remotely resembled the "new look"—no dresses with fullish skirts and mid-calf hemlines—and my prewar dresses were by now pretty scruffy. I had only one decent dress (bought during wartime), a thing of a troubled yellow that couldn't make up its mind what color it was. Like Lucky Strike, which before the war had been in a green package and during the war was in a white one and whose advertising proclaimed that "Lucky Strike green has gone to war," the color

of my dress had apparently gone to war as well. At any rate, I wore it, and
Bobby wore her gray wool dress with her pearls.

The professor's place was a bit outside Gainesville, and when we drove
up to it, it appeared to us to be a country estate, with the house at the
end of a long driveway. We made jokes about it, about maybe we were in
England or maybe we were in some kind of English movie produced by
J. Arthur Rank. Well, George and Bobby made jokes. I was a little unsettled
at this splendiferous vision, and I didn't make jokes. Jack didn't make any
either. If the owners were trying to project the image of a lushly forested
English estate, the profusion of Gainesville's matchstick pines in the front
yard fought them hard. But the house itself—a two-storied red brick, with
a few ornamentals clustered near the door—was English to the last leaded
window.

When the professor came over to us, he talked softly and easily, and
used words not ordinarily heard in conversation, not big ones especially,
but words typically read and not said. He explained, for example, that the
"erstwhile" owner of the house had been another English professor, and he
said, yes, the pair of corgis scampering around us were "engaging" but one
was more "taciturn" than the other. I wondered if Jack would eventually
pick up on this way of speaking. Would he turn in his endearing New York
"beauteeful," in favor of—oh, say not so—"beauteous"? What comforted
me was the thought that Jack didn't do anything just because everybody
else was doing it.

Other students joined us and immediately started talking about the
professor's course, which the professor referred to as the one "you boys are
suffering through." He said this with a little laugh—a "chuckle," he would
have called it—seemingly confident that "you boys" would offer a protest.
And some, no doubt non-GIs, did. The boys talked about the course, which
was apparently now concentrating on Lord Byron, and they seemed to take
pleasure in pronouncing the name of his protagonist as "Don Joo-ahn,"
and not "Don Wan," as I would have said. "Don Joo-ahn" was apparently
how the British did it, and how the British did it, as I was continuing to
learn, was for English majors the one and only true way.

It seemed obvious that for many of the students at the professor's party,
literature was a passion of long standing, and their speech—their choice of
words, their turns of phrase—reflected this. I may have waited for Jack to
join in, but if I did, I waited in vain, for Jack, usually so eager to enter into
any discussion, was offering nothing at all. And as I continued to listen to

the conversation, to the "I daresay's" and the "Quite right's," I realized that Jack was reacting to the fact that he did not speak in a literary manner.

As we rode home in the "Chivy," back down the long driveway and into the Gainesville streets, I tried to assess the afternoon, up to and including how it meshed with Professor Lyons and his role as English don manqué and his class as an Oxford tutorial manqué. The afternoon had been all English style all the time, and I had to think that those in the English litera-ture business were straight out of an English novel of manners; and I had to also think that if Jack was going to be a professor of English literature, he was going to have to work hard to make it a fit.

I tried to envision it. A New York Jewish boy among gentile Anglophiles? An athlete among the aesthete? And how about me? A daughter of Russian Jewish immigrants who spoke English with accents and who didn't know a Ph.D. from the man at the causeway bridge catching fish? How was all this going to work?

At home, after we had gathered Rick from the Bells and after we had gotten into bed, after we had listened for a while to the thumping of the palmetto bugs on the back of the mirror, we talked about it. Jack said it might not work at all, and I listened as he ran through all his negatives. First of all, he, like me, had been unsettled by the other students and their easy familiarity with the language and the literature, and when I tried to put a better light on it, "You don't understand," he answered me. "They act and sound as if they're born to it, and I don't." Well, I did understand, and when I reminded him that George wasn't "born" to it, Jack said in a jokey way, "Ain't you noticed that George is a Wasp? He don't have to talk so good, see?" And then Jack laughed, and I laughed with him.

As I went to sleep on that night after the party at the home of the el-egant professor, despite Jack's misgivings I had every feeling that it was going to be all right, that we were doing okay. With the GI Bill providing the power, I felt we were going forward, moving in a positive way. I only hoped that Jack felt this way as well.

FINISHING UP THE B.A.

At this particular moment time was charging toward Jack's graduation and Rick's birthday. Rick turned three and his absolutely best friends— the fraternity boys—gave him a party. The fraternity boys stood Rick on a table, all sixty-five of them gathered 'round, each gave him a gift, and

Rick pointed to each boy and thanked him by name, thus showing an early talent for a political life. Was I seeing the first Jewish president having his third birthday party?

In a couple of months Jack finished his courses for his bachelor's degree and we went to commencement exercises, where Jack was handed his diploma by President John J. Tigert, whom Rick confused (loudly) with President Truman in one of the afternoon's more diverting moments in an afternoon badly in need of diverting moments.

If the afternoon was not exactly fascinating, it was not the afternoon it might have been a few years earlier when Jack would have looked down at the diploma in his hand and wondered what he was supposed to do with it. Now, thanks to the GI Bill, he knew. What he specifically knew was that this diploma would lead him to the next one—the master's one. And from there?

There was also a disconcerting moment: the afternoon kept reminding me of how many of the boys who had started the GI Bill journey with us were not there and would not be there next year or the next, the ones who had dropped by the wayside. "It's too much of a grind," they had said. "Too much for an old fogy like me." So the list of the GI Bill boys still with us was little-jack-little winnowing down to the few. What the dropouts had apparently discovered was that nobody was standing at the tollgates waving them through.

To reward Jack for his achievement, I went down to Silverman's Men's Store and bought him a tweed jacket, along with a pair of suede patches for the sleeves. After some deliberation, however, I decided not to put the elbow patches in place; they would stay in their package. The tweed jacket would symbolize the first step, and the patches would be awarded for the second. Was I doubtful? Was I becoming unsettled by the defection of some of the GI Bill boys? Maybe I was.

At the same time that Jack was finishing his B.A., George Harper was finishing his master's degree and departing Gainesville. With the GI Bill in his suitcase and a choice of places for his doctorate, George decided on the University of California at Berkeley to study there with a particular professor. So across the country George and Bobby went, and we received a letter from George almost at once. "That I'm studying with the eminent Mark Shorer is hard to believe. It seems like some kind of magic put me in his classroom. I'm still wondering at the largesse of the GI Bill." And when Jack wrote back, he said, "I don't know if I'm ever going to study with anybody 'eminent' or not, but I'm glad you have the chance." I didn't much like the sound of Jack's answer. Was there a discouraged note in there somewhere?

Our friends were dispersing in various directions like fans after a foot-ball game. I did, however, have a small, very small, consolation: When Harold and Margie Retman left, Margie gave me her recipe for the vaunted tuna casserole, which turned out to be a can of tuna united with a can of Campbell's mushroom soup.

Things kept changing. Jack's brother Irwin and his wife Ruby came to Gainesville and moved in with us. Irwin was now eager about a degree in engineering, having some feeling that the field, if it did not exactly put the welcome mat out, did not have a sign out front that said, "If you're Jewish, don't even think about it."

My sister Ruth and her husband Phil came, along with two-year-old Dale, and they lucked out with an apartment in the now-available housing for veterans called Fla-vet Village, which was basically a reassembling of the two-story barracks that had been in use at Camp Blanding during the war and was now fitted out with kitchens and bathrooms and rented out to veterans' families. Phil didn't know what he was going to do with his GI Bill. He was going to shop around, he said. "I feel like a do-it-yourselfer in a hardware store," he said to us, "and I want every shiny tool on the shelf." I'm not sure that Phil, a Bronx apartment dweller all his life, knew any-thing about a hardware store and shiny tools, but we got the message—Phil was excited.

Irwin and Ruby were now in Rick's bedroom, and Rick's bed was now in the corner of the "sunroom," an afterthought of a room that never got any sun because it was in the wrong part of the house, but it didn't matter because Gainesville had precious little sun anyway. Jack still did his work in the corner of our bedroom, and I used the kitchen table for typing.

I typed with the radio turned low, and I listened to news and music. My father was probably still listening chiefly to Gabriel Heatter, but my news came likely as not from H. V. Kaltenborn, the moment's prime newscaster, and I became very familiar with his clipped delivery and his Germanic overtones. Edward R. Murrow was still giving the news, though he was no longer the spellbinder he had been when he was broadcasting from England during the war. Then we had known him as a broadcaster so intrepid that we could hear a "blitz"—a London air attack—booming all around him as he gave his radio report. Murrow was also the reporter who gave us the first news of Buchenwald, and when he described "bodies stacked up like cordwood," it was the metaphor we imprinted on. In a few years Murrow would report to us during a different kind of blitz, one that did not involve bloodshed but would seize us nonetheless; and Edward R. Murrow would again become a spellbinder.

Radio music sometimes came from big bands, though they no longer dominated. Now, music described by the disc jockeys as "rhythm and blues" was giving the big bands a run for their money, and something called "rock and roll" was making itself heard. I wasn't sure I liked the new music. It was different in so many ways: smaller groups of musicians, and the guitar—hitherto little seen or heard—the featured instrument. The new music seemed to me a combination of country music and the blues and even a little gospel, all of which I had heard in Union City, though not, I have to say, all in the same piece of music.

I was still clinging to my favorites, and for those of us accustomed to our idols of the 1930s and 1940s, it was a time for taking sides. Bing Crosby or Frank Sinatra? The rivalry was intense. The Crosby disciples described Sinatra's voice as thin and whiny; the Sinatra ones held that Crosby had a voice only your mother could love. I myself couldn't choose. How could I when they had both gone through the war with me?

DR. LYONS DEPARTS

Soon there was another loss: Professor Lyons announced he was leaving. This was something of a blow to Jack, but Dr. Lyons was going to the University of North Carolina in Chapel Hill, and as he said to Jack, "When the University of North Carolina sends for you, you grab your helmet and get in the game. Nobody turns Chapel Hill down." He had said "Chapel Hill" to mean the university, and I was beginning to understand that "The University of North Carolina" and "Chapel Hill" were one and the same, and I was beginning to understand that there was a commonly held perception that the English Department at the University of North Carolina was number one in the South. So who could argue with Dr. Lyons when he accepted Chapel Hill, especially when he was to be their English Department chairman?

I knew a few things about the state of North Carolina, chiefly through my father's subscription to the *Carolina Israelite,* a Charlotte newspaper edited and published by an ex–New Yorker named Harry Golden. My father was ever interested in the doings of southern Jews, and he found a rich source in Harry Golden. Whenever he found a particularly meaningful item, he would clip it and send it to us in Gainesville.

The *Carolina Israelite* called North Carolina a "philo-semitic" state, and after my father found out what "philo-semitic" meant, he understood that Harry Golden shared his feelings that the South was a relatively good place for Jews. And when he read that E. J. "Mutt" Evans, a Jew store proprietor in Durham, North Carolina, had been six times elected mayor of that city, he felt it confirmed this. Mutt apparently held the view (and was quoted as saying so, if not in so many words) that southerners didn't care if you were Methodist or Jewish or Polka Dottish so long as you were religious, and Mutt maintained that he had made it clear to the townspeople that he was a staunchly religious man. Of course my father was not a religious man, staunchly or otherwise, but he thought that what Mutt was saying was "good for the Jews."

Jack liked to call Harry Golden the American Jonathan Swift. Like Swift, Harry Golden was famous for offering seemingly zany solutions to serious issues, and in later years he had several profoundly zany ones. One, the Vertical Negro Plan, took off on the white southerner's problems with school integration, specifically the objection to black children sitting alongside white children in the classroom, and Harry Golden said that since *standing* alongside blacks offended nobody, his solution was to get rid of the chairs.

In later years he also proposed the White Baby Plan, in which black women carrying white babies could ignore the "whites in front, colored in back" custom. I was familiar with this plan, having been carried to many a town event in Union City in the arms of my mammy Willie Arnold to the front of the crowd when she wanted a better view. A workable custom, Harry Golden thought it was, and if a black woman had no white baby to carry, a white baby would be provided.

Harry Golden always had kind words for the University of North Carolina, and he clued us in to how the UNC president, Frank Porter Graham, as a U.S. senator, had managed to distance himself from the typically arch-conservative views of his southern colleagues. For those of us with a liberal sensibility, when we compared Dr. Graham with the University of Florida president, John James Tigert, a former basketball and football coach at the University of Kentucky, the difference was striking. President Tigert did indeed look the part of a university president, and, according to his pictures, Frank Porter Graham did not, but if President Tigert held any progressive views, he didn't tell anybody.

And so, Chapel Hill was ever out there, ever beckoning to English majors and graduate students and faculty. George Harper, that serious scholar, wanted to end up teaching there; Jack thought of working there for his Ph.D. I figured George would make it; about Jack I was not so sure.

In honor of Professor Lyons's coup, I thought to invite him and his wife Gladys to our house on Hernando Street "for drinks," as I had learned the practice was described. Did I think of it as a rehearsal? If I did, it didn't take me long to find out I had a lot of rehearsing to do.

Where when I needed her were Bobby Harper and her familiarity with "scotch and sodas"? I asked around for suggestions for proper hors d'oeuvres, and though the women vetoed tacky old potato chips and pretzels, they thought it would be all right to serve Ritz crackers topped with Velveeta, and someone advised me to put a slice of pickle on it. I finally settled on peanut butter stuffed into celery sticks with a dish of nuts on the side.

Professor Clifford Lyons was, as Jack had described him, a "tank of a man," and Mrs. Lyons was mature-lady pretty, ever smiling, with very white hair, very blue eyes, and a look of being very Episcopalian. As I found out later, I had it right: English professors and their wives were almost unanimously supplicants in the Episcopal Church because it was the closest church to the mother Anglican one, and Dr. and Mrs. Lyons were no exception.

We sat around the living room, Jack got drinks (he remembered how!), and as I passed around the celery sticks, I was very much aware of the dynamic of "Faculty member and wife socialize with graduate student and wife." The Lyonses were unfailingly polite and Dr. Lyons announced that peanut butter was his very favorite snack. "Ask Gladys," he said, and Mrs. Lyons smiled and nodded, and said, "Cliff just can't get enough." Did I believe her? Well, it sounded nice.

After a while Jack and Dr. Lyons talked with each other, and Gladys Lyons and I were left to our own conversation, and I knew only too soon that we were badly in need of help. I still had that southern attitude that holds that a train wreck is preferable to a gap in conversation, but I felt it just wouldn't do to "interview" Mrs. Lyons. She did her best, but we were not a comfortable fit. She was gracious, seemingly interested, and careful—too careful—and I soon knew that the gulf between us would not be navigated smoothly.

I tried for something. As I had learned in Union City, when all else fails, you compliment your lady guest on her dress, and I did this. Mrs. Lyons laughed and said she had owned it for years. "The Depression, you know," she said. It had not occurred to me that the Depression had hit the universities, and I told her this.

It was the first easing of the conversation, and if Mrs. Lyons was think-ing, "At last, a crust of bread for a starving soul," she didn't show it. She just slid gracefully into a humorous telling of how during the Depression the University of Florida had been broke because the state itself was broke, and the state had paid the faculty and staff with scrip. Mrs. Lyons did a little amused laugh and said, "After a while, scrip began looking more real than dollars, don't you know."

I offered that Mrs. Lyons had taught me something about the Depres-sion, and I said to her, "The idea of scrip pay is certainly an intriguing piece of history." After that small, and awkward, offering, my southern gift for nonstop chatter totally deserted me, and Mrs. Lyons and I reverted to talk-ing in fits and starts until she and Dr. Lyons left.

Gladys Lyons, in demeanor and in style, was, I convinced myself, the very model of the upper-level faculty wife, given as she was to kindness and tact and ultimately to an impenetrable reserve. Bobby Harper might find a way to play this role, but I wasn't sure I could.

THE EPISODE

In the meantime, Jack's master's degree was within striking distance. All assigned papers had been written, classwork requirements fulfilled, pass-fails awarded. All that remained was for Jack to pick a subject for the thesis. And Jack's special problem in this area—that inability to go along with the crowd—turned what should have been an easy decision into a predicament.

To get the master's degree, Jack would have to slough off that third foot—the one that his drill sergeant had pointed out with such despair—and get into the rhythm. He would have to decide on a thesis topic that the faculty would okay. The trouble was that Jack knew that his ideas, drawn as they were from a New York life and, more lately, from a war, would not conform to faculty ideas. What Jack wanted was a topic that dealt with contemporary people and societal problems, and what the faculty wanted was a historical approach. If George Harper had still been around, he would have given Jack his speech about sticking with the "good stock," and never mind "the new guys."

Jack knew it would be an uphill fight. The American literature faculty was just about embodied in a single professor, Herman Spivey, and Jack was not surprised that Professor Spivey was unsettled by Jack's idea of a topic. The professor was of a mind that a thesis that carried the imprimatur of the University of Florida English Department should be within the mainstream. Perhaps someone like Emerson?

In return, Jack proposed John Steinbeck. Surely, Professor Spivey said, Steinbeck was a spokesman for a particular moment and would be forgotten in the very near future? John Dos Passos? "An innovator attractive to young writers who will no doubt fill the shelves with bad imitations," Professor Spivey said.

Thomas Wolfe? Herman Spivey admitted, grudgingly, that Thomas Wolfe might have some lasting value and agreed to act as Jack's advisor for a thesis devoted to him. It was not to be called, however, "The Social Idealism of Thomas Wolfe," as Jack had proposed, but "Idealism in Thomas Wolfe," which apparently better suited Professor Spivey's more careful sensibilities.

I too liked Thomas Wolfe, though after typing a couple of hundred pages filled with Wolfe quotations, I began to understand what the critic Bernard de Voto had meant when in a review of Wolfe's work he said, "You can't cure America by throwing adjectives at it." And oh, Mr. de Voto, many thousands of thrown adjectives did I type.

Still, it was through Thomas Wolfe that I was drawn to the town he wrote about—a small college town he called "Pulpit Mount," which was obviously Chapel Hill, North Carolina. Was I drawn to it because I was prescient, because I sensed that "Pulpit Mount" would play an important role in our lives? I think probably not.

If Jack had a hard time getting approval for a topic, it was only the beginning of his thesis travails. Each step of the writing had to be run through the filter of Dr. Spivey, and Dr. Spivey, like other faculty advisors dealing with master's degree candidates, was extremely strict. "They can afford to be strict," Jack said, "They're up to their butts in quality students."

Getting a master's degree was, then, not a walk in the park. If graduate students before the war had taken a less than a serious approach to getting their degrees, the GI Bill boys were serious down to their army boots; and even if, like Jack, they knew they wrote well and knew that their thought processes were in good working order, they also knew that the standards were now perilously high. Moreover, the thesis not only had to be ship-shape, but the boys also, after turning it in, had to face a faculty committee, or as the boys called it, "the team of assassins." Jack said that facing the faculty gauntlet was like being over Japan. "There I am, dodging and trying to get my guns aimed," he said to me, "and all the while they're trying to bring me down."

Still, had the GI Bill said that you could just take the money and run? No, it had not. It said you could take the money and work like the dickens. And so, in the end, Jack and most of the other candidates got their master's degrees, but by the time they did, I (and no doubt the other wives) had ceased being the innocents about what it took to get them. But wasn't the rose of Sharon bush blooming again? Yes, it was, and that was a good thing.

* * *

When Jack managed to slough off that third foot long enough to finish his thesis and get his master's degree, I had not anticipated that he would need to make a further career decision. Like all wives whose husbands were in the master's program, I had assumed that my husband would segue without a ripple into becoming a Ph.D. candidate. That the University of Florida still did not offer the Ph.D. and that the degree would have to happen at another university seemed to me not a problem. As it turned out, however, Jack was working another side of the street.

The rumor was rampant that teaching jobs on the college level were available for those with master's degrees, and Jack told me that some of the boys were talking about going after them. I had every feeling that this was more than a casual aside. As I was to find out, and very quickly, Jack had decided to look for a teaching job. *Teach? With a master's degree? With time left on the GI Bill?* I sensed a fit beginning to percolate, and the tail was coming into view.

I tried to stay calm. I figured that the struggle with the master's degree was playing a big part in Jack's decision and, like some of the other boys, he was feeling that those who had endured combat—in the air and before the "team of assassins"—had endured enough and were entitled to begin their real lives. It was something hard to argue with. I knew that if consulted, however, the authors of the GI Bill would tell him to use the bill until it, not he, gave out.

I let Jack know what I thought. What I thought wasn't new to him, but I figured it wouldn't hurt to say it again. So, in a voice louder than usual, I said, "I want you to get your doctorate. I want you to realize your potential." And I said, as if I had it all figured out, "You can't know your potential with just a master's degree." And Jack answered, "I know I can't. But who says I have all this great potential?"

I had not convinced Jack of anything. All I had done was to set him remembering the party at the professor's estate. "Those guys are my competition," Jack said to me. "You think that even if we all had the same qualifications, they'd choose me over them?"

My fit showed up in a couple of ways: I didn't sew on Jack's patches, and I didn't type his query letters, the result being that Jack didn't ask about the patches and he wrote the letters himself in longhand. The letters, which I read surreptitiously, were all the same and simply included his experience and achievements, and they were sent to small colleges and to one or two southern state universities where a doctorate might not be essential. Undoubtedly filled with memories of quotas and discrimination, Jack didn't mention in his query letters that he was Jewish. And he didn't discuss the letters with me. I had been kicked off the team.

Answering letters appeared, and having no doubt that I would read them, Jack left them around. The ones from the small colleges said nothing about Jack's qualifications but asked, without explanation or apology, about his religion. Jack answered by saying he was "a neutral observer of religion," and the answers to *that* were, as one letter put it, "We were hoping for more than neutrality."

Throwing my fit aside for the moment, I had to wonder if the rebuffs were simply a subtle bit of bigotry. Did these colleges have an interest only in those with strong religious feelings? This would definitely be true of the numerous colleges whose support came from religious groups, and to me, that demurral would have been more or less acceptable. Still, I knew Jack's feelings on *that* subject—that colleges stressing religious learning were just a distraction from the main goal of getting an education.

There was another possibility: had the college people made the assumption, despite Jack's not having declared himself, that he *was* Jewish? And were they using "hoping for more than neutrality" as an excuse to disqualify him? Would Jack have been better off simply to say he was Jewish and take a chance? I had learned where I grew up that if you were Jewish, everybody knew it, and the chips fell whichever way. But in New York where Jack grew up? Up there, did northern Jews accept there were times when you were allowed to dissemble? Like Herschel Walcoffsky—er, Harvey Walcott?

Then, surprisingly, the University of Georgia came through with an offer. Apparently the University of Georgia was so loaded with students that if it had ever considered religion a prerequisite, it didn't any longer. It needed teachers; it needed them bad, and it needed them now. The position it offered was an instructorship in freshman English at a salary of $2,400.

Even if it was not much, I knew we could live on it, but would I admit that to Jack? I would not. I was in that fit, and the tail was growing.

By now Jack and I had stopped speaking, and I was deep into frustration. I kept thinking that we hadn't reached our destination, that there was another leg to our journey. What we were about to do, I thought, was neither the beginning nor the end of anything, just an unsatisfactory disengagement. Well, it was a beginning of sorts, but not the luminous beginning we had in Gainesville. And it was also the end of something—the GI Bill would be out of our lives.

And so as we set ourselves to go to Athens, Georgia, I packed our things with as much enthusiasm as I had in Union City when I had to go to school on a snowy day and the snow was perfect for sledding. Anxieties were flying about us like a swarm of lovebugs, those pesky things Florida knew so well. But lovebugs Jack and I were definitely not. We had retreated to our separate corners and were nursing our wounds. And the tail on my fit was switching around like mad.

* * *

During the war, when Jack received his orders to go overseas, we were stationed in Salina, Kansas. I had to get Rick and me back to Miami, and I did it by means of a long, arduous automobile trip. And it was on this trip that something remarkable happened. It was early afternoon, the sun was shining brightly, and I was feeling in control: I had gasoline, we had gotten through Texas, Louisiana, Mississippi, and Alabama, and we still had some of the food—fruits and cookies that the Cajun café owner in Lafayette, Louisiana, had put in a bag for us ("Just a leetle somethin' for you voyage, ma chère," he had said). I was driving down U.S. 1 between Jacksonville and Daytona Beach, the roads were clear, and to add to my feeling of well-being, Rick had settled in for an afternoon nap.

Well, it turned out that the roads were clear except for the lovebugs, and at that time of the year, these swarming male-female duos were crashing with abandon into any automobile that came their way.

Lovebugs weren't called lovebugs for nothing: they were locked in embrace both in life and in death. And on this day, seemingly impassioned senseless and in what was probably a ritualized love display, vast numbers were committing suicide on my windshield, which soon became a sticky, gluey, smeary mess of dead *plecia nearctica*. In no time at all I could see nothing. The road ahead became a thing of mystery, and the diminution of sunlight turned the interior of the car into a cave. There was only one thing to do—take a rag from the glove compartment, get out of the car, and start wiping at the windshield. Who was I kidding? That windshield needed a blowtorch. I would settle for a chemical solvent, but *what* chemical solvent? Out here in these empty fields there was no filling station, not even a house. Could I possibly hope for some help from the skies, perhaps an ocean or two of rain?

Fat chance. The sky was glittery with sun. Well, to be honest, miles away was one little cloud. I got back in the car, and while Rick slept, I sat. I sat, I worried, and I finally stuck my head out the window and took to watching the little cloud. Was I imagining that the cloud was moving toward me? Yes, it was, and what's more, it was moving *inexorably* toward me. And suddenly it was over me, and suddenly it was pouring rain on my car. That cloud had obviously been programmed to target something, and it seemed to be me. The cloud sat up there and pelted the car with rain for about twenty minutes, and then, its job done, my windshield again clean and clear, it gathered itself up and left.

I never forgot that little incident. I don't believe in miracles, but I do have a healthy respect for marvels, and that cloud and what it wrought was definitely a marvel of the first order. Still, compared with the marvel that came to us as we were preparing to leave for Georgia, it was not even in the competition. This new marvel originated in Chapel Hill, North Carolina, and Professor Lyons was my rain-filled cloud. Dr. Lyons was on the phone, and what he had in mind was not only a marvel, it was a life-changer.

The conversation had started out innocently. Dr. Lyons had apparently asked how Jack was doing and what his plans were. "I hear you're going to the University of Georgia," he said. And when Jack said he was, Dr. Lyons responded with, "They may have their way in football, but we can beat 'em out on this one."

I stood by listening to Jack's side of the conversation, and I held my breath. Was Dr. Lyons was offering Jack a job? Yes, it turned out that he was. "Want to come up here as a student assistant?" he asked Jack.

Could Jack have done a little stagger? I thought he did. And I thought his voice came out as a little croak when he said, "You mean in Chapel Hill?"

And when Dr. Lyons said, "Well yes," and "Do you want me to pursue it?" Jack turned and gave me the thumbs-up sign. Then, summoning as much voice as he could, he said, "Please do pursue it. And thank you for thinking of me."

"I've been thinking you were about to do something really dumb," Professor Lyons said to Jack. "I've been thinking you were about to let the GI Bill go to waste, and I wasn't going to let that happen." There was more! "And while you're here, you can work on your doctorate," he said.

Did I think that Dr. Lyons was taking special pains with Jack because they shared an athletic bond? Or had my peanut butter–filled celery sticks made such a lasting impression? Or did Dr. Lyons think to do something nice for a minority who knew discrimination? None of those explanations suited me, and I clung to the thought that Dr. Lyons did it because he had spotted someone he would be proud to share his profession with.

So Jack and I emerged from our corners, met in the middle of the ring, and hugged for a long time. To seal the deal, I sewed on Jack's patches and got on with typing his stuff. And almost immediately, the tail on my fit— and then the fit itself—fell away.

I typed a letter to the admissions office at UNC, and back came the answering letter from the English Department with an offer of an assistantship and forms to fill out. Again, there was a slot for writing in your religion and this time Jack groaned, bit the bullet, wrote in "Jewish," and gave me the look that said "who knows?" Would it matter that he was Jewish? It apparently didn't, for there was an answering letter with a welcome in it.

I had to wonder: after Professor Lyons's good offices on his behalf, did Jack still think that all gentiles—with the pointed exception of George Harper—harbored traces of anti-Semitism? Hadn't the action of Dr. Lyons proved otherwise? I put it to Jack. "Don't you think you can revise your thinking on the subject?" I asked him. I wasn't surprised that Jack's answer was an unsatisfactory "Maybe." Still, with the body and soul of a New Yorker overlain with a slight patina of Miami Beach, Jack would find it hard to say anything else.

GOODBYE TO GAINESVILLE

We said our goodbyes. Jack had said his to the guys who had been in two kinds of trenches with him—the war kind and the class kind—and no one, Jack said, failed to mention how lucky he was to be going to UNC. Rick had gone over to the fraternity house and said goodbye personally to each of his best friends, got a couple of freshman beanies as going-away presents, and played one last time with Travis Bell in the sandbox in the Bells' front yard.

Although we were leaving Ruth and Phil behind, we knew they were proceeding nicely. Phil had picked his first shiny tool—accounting—and he was hard at work on it. We were also leaving Irwin and Ruby, but Irwin would be finished soon, and then . . . well, and then he would cross his fingers and hope for openings for Jewish engineers.

I knew I was saying a final goodbye to the women who had been with me in the last years, those who had variously suffered, breezed, or stumbled through with me. We had learned things together, chiefly how to be a helpmeet and not a drag. I expected that I would find other GI Bill wives in Chapel Hill, but my Gainesville ones were my first GI Bill sisters. It was true we would no longer have each other, but our memories would be like Gainesville clay that dyed your clothes forever. So unlike the manner in which we had left Montgomery, which was with a cry of "Goodbye forever, hope never to see you again," we departed Gainesville with good feelings. We had momentum in Gainesville, and it was building.

We drove up to Chapel Hill in Jack's father's car. He had given it to us when he managed to get himself a Hudson, which, even if it looked like a rhinoceros, was managing currently to roll off the lines. We were therefore in our own "wheels," as the boys called anything that you could ride in or on, and our wheels were a 1940 Ford. It was fine with us—deluded, demented Henry Ford and his Protocols of Zion be darned. In the car with us were, besides our clothes, the little radio, Elsie the typewriter, Jack's books, and Rick's tricycle.

As we drove, as we set off for North Carolina, up U.S. 1 and U.S. 17, and then from the coast road over to Chapel Hill, Jack and I were having very different dreams. Jack was envisioning his life as a Ph.D. candidate and an assistant instructor. I was envisioning his actually holding the ultimate diploma, and I was thinking of what had started it all—the brochure that we had found at the Miami post office, the one that told us that the Servicemen's Readjustment Act was out there and ready to be of service.

* * *

The Servicemen's Readjustment Act—the GI Bill—had taken Jack and me, and the majority of GI Bill boys and their families, through the late 1940s, and as we rolled into Chapel Hill, the 1950s were upon us. And though the 1950s are often spoken of as years of quiet calm, as a peaceful postwar period, if you asked a returning veteran, he would tell you that those years were filled with a lot of high drama and low comedy. The veterans had matured during the war years, and the world of the 1950s, as they saw it, was anything but humdrum.

The GI Bill veterans saw the fifties not as tranquil but as roiled about, sometimes with huge swells and crashing waves. It was in fact a time when the country was hard tested in many ways. In just five years after the end of the war that came after the war to end all wars, another one came to us. And then in our gratefulness to a brilliant general, we made him our president, not bothering to find out if a brilliant general would make for a brilliant president. In fast order we would find ourselves in the sway of another man who from his high office would manipulate and bear false witness and go his way unchallenged for too long a time, and we would know government committees that would grow ever more powerful and stoke fears in us, and we would find few leaders brave enough to call them to account. We would struggle through changes in traditions, through foolish laws and dangerous ones. And in personal ways, we would be confronted with marriages in trouble, often those of close friends who had married in wartime haste and were repenting not at leisure but in a couple of years.

So there were challenges aplenty in the 1950s. And through it all the GI Bill boys and their families watched, learned, and prepared themselves. The GI Bill boys were getting ready to make a difference.

THE UNIVERSITY OF NORTH CAROLINA

Chapel Hill's emphasis on tradition was new to me, accustomed as I was to traditionless towns. In Union City we had no significant traditions unless it was the "dog days" of August, when stray dogs suspected of being rabid were rounded up and summarily put down whether they were rabid or not. Or maybe "tradition" might apply to the annual event at the U-Tote-'Em grocery store when we counted beans in a jar and competed for a baseball or talcum powder. I could think of no old and treasured Union City buildings, Union City buildings being just the usual red brick edifices with the name of the first occupant—"Manning's Hardware, 1908"—set in stone on the fascia. As to traditions in Miami Beach, there was no Miami Beach until around 1870, and it wasn't actually a town then but a farm for planting and harvesting coconuts, and even this little enterprise soon disappeared.

But Chapel Hill had traditions. Why not, considering that it was founded in 1789 and still had buildings dating from that period? As we drove through the treed—more like "forested"—campus, I felt the presence of Thomas Wolfe, with whose writings, and adjectives, I had come to know so well when I had typed Jack's master's thesis. Descriptive passages about

Chapel Hill flowed through his books, and I now understood why he had been under the spell of this verdant town.

It was in Chapel Hill that we became government double-dippers. This was another college town where housing was extremely tight, and the dwellings for veterans—Victory Village—were full up. A real estate agent showed us a new development where we could either buy a four-room house for $4,200 or a five-room one featuring a dining room shooting off to the side for $5,100, and since the lower price had seemed astronomical enough, and because our minds had shut down after hearing it, the $4,200 house was the choice. The man at the bank looked at Jack's papers, gave him a form to sign, said "Your mortgage payments will be forty dollars a month," and wished us well in our new home. The GI Bill had provided again. The housing clause, in conjunction with the Federal Housing Administration, had bought us a house, and we were now GI Bill double-dippers.

We settled in. Jack, as an assistant instructor, found himself with a lot to do besides the usual. He had also to prepare classes and keep office hours for his students. And his own classes, I gathered, were more demanding than ever.

Rick had no trouble making himself at home. In our development were many families like ours, with children all over the place. So Rick put the Pi Lam fraternity boys and Travis Bell into his memory bank and went about making new best friends. Exchange babysitting having been established among the Chapel Hill mothers of the GI Bill persuasion, I went to work on the campus as a "temp." It was a job, I quickly learned, that covered all the tasks the permanent staff had said in no uncertain terms was "not my job." As a result, I did a lot of filing and mimeographing and whatever else was nobody's job.

When I was assigned to the English Department, however, the job got a bit more interesting. As "temporary clerical," I was Queen of the Files and could rummage among them to my heart's content, including in Jack's folder. I found nothing earth-shattering there, just the forms Jack had filled out and a letter from Dr. Lyons in support of Jack's joining the department, in which only two comments held any real interest—one of them that Jack was "hearty," which I supposed was a positive attribute, and one that Dr. Lyons thought would appeal to the admissions committee in case the committee had been looking for "hearty" types to counterbalance the "unhearty" ones. The second was that Jack was Jewish, and, doing my usual reflexive checking, I found no "Yes, he's Jewish, but. . . ."

POLITICAL MATTERS

On the front burner currently—one that had turned up the moment Jack and I had crossed the border into North Carolina—was the presidential race between Truman and Dewey. But wait. There was also a third and a fourth party in the race—the Dixiecrat and the Progressive. Truman was favored by most of the boys, chiefly for his plans to help out financially distressed European countries, and some of the boys—certainly not all—liked that he had desegregated the troops (even if a lot of military installations paid no attention whatsoever, including, as we heard from friends, Maxwell Field in Montgomery).

Passions for and against the third and fourth parties ran very high, and at the usual Saturday night parties, which were much like the ones in Gainesville down to the last drop of Southern Comfort, they ran very high indeed. There was again "plantation twaddle," as there had been in Gainesville, and twaddlers announced they would vote for Strom Thurmond and the Dixiecrats. Some tried to make a case for Henry Wallace, the standard-bearer for the Progressive Party, and I for one was impressed with some of the things Wallace-ites were saying, especially Wallace's caution against what he called "American fascists," those who wanted, as he said, "to poison the channels of public information." Not everybody saw Wallace this way, and those who didn't said, "He's just spouting Communist propaganda. By damn, he's so pink, he's almost red." When Jack and I went to bed after one of these parties, we felt we had escaped from a bloody shoot-'em-up.

It was not a fun election: by this time most of the boys were beginning to question Truman's wartime decision to drop the atom bomb and some were questioning his support of civil rights. The most fun we got was after the election, when H. V. Kaltenborn prematurely called the race for Dewey, and Truman, in a dead-on imitation of Kaltenborn's delivery, managed to make this self-important man sound very foolish indeed. Of course in the end, neither the Dixiecrats nor the Progressives got much of a vote, though I was happy to see that the Progressives got more than the Dixiecrats.

News of the SS *Exodus* broke, and with it talk of where to locate, yes again, displaced European Jews. The *Exodus* had been trying to ferry some four thousand Jewish war refugees to Israel, and had been intercepted by the British, who sent its passengers back to Europe. It was a little different from the SS *St. Louis* episode. That ship had been carrying German Jews trying to stay out of death camps, and the *Exodus* was carrying what were called "displaced" persons. Still, the incidents were similar in one way: both ships had been denied entry. The *Exodus* had an additional horror story: the native lands of its displaced persons had made clear that they didn't want "their" Jews back, so these once-German, or once-Polish, or once-something Jews were returned to the refugee camps from which they had come.

I was not the only one puzzled; all the GIs were puzzled. They thought they had fought that battle. They thought they had fought a war to allow European Jews to live free. The boys would shake their heads and say, "Can't believe this thing is still happening." And Jack would answer, "Why not? Anti-Semitism is nothing new, you know."

When in 1948, after the Arab-Israeli war, Israel declared itself a state, nobody, it seemed, wanted any displaced Palestinians either. My father had been coming to our Chapel Hill parties in the guise of letters, and he was still writing many a letter containing many an opinion, and in 1948 he was going on about the Arab-Israeli war in which more than 700,000 Palestinians were displaced and how nobody wanted them, certainly not the surrounding Arab states. My father wrote, "What the Arab states want is for Israel to disappear and for the Palestinians to go back so they can call it Palestine again. The Israelis may like having a country of their own, but believe me they got nothing but *tsores.*" *Tsores.* Trouble, nothing but trouble.

When the boys talked about this, they were reluctant, perhaps feeling that any criticism of Israel would not sit well with us. Jack's take on this was that it depended on how informed you were: "Be my guest to criticize Israel if you know the issues," he would say to the other boys. "But if you don't know anything and you still criticize Israel, you're just an anti-Semite." And when the non-Jewish boys would ask, "Aren't Jews and Arabs supposed to be cousins?" I would quote my father when he said, "With cousins like these, you don't need strangers."

Hot on the heels of this came Korea. The cold war between the United States and the Soviet Union had suddenly gone past cold to very hot, and Senator McCarthy, the man my father had advised me to keep an eye on, was making a name for himself as the point man in the hunt for Communists, and he didn't hesitate to accuse Truman of being "soft" on Communism. Any of us who had been reading a newspaper—and we all had, more or less—knew that North Korea was a client state of the Soviet Union, and this put Truman on notice. So when North Korea crossed the dividing line between the two Koreas—the portentous thirty-eighth parallel—there was little surprise when Truman ordered the navy and the air force into battle. No surprise, but also no huzzahs, and definitely no "let me at 'em."

Still, we were again at war. And now even those boys who believed in the domino theory—the one that held that if Korea fell to the Communists, the other states in the area would follow—were stunned, and they asked, "Didn't we just have a war?" Yes, we did, but it appeared we were having another one. And the GI Bill veterans who had signed up for the reserves had to pack up their books and put on their uniforms. Jim Galloway took it hard. "I'm just getting started on the dissertation," he said to us. "When—and if—I come back, I doubt I can start all over again." My father, the superpatriot, wrote to say that, sorry as he was that more of "our boys" would be in harm's way, it couldn't be helped. "Our country is calling again," he said. And he finished with a flourish: "And now when the boys come home, they'll have the GI Bill. Not like the doughboys."

When I read his letter, I dismissed the thought that our country would be "calling again" on Jack. A few days later, however, the thought returned when a couple of men in officers' military uniforms were standing on our front steps, and one of them was saying, "Captain Suberman?" I looked at Jack and thought that "Captain" was a curious appellation for a guy in blue jeans and a sweatshirt, but that's what the man said.

The uniformed man had called Jack by his military title because he was from the Officer Recruitment Office and he and his fellow recruiter were looking for men who could be talked into reenlisting. Jack knew—we all knew—that our armed forces were severely depleted, and the men at the door in fact freely admitted that they had been beating the bushes looking for veterans willing to go back in. Jack listened while the military men promised things. A promotion? Most definitely. Pay? Yes, sir, the pay scale has gone way up. Jack said he'd think about it, and the men left.

At least Jack had a choice, one he would not have had if he had signed up for the reserves when he found that invitation among his separation papers at Camp Blanding. If he had put his name on it—which he had almost done—he would now not have the luxury of "thinking" about it. He would now be back in. The reserve—inactive and active—was being called up without ado.

Why was our country "calling again," as my father had written? Was this a war where we had been attacked? A war to vanquish a madman? What was this war *about* anyway? Was this a "good war" as the last war had been? Or was it a power struggle between communism and capitalism, maybe even between Joseph Stalin and Harry Truman?

Still, Jack actually did give thought to the offer. The men had made him feel sought-after, as if somewhere he could be a significant presence. He did not feel like a significant presence at this moment in time. The "writtens" were just ahead, the dissertation a lurking monster. Nevertheless, in the end, Jack said no to the military men who had come to our door. And if a fit had begun to make itself known to me—and it had—it went away.

THE YEAR 1952

The 1952 presidential election was upon us, and it was General Dwight D. Eisenhower versus Adlai Stevenson. Whom to support? On paper Adlai Stevenson was by far the better candidate. But the Korean War was still on, and when Eisenhower said, "I will go to Korea," so great was the feeling among the boys that the Korean conflict should be brought to an end that they wanted to believe a reconnoitering trip by the country's top military man might do it. There were other reasons for supporting Eisenhower. "Look, you guys," some of the boys would say, "he's *Eisenhower*. He's our big guy. How can we vote against him?"

Jack and I were definitely Stevenson supporters. Could Jack resist a man who wrote books and sprinkled his speeches with literary references and fine phrasing? Could he resist the man whose acceptance speech for the nomination contained such sentiments as *"When the tumult and the shouting die, when the bands are gone and the lights are dimmed, there is the stark reality of responsibility in an hour of history haunted with those gaunt, grim specters of strife, dissension, and materialism at home, and ruthless, inscrutable, and hostile power abroad"?* And when Stevenson said, *"There are no gains without pains . . . and we are now on the eve of great decisions,"* Jack was a goner. And how could I resist a man who was on the side of civil rights, who had indeed won out over the candidacies of archconservative southern Democrats who proclaimed civil rights to be a blow to liberty?

Jack was so satisfied with Stevenson that he put together a little essay in which he said, "Even though we admire General Eisenhower, this is not a popularity contest." He went on to say that "an election revolves around issues, and Adlai Stevenson understands the issues." I thought what it said was just right, and acting out my role as the daughter of a man who had served on the Democratic Party Committee of Obion County, Tennessee,

I thought to have a bigger audience than just our Saturday nighters, so I mimeographed the essay (in the political science office, which I reasoned was the appropriate place to do it), and Rick and I handed them out to passers-by in front of the post office, which I thought was the appropriate place to hand them out. And I sent one to my father.

My father was one of those in a bind. Perhaps forgetting his rage at Eisenhower when the general had run the veterans out of Washington but remembering that Eisenhower had led the battle against Hitler, he wrote to me, "How can I vote against Eisenhower?" And then, in the next sentence, he wrote, "But how can I vote against my party?" Fevered Patriot was confronting Fevered Democrat. Jack said it was no contest, that in the end Fevered Patriot would win out. And he did.

Eisenhower was elected, he went to Korea, and the "conflict" ended. Did he influence it? How could we know? At any rate, after Korea, it seemed that little of importance remained on the national agenda. We all, however, kept our eyes on Washington, and though we sometimes had to settle for taking note of Eisenhower's golf scores and Mamie's bangs, we thought that, all in all, Eisenhower was adequate for the times. But then HUAC and Joseph McCarthy began to make serious noise, and we again had an issue calling for attention.

Senator McCarthy had joined forces with HUAC and together they were busy ferreting out "Commies" and "pinkos." When the committee hearings were televised, the one campus television set—in the Student Union building—was crowded around with GI Bill boys. We had been promised that a lot of Hollywood celebrities would be testifying, so who could resist? Certainly not us, not us lifelong movie addicts.

The majority of celebrity witnesses, like the actor Ronald Reagan, were friendly to the committee, though it was later said that Reagan saved his juiciest information for the FBI. Walt Disney was very friendly indeed. Among gestures of friendliness, he provided name after name, and about one he said, "I looked into his record and I found, Number One, that he had no religion and, Number Two, that he had considerable time at the Moscow Art Theater studying art direction or something." He also recommended outlawing labor unions for their un-American tendencies, and I thought of our friend Ben Levin, that staunch union supporter we had known in Gainesville, and I wondered how Ben was taking all this. I could see Ben pointing a finger at the television set and yelling, "Why don't you just stick to your mouse and your duck, Mr. Disney?" I also thought of the retired garment workers in Miami Beach and how they were no doubt this minute boycotting Walt Disney movies.

If the boys discussed HUAC and McCarthy endlessly, in the U.S. Congress little was being said. Only Senator Margaret Chase Smith of Maine had spoken up, and when she was joined later by six other senators, Senator McCarthy promptly derogated them as "Snow White and the Six Dwarfs," and a lot of people laughed at the joke of it all, of a woman trying to impugn the patriotism of burly, manly Joseph McCarthy. But many of us were proud of Senator Smith, and I for one forgave her for being a Republican.

Repercussions from the HUAC and McCarthy witch hunts abounded: Unfriendly witnesses were harassed and discharged from their jobs. A slight connection to the Communist Party—a car pool with a Communist neighbor, book from the library written by a Communist—were grounds for being charged with Communist activism. When I wrote to my Communist friends in Miami Beach to learn how they were holding up, at this moment they chose not to reply.

Eisenhower was not speaking out, and his remark—"I will not get into the gutter with that man"—was not well received, certainly not by many of the GI Bill boys who asked, "When he wanted us to get into the gutter with that man named Hitler, did we choose not to?" The same atmosphere that prevailed in Chapel Hill prevailed at other places where GI Bill boys gathered. We had letters—angry ones—from friends all over the country. George Harper wrote that California had taken a cue from HUAC and McCarthy and had imposed a loyalty oath for all government workers, including university faculty. "We're all mad as blazes out here," George wrote to us. "We have to get rid of guys like McCarthy. Why are we letting him turn us into something we're not?"

At last someone rode in to right things, and it was that old World War II hand, Edward R. Murrow. The same man who had informed us in 1945 of the London blitz and the horrors of Buchenwald stepped once again to the microphone, this time to talk of a blight named Joseph McCarthy. With Murrow's attack, others spoke out, and President Eisenhower finally decided that he could get into the gutter after all. Still, it wasn't until sometime later that the nation could finally exhale, and then the Senate, having at last had enough of McCarthy and his "Red Scare," issued a strong censure. It might have appeared that America had regained its balance, but the rose of Sharon blossoms were barely blooming: the race issue was still swirling round.

EXAMINATIONS OF ONE KIND AND ANOTHER

The ills of the world notwithstanding, Jack had his own world to think about, and it was true that though important things were happening on the national and international scene, most of the boys were not distracted or deterred. Their first loyalty was to their studies and they knew it. Jack indeed stayed on track, although he definitely had his ups and downs. And when he was preparing for his language exams—in French and in German—he felt a down coming on. French was not easy for him, and neither was German. We gave a "whew" when Jack passed both of these exams, although the relief didn't last long. Immediately behind was the second hurdle—the "prelims"—the oral exams to determine that the dissertation topic was faculty-proof and, above all, to test the student's appropriateness as a doctoral candidate.

First things first: a dissertation topic had to be arrived at before the prelims could be scheduled. This time Jack didn't hold out for writing on, say, the black writer Langston Hughes (who, among other things, interested Jack because his paternal great-grandfather had been Jewish), but yielded to reality and chose the noncontroversial, the tried and true, the all-time favorite—Shakespeare. He anticipated no fuming about the subject being "doubtful" or "untested." It was, after all, Shakespeare. But Jack, an ardent Platonist, was more than pleased by the fact that the dissertation would deal with Shakespeare's use of Platonic themes and phrases. That Jack had quote/unquote yielded to reality was to me a very good sign that the third foot was not going to show up.

It would be almost impossible to say that Jack studied extra hard in preparation for the prelim exam, because he was always studying extra hard. Still, the exam was to be an oral one, and because Jack had never felt he was blessed with that gracefulness of language that most of his fellow candidates possessed, he was unsettled. What could he do about it? Well, nothing. But he could try to explain it, at least to me, and he explained that he and those more graceful others were born in different places, to different parents, among different ethnic groups. "Can't be helped," he would say. "The committee will just have to love me for myself."

Evidently the committee did love him because he passed, and Jack could proceed with his work. The "writtens"—a truly momentous exam— was now imminent, and the battle joined. Jack did not a little worrying. "Writtens" meant you were going to do a lot of writing, and he had to wonder, among his many things to wonder, if his writing skills were good enough. The faculty, when referring to writing style, threw around the word "felicitous," which made Jack wonder if his writing was *felicitous*. He hoped the faculty would settle for "workmanlike."

The day finally arrived, and I took Jack to the campus. When he got out of the car, getting out with him were dozens of blue books and a goodly supply of No. 2 pencils. My kiss as he left was not so much one that said "so long, see you later" as one that said, "I'm with you in your moment of do or die."

A week later we knew that Jack had not died but had "dood" it. I was still using that word—that word "dood"—though the time of its original use was long in the past. But that word had meant something to me—something to us all—when General Doolittle had led the first bombing attack on Japan, and a newspaper headline read, DOOLITTLE DOOD IT. Because the word connoted daring, know-how, and success, to say that Jack had *dood* it seemed profoundly appropriate.

With the "writtens" over, Jack could now concentrate on the dissertation, which turned out to be "Shakespeare's Debt to Plato." George and Bobby Harper were now in Chapel Hill and living in the veterans' housing complex called Victory Village, and when Jack had run his topic by George, George had put his stamp of approval on it. "It's 100 percent USDA Prime beef," George had said. "You can't do much better than this."

By now Jack's GI Bill had run out. But not to worry. The GI Bill had arranged for this contingency by seeing Jack into the teaching job he was now holding. The job not only paid tuition fees, it gave Jack a stipend as well, and, modest though it was, it enabled us to get by. And that was good enough.

So Jack didn't have to worry about how long the dissertation would take to write, and he gave himself over to the writing. He wanted to write a good dissertation, and he knew he could do it. If there was one German word he was fond of, it was *setzfleish*, literally "sit meat," and he was eager to *setz* his *fleish* on his desk chair. There would be no problem there. In his upbeat mood Jack figured he would need no glue. *Setzfleish* was easy.

In time, Jack finished the dissertation, and the faculty committee was satisfied with both the dissertation and Jack's later defense of it. At the final oral examination, they were in fact merry with contentment. After the usual cloud of chalk dust had escaped from the manuscript, and after somebody had asked, "What the devil *is* all this stuff?" they all laughed and it was done.

Jack called me with the news, and I thought I took it well. I didn't scream the house down; I just gave a whoop and a holler. And then Jack left me to my noises and joined the committee for lunch. The group being faculty, they went Dutch treat, and being English Department, they didn't go for lunch, they "repaired to the Carolina Inn for a small collation."

When Jack came home, there was one thing left to do—call his father, expensive day rates be damned. After his father came on the phone, Jack said to him, as if he'd been waiting to say it, "It turns out that I'm not too light for heavy work after all." Although I still didn't know just how that worked, Jack said his father gave him a big pre-Depression laugh.

14

Mission Accomplished

In a ceremony at the University of North Carolina in the spring of 1955, Jack received a diploma that proclaimed he had "fulfilled the requirements" for a doctorate in philosophy. And if it seemed too cool a declaration for so hot an achievement, if the wording seemed too official for all the drama that had gone into it, it was nonetheless imparting something meaningful. It was saying that a gauzy fantasy had become solid reality. What had been a fantasy man in a tweed jacket with patches on the sleeves was now a flesh-and-blood one wearing a black academic robe and a hood that bore the blue of the University of North Carolina and the white of literature, and his sleeves were glowing with the three velvet chevrons that signified the doctorate.

And so it was fantasy fulfilled: And fantasy fulfilled meant that the GI Bill had kept its promise to Jack and that Jack had kept his promise to the GI Bill. Franklin Delano Roosevelt could not have asked for more.

EPILOGUE

Jack took a job at North Carolina State University in Raleigh, soon became chairman of the freshman English program, and in no time had published a remedial English handbook called *Basic Composition*, which the publisher Prentice-Hall called "an indispensable book for these times." At NC State, what Jack had realized was that he was now in the role of teacher to country boys going to college under the GI Bill who were woefully underprepared by their rural high schools. Feeling a brotherly responsibility to do better by them, he had written the book with those freshmen in mind.

(Having worked on the book with a Jewish colleague, Henry Rosenberg, and sharing with Henry the same sense of the ridiculous, they were soon calling it between themselves, *The Jew Book for Southern Youth*.) It was a very popular handbook that went into numerous printings, and Jack would say that its success meant that many state universities, and some private ones, were feeling the obligation to educate every veteran who chose to be educated, no matter how ill educated they had been.

It was while we were in Raleigh that the race issue came off the back burner. It made its move in a surprising place—Montgomery, Alabama, the very same Montgomery, Alabama, whose racial attitudes I had so deplored. When we had lived there, those attitudes seemed encased in a shell as thick as the shellbark hickory nuts on our backyard tree in Union City. But there was a difference. Inside the nut of that shellbark hickory was meat as sweet as honey, and Montgomery had seemed to me as bitter on the inside as on the out. And yet, of all the cities in the South, Montgomery was the first to take the step to desegregation. The step was all about buses, actually about a very organized boycott of them.

I thought back. Hadn't buses figured in the plans being hatched in that black church in Montgomery? Hadn't the women been talking about how the buses were the symbol of all that was wrong in their city, and hadn't they thought about a boycott? I seem to have remembered that they had. So when racial discrimination in the South began to lose ground, would I be wrong to say that it started in the basement of a black church in Montgomery, Alabama?

*   *   *

In the sixties, we went back to Florida but now to Boca Raton, where Jack, as a professor of English, was dean of the College of Humanities at Florida Atlantic University, a new upper-level addition to the state university system. Once back in south Florida, we were able to pick up on those other GI Bill boys who had been with us in Gainesville and/or on the Suberman porch as we waited for deliverance.

The family's GI Bill boys had done well. Jack's brother Irwin had found that Jewish engineers could find a place in the profession and eventually became a successful building contractor. Ruth's husband, Phil Heckerling, who had all those shiny tools on the shelf to pick from, had added one to his accounting degree and it was the law. He found a way to practice both, and to teach at the University of Miami, and to establish the prestigious

Heckerling Institute on Estate Planning. The majority of boys who sat on the Suberman porch struggling to find ways to the future became lawyers, and we noticed how they now made up a substantial number of Dade County's protectors and defenders. Many others, porch-sitters or not, went into elective politics and made up a sizable chunk of Dade County's judges and mayors.

I don't know if Jack Rubin stopped answering questions about being a Nazi prisoner of war, but I do know that he had asked for and got that GI seed money so he could buy a printing press, which he nurtured until it became a small publishing house called All-Miami Press. Bill O'Connor, up there in Boston, had written us that GI Bill funding got him his own bar. Bill's enterprise may not have fit the typical definition of "making a contribution," but it took care of the kids.

The Harpers had done just what we had expected them to do. George became one of those eminent scholars he had so admired and was soon considered by all to be the star of Irish literature studies. And, as I had predicted, Bobby Harper was the classic diplomatic, tactful academic wife, though, as I also expected, in her private moments, she remained the same entertaining, clear-eyed woman I had always known. I was also an academic wife, though I was not the Gladys Lyons wife of utmost propriety and deference. It was, after all, the 1960s to 1970s, and I worked. And no, much to my own surprise, I did not work in places with social and/or political agendas; I worked in art museums. Sorry, Dad.

And Cyrus, our Montgomery seatmate in that Lincoln Zephyr? Having taken an undergraduate degree at Alabama State College for Negroes in Montgomery, he had found the nerve to apply to a northern university for graduate work and he had been accepted. "I'm in class with whites and coloreds," he wrote to us. "I still haven't gotten used to it, but I'm working on it."

In the sixties came upheaval. Yet another war—the war in Vietnam—descended upon us, and with it came a cosmic shifting of priorities and attitudes. And it was at that moment that the GI Bill of World War II demonstrated its power and influence. A new generation was now out in front. They were the children of the GI Bill boys, and the children had taken their fathers' lessons to heart.

What they learned was that their fathers, those returning World War II veterans, as beneficiaries of the GI Bill had lived lives of security. They were confident and self-assured, and because they were, they had determined never to be underestimated, never to be taken for granted. When the big issues were out there, they gave themselves permission to speak out however they chose. It was not the 1930s anymore.

It seemed that , if the men of World War II no longer wished to go along with convention or custom, they didn't. If they wished not to restrict themselves to the dictates they had grown up with, they cast those bonds aside. And it was this message, this gift, that their sons and daughters understood.

If, therefore, GI Bill children wanted to speak out against the Vietnam War, they did. By now they had learned that not all wars were good ones, not all wars were a matter of "fighting for your country." Some wars, they had also learned, were not fought because your country was in danger but because your country was being influenced by selfish interests. Was this or was this not shades of my old mentor, Henry Wallace? Still, unlike at earlier periods of national stress, at this time trusted public voices were heard, and often the voices of sons and daughters of the GI Bill boys.

The new-generation sons and daughters furthermore knew from their earliest years, as their fathers had not known, that college was no longer the preserve of the moneyed ones; it was for all, for anybody who wanted a good life, who was striving for success, who wanted to make a contribution. For them, college was not a dream; it was taken for granted.

For Jack and me personally, our son Rick gave a warm welcome to the GI Bill gift that ultimately came to him. Although he did not become the first Jewish president, he had, like his father, a solid college career and, like his Uncle Phil, became a professional in two disciplines—in Rick's case, medicine and law—and he practices both in Chapel Hill. And if his grandfather was still alive and asked him if he remembered the difference between a Democrat and a Republican, Rick would reply, "Yes, Grandpa, I do."

* * *

Although Jack might quote William Faulkner's words—"The past is never dead. It's not even past"—the particular ills I knew are no longer with us. Other ills have disappeared as well, even if, in the natural scheme of things, different ills have popped up to take their place.

Those of us who remember the spirit engendered by the old GI Bill are saying we need something similar for the many problems of these times. We want to make sure that the "idea of America"—America as an open, optimistic, and just society—will endure.

Still, we who remember are not despondent. We keep the faith that when America suffers setbacks, it finds ways to come back, often stronger than ever. So when I pick up *The New York Times* and read how the world is going to hell in a handbasket, I take a deep breath and remind myself of the ways of the rose of Sharon bush and remember that when the rose of Sharon sheds its blossoms in the evening, we have only to wait through the night for other blossoms, sometimes more beautiful and more abundant, to show themselves in the morning. And so I say to myself that the rose of Sharon bush that is America will bloom again. Don't I have evidence that it always does?

The GI Bill Boys was designed and typeset on a Macintosh OS 10.5 using InDesign CS5 software. The body text is set in 10/13 Meridian and display type is set in Cronos Pro. This book was designed and typeset by Barbara Karwhite and manufactured by Thomson-Shore, Inc.